WRAP CONTRACTS

Wrap Contracts

FOUNDATIONS AND RAMIFICATIONS

Nancy S. Kim

OXFORD
UNIVERSITY PRESS

OXFORD
UNIVERSITY PRESS

Oxford University Press is a department of the University of Oxford. It furthers the University's objective of excellence in research, scholarship, and education by publishing worldwide.

Oxford New York
Auckland Cape Town Dar es Salaam Hong Kong Karachi Kuala Lumpur Madrid
Melbourne Mexico City Nairobi New Delhi Shanghai Taipei Toronto

With offices in
Argentina Austria Brazil Chile Czech Republic France Greece Guatemala Hungary
Italy Japan Poland Portugal Singapore South Korea Switzerland Thailand
Turkey Ukraine Vietnam

Published in the United States of America by
Oxford University Press
198 Madison Avenue, New York, NY 10016

Library of Congress Cataloging-in-Publication Data

Kim, Nancy S.
Wrap contracts : foundations and ramifications / Nancy S. Kim
pages cm
Includes bibliographical references and index.
ISBN 978-0-19-933697-5 ((hardback) : alk. paper)
1. Contracts. 2. Adhesion contracts. I. Title.
K840.K55 2013
346.02'2—dc23
2013000756

9 8 7 6 5 4 3 2
Printed in the United States of America on acid-free paper

Note to Readers

This publication is designed to provide accurate and authoritative information in regard to the subject matter covered. It is based upon sources believed to be accurate and reliable and is intended to be current as of the time it was written. It is sold with the understanding that the publisher is not engaged in rendering legal, accounting, or other professional services. If legal advice or other expert assistance is required, the services of a competent professional person should be sought. Also, to confirm that the information has not been affected or changed by recent developments, traditional legal research techniques should be used, including checking primary sources where appropriate.

(Based on the Declaration of Principles jointly adopted by a Committee of the American Bar Association and a Committee of Publishers and Associations.)

Dedication

To my parents,
Yeun Soo and Mi Wha Kim,
with gratitude.

Contents

Acknowledgments

THIS BOOK IS the culmination of years of research and writing in the area of contracts and technology. The analysis and ideas in this book build upon and further develop work which previously appeared in the following publications:

The Duty to Draft Reasonably and Online Contracts, in Commercial Contract Law: A Transatlantic Perspective, ch. 8 (Cambridge University Press, 2013)
Contract's Adaptation and the Online Bargain, 79 U. Cin. L. Rev. 1327 (2011)
Wrap Contracts and Privacy (Proceedings of the Intelligent Information Privacy Management Symposium, AAAI Press, 2010)
Bargaining Power and Background Law, 12 Vand. J. Ent. & Tech. L. 93 (2009)
Website Proprietorship and Online Harassment, 2009 Utah L. Rev. 993
The Software Licensing Dilemma, 2008 Byu L. Rev. 1103
Internet Challenges to Business Innovation, 12 J. Internet L. 3 (August 2008)
Mistakes, Changed Circumstances and Intent, 56 U. Kan. L. Rev. 473 (2008)
Clicking and Cringing, 86 Or. L. Rev. 797 (2007)
Martha Graham, Professor Miller, and the Work-for-Hire Doctrine: Undoing the Judicial Bind Created by the Legislature, 13 J. Intell. Prop. L. 337 (2006)
Evolving Business and Social Norms and Interpretation Rules: The Need for a Dynamic Approach to Contract Disputes, 84 Neb. L. Rev. 506 (2005)

There are many people who have helped in different ways with this book.

I benefited a great deal from the feedback of participants at forums, conferences, and faculty workshops hosted by various institutions, including the American Association of Law Schools, the American Bar Association, American University, Brigham Young University, California Western, McGeorge, The Ohio State University, Stanford University, Stetson University, Southwestern, University of Akron, University of Cambridge, University of Sheffield (UK), University of Nevada–Las Vegas, and Wake Forest. For providing comments or suggestions on chapters of this book, the aforementioned articles, or for helpful conversations and insights, I thank Tom Barton, Curtis Bridgeman, Ryan Calo, Larry Garvin, Danielle Kie Hart, Woody Hartzog, Cynthia Ho, Tom Joo, Mike Kelly, Jacqueline Lipton, Steve Macias, Juliet Moringiello, Cheryl Preston, Keith Rowley, Amy Schmitz, and Yana Welinder.

For her diligent and thorough research assistance, I owe a tremendous amount of thanks to Alyn Beauregard. For help in citechecking and locating sources, I also thank Ashley Dudley and the excellent California Western library reference desk staff, especially Brandon Baker, Bill Bookheim, Barbara Glennan, Ian Kipnes, and Bobbie Weaver. For help in preparing this manuscript, I thank Joyce Stallworth and the California Western faculty support staff.

My current and former students at California Western School of Law, Rady School of Management, University of California–San Diego; The Ohio State University Mortiz College of Law; and Victoria University, Wellington, New Zealand helped me see a familiar topic with fresh eyes and energized me with their curiosity.

My former professor, Herma Hill Kay, has been a mentor and an inspiration to me as she has been to many other women in the legal profession. Her kind words of encouragement gave me the confidence to pursue an academic career and her wisdom has guided me through the years.

I have the good fortune to work at California Western School of Law, where my fledging ideas were nourished by helpful colleagues and an accommodating and supportive administration. Victoria University, Wellington, New Zealand, provided me with a welcoming home for several months where I was able to write portions of this book, and I thank my colleagues there, especially David McLauchlan, for their hospitality.

Thanks to Alden Domizio, Maria Pucci and the production team at Oxford University Press for doing the hard work needed to turn these pages into a book, and special thanks to my former editor, Matt Gallaway, for his faith in this project and his support throughout the publication process.

I thank my parents for teaching me the value of keeping promises.

Most of all, I am incredibly grateful for my home team, Seth, Mina, and Amelia. They adopted this project as their own and helped find many stories and examples of contracts that informed my research. I thank them for allowing me to commandeer their computers, their cameras, and their phones in the name of contract law. Their encouragement, support, and understanding sustain and motivate me.

1 Introduction

HAVE YOU ENTERED into a contract today?

Or rather, *how many* contracts have you entered into today? If you are like me, you have agreed to the terms of a contract several times today. I entered into a contract with my bank when I went online to pay a bill. I entered into a contract with my e-mail service provider when I sent an e-mail to a friend. I entered into a contract when I purchased a song from a digital music retailer. I entered into all of these contracts without even uncapping a pen.

My experience is not atypical, yet when I ask my law or business school students whether they have entered into any contracts in the past week, few raise their hands. When I ask those who do raise their hands what kind of contracts they have entered into, they usually tell me that they signed a lease for an apartment, or a loan agreement for a car, or some paperwork for a student loan. Occasionally, one of my business school students will have signed a commercial contract.

But when I ask whether they have checked their online banking account, or downloaded software or music, or posted to their Facebook or Twitter accounts that week, nearly every hand in the room goes up.

"Then you have all entered into a contract," I say, pausing for dramatic effect.

But have they *really*? And if so, how to explain this disconnect between perception and reality? Is it possible for someone to enter into a contract and not know it?

The answers to the first two questions are complicated, and this book devotes many of its pages to them. The answer to the third question is more straightforward: Yes.

As strange as it may seem, under contract law you can legally bind yourself without knowing it. This is especially true online. Sometimes online agreements require that a user click using a computer mouse on an "I agree" icon, but clicking doesn't register in many people's minds the same way that signing on a dotted line does. Often, you don't even have to click to be bound. In many cases, you can be deemed to have entered into a contract simply by visiting a website.

How is that possible? And how did we get here?

When most consumers think of contracts, they think of a multipage document with fine print that they sign when they want to rent a car, apply for a credit card, or enroll in a cell phone plan. They may think that in order for a contract to be legally binding, it needs to look like a legal document. In other words, a contract, in their minds, should be typed, dated, and signed by both parties. It should contain legalese and unnecessary words such as "wherefore" and "henceforth."

But they are wrong. A contract generally does not need to be signed by both parties in order to be legally enforceable. In fact, barring a few exceptions (e.g., personal guaranties, contracts for the sale of goods $500 or more, contracts for the sale of real property, and a few others), a contract does not even need to be in writing in order to be enforceable.

To be sure, many contracts are printed up on nice paper and signed by both parties and too many of them contain unnecessary words and legal mumbo jumbo. But often contracts, even when written, do not announce themselves on legal-size paper, nor do they arrive under wax and seal. Sometimes they sneak into the transaction unnoticed, slipping into the consumer's hands after money has already been exchanged. Sometimes they simply hang out on the edges of a website, outfitted in a modest hyperlink to mask the unsightly terms contained within. Even when an agreement precedes the transaction, consumers feel powerless to negotiate standard form contract terms. To these consumers, it makes no difference whether the terms come before or after the transaction because the terms are offered on a "take-it-or-leave-it" basis. These contracts are known as "contracts of adhesion." This book is primarily concerned with a certain type of contract of adhesion—wrap contracts.

So what is a wrap contract anyway? This book uses "wrap contract" as a blanket term to refer to a unilaterally imposed set of terms which the drafter purports to be legally binding and which is presented to the nondrafting party in a nontraditional format. Nontraditional in this context means that the contracting form wasn't commonly used prior to 1980 and includes electronic media and offline mediums. The single common characteristic is that the adhering party does not have to use a pen in order to accept the terms. (Under a federal law, Electronic Signatures in Global and National Commerce Act, known as ESIGN,[1] an electronic signature or contract cannot be denied legal effect simply because it is in electronic form. In addition, most states have adopted some version of the Uniform Electronic Transactions Act known as "UETA" which also permits electronic contracting).

Wrap contracts include shrinkwraps, clickwraps, and browsewraps. Shrinkwraps are pieces of paper wrapped in plastic wrap that come with software compact discs. Clickwrap and browsewrap agreements are digital and can be found on nearly every website. A clickwrap requires clicking with a computer mouse on a box or icon that says, "I agree," or something similar, whereas a browsewrap requires no affirmative act and is accessible via a hyperlink, typically located at the bottom of the home page and identified with wording such as "Terms of Use." Other forms of wrap contracts have started to emerge. "Tapwraps" pop up on mobile devices such as smart phones and require a tap of the finger rather than a click of the mouse to indicate acceptance. This author recently encountered a "ripwrap" when her new laptop arrived in a plastic bag with legal terms on a sticker which were deemed "accepted" by tearing open the sticker (which was required to open the bag containing the laptop). It seems there are as many ways to present contract terms as the imagination and technology allow.

Which may lead you to wonder: Given that many of the problems pertaining to wrap contracts also apply to other types of consumer contracts, is there any need to distinguish wrap from other contracts? Is there a difference between online and offline, traditional and nontraditional standard form contracts? Negotiating or "bargaining" disparities exist with both wrap and other standard form contracts.[2] Consumers routinely "accept" the terms of both written and digital agreements without bothering to read their terms. Some commentators even speculate that the electronic contracting environment may be a better one for consumers than the offline one for several reasons. They argue that consumers have access to information about a company's contract on its website.[3] They note that time pressures may be

---

[1] Pub. L. No. 106-229, 114 Stat. 464 (2000) (codified at 15 U.S.C. § 7001 *et seq.*).

[2] Juliet Moringiello and William Reynolds, for example, argue that contract law is malleable enough to address electronic contracting issues. *See* Juliet M. Moringiello & William L. Reynolds, *From Lord Coke to Internet Privacy: The Past, Present and Future of Electronic Contracting*, 72 Md. L. Rev. 542 (2013).

[3] Christina L. Kunz, John E. Ottaviani, Elaine D. Ziff, Juliet M. Moringiello, Kathleen M. Porter, & Jennifer C. Debrow, *Browse-Wrap Agreements: Validity of Implied Assent in Electronic Form Agreement*, 59 Bus. Law 279, 290 (2003) (noting that "in an electronic setting, a Web site can be designed to provide a customer with detailed information about the contractual terms through the use of Frequently Asked Questions (FAQ) pages or by providing a method of contacting the Web site provider with questions.").

diminished when the user is shopping from home.[4] The user can comparison shop and interrupt online transactions more readily than offline ones.[5]

Why then devote a book to the subject of wrap contracts in particular, rather than mass consumer contracts generally?

Wrap contracts are different from paper contracts in both their form and the environment in which they are presented. This book explains how businesses, courts and technology create a coercive contracting environment where one-sided legal terms are imposed upon non-drafting parties who literally have no choice but to accept them if they wish to participate in modern society. It also explains how contracting form (i.e. digital or paper) significantly alters the behavior of contracting parties, which in turn creates seismic shifts in both methods of contracting and the substance of the contract itself. Wrap contracts are insidiously shaping the development of online activity by, for example, legitimating privacy-eroding practices.[6]

Furthermore, what happens online doesn't stay online. As our online and offline worlds merge, and as products become more digital and less tangible, contracting practices that were tolerable in the context in which they originated become much more ominous. As consumers become acclimated to "clicking," they are made to do so in physical spaces and for transactions which were formerly free of contracts. A consumer now can walk into an Apple store, have the "Genius" salesclerk charge her credit card, and then be required to accept the terms of Apple's agreement on her new iPad before being allowed to take possession of it. Perhaps even more troubling, offline and online contracting methods can be used in a way that aggravates certain legal burdens on consumers. For example, one court held that a consumer was bound by the terms of an online agreement because she had received a notice in the mail that the terms were available online.[7]

The problem with wrap contracts is not solely their novel forms and their aggressive terms; it is also the stale formalism that rationalizes them. In a society where contracts are ubiquitous, do traditional doctrinal rules make sense? How can contract law balance the needs of an evolving marketplace with the realities of consumer behavior?

Modern contracts befuddle critics who view them through the prism of traditional contract doctrine. Others argue that mass consumer contracts are not contracts at all

---

[4] *Id.* at 15.

[5] *Id.*

[6] This book examines many provisions from actual contracts which were current as of the date indicated in the associated footnotes. But given the ease and frequency with which digital contracts are updated, the terms of the cited contracts may have changed. Similarly, some of the associated issues in this fast moving area may have changed due to legislative reform efforts and regulatory action.

[7] Briceño v. Sprint Spectrum, 911 So.2d 176, 180 (Fla. Dist. Ct. App. 3d Dist. 2005).

because they lack a critical doctrinal requirement, such as consideration or offer and acceptance. Some argue that even if these contracts are validly formed, they should not be enforceable because they are contrary to public policy.

Wrap contracts have their defenders, too. They argue in favor of innovative contracting forms, such as browsewraps or clickwraps, sometimes on the grounds of autonomy but more often economic efficiency. In doing so, these defenders narrowly rivet their attention on ways that wrap contracts are similar to traditional contracts and blithely overlook the many ways in which they are not.

In this book, I explain why traditional contract law is insufficient to address modern contracting needs. The rigid rules of traditional contract law simply ignore the reality of modern day transactions. Realizing the limits of playing by formalistic rules, courts have twisted contract doctrine to uphold certain agreements that made sense given a particular business environment. Unfortunately, they did not limit the applicability of the doctrine to those business environments. The result is undesirable and harmful legal precedent that shifts the balance of power away from consumers and toward businesses, which now have the ability to set and shape norms through their contracting methods.

In the dynamic online and mobile computing environment the aggressive practices of businesses—accomplished in large part through wrap contracts—threaten to reshape societal norms and values such as privacy and property ownership. Social change is inevitable and often desirable but process matters. Where the change occurs organically and through the desires of a population, it represents the progress of a civilization; on the other hand, where it is instigated by self-interested businesses without the approval or awareness of the masses—through the vehicle of stealth contracts—it reflects coercion and exploitation.

The first half of this book explores the differences between wrap and other contracts, lays out the foundations for wrap agreements, and traces their origin, rise, and influence. The second half of this book focuses on the social and legal ramifications of using wrap contracts, and concludes that while a specialized body of law is unnecessary, doctrinal adjustments should be made to address the problem of wrap contracts. These adjustments reallocate the balance of burdens on the parties by recognizing contracting realities such as the power of the drafter to present terms and the futility of shopping for alternative terms.

2 Why Enforce Contracts?

AN EXAMINATION OF the enforceability of wrap contracts requires examining why any contract is enforced. Contracts scholar Steven A. Smith writes that contract theories are either "analytic" or "normative."[1] Analytic theories explain *what* contract law is, whereas normative theories explain *why* contract law is (and why it should be). Smith explains that theories that aim to answer the "analytic question" about the nature of contract law fall into one of three categories: promissory theories, reliance theories and transfer theories. Promissory theories understand contractual obligations as promissory obligations which are essentially self-imposed. The intent of the parties is therefore essential as the contractual obligation is a duty to perform what was promised. The second category, reliance theories, regard contractual obligations as imposed by law in order to ensure that one is not induced to rely upon the actions of another and thereby made worse off. Under the third category, transfer theories, obligations are incurred by the intentional transfer of a right to a

[1] STEPHEN A. SMITH, CONTRACT THEORY at 43 (Oxford 2004) ("The first question that a complete theory of contract must answer is an *analytic* question about the nature of contractual obligations. The second question is a *normative* question about the justification, if any, for contractual obligations.").

beneficiary. The obligation then is one to respect the property-like right to receive performance held by the beneficiary.[2] Smith concludes that "promissory theories provide the best answer to the analytic question about contract law."[3]

Promissory theories align with how contract law actually operates. Numerous courts and the Restatement (Second) section define a contract as a legally enforceable promise.[4] A contract must be supported by at least one express or implied promise, but not all promises are contracts. Contracts then, concern a particular kind of promise or promises. But what kind? If contracts are legally enforceable promises, what makes a promise legally enforceable?

The legal enforceability of promises has two aspects to it. The first has to do with formation. A promise is not enforced as a contract if the contract has not been properly formed. Proper contract formation requires offer, acceptance, consideration, and mutual assent. These formation requirements are necessarily intertwined. Consideration is a bargained-for exchange, which means that each party is induced to make his or her promise because of the other party's promise (or in the case of unilateral contracts, in order to get the other party's performance).[5]

But consideration means more than a bargained-for exchange; it also refers to the substance of the bargin. Some promises, even if bargained for, do not constitute sufficient consideration. These are promises made for affective reasons, meaning that if the promise is made in exchange for somebody's love or gratitude, it is not recognized as consideration. The law concludes, in those situations, that the promise is being made for altruistic reasons, even if in reality, it is being made to induce the other party to act in a more affectionate or loving manner. Contract law does not recognize that the promise of affection can induce other types of promises (and promises of certain kinds of affection in exchange for promises of payment are illegal in most jurisdictions).

In addition, the parties must—at least in the abstract—share the same understanding of what is being offered and accepted, which is referred to as mutual assent. Mutual assent does not mean that the parties *actually* shared the same understanding. It would be too awkward, difficult, and time-consuming for courts to decipher the subjective motivations and beliefs of the parties. The courts apply an objective standard to the contract dealings, meaning that they will assume that the parties were reasonable people and believed and acted the way reasonable people believe and act.

---

[2] *Id.* at 43-45.

[3] *Id.* at 103.

[4] Restatement (Second) of Contracts § 1 (1981) ("A contract is a promise or a set of promises for the breach of which the law gives a remedy, or the performance of which the law in some way recognizes as a duty.")

[5] *Id.* at § 17 and § 71.

Offer, acceptance, consideration, and mutual assent are often referred to as formation doctrines. There are other formation requirements having to do with the form of the contract itself. The statute of frauds requires that certain types of contracts must be in writing, for example. Other contracts may, by legislation or other law, be required to be in a particular form. As previously noted, however, most contracts do not have particular requirements of form and do not even need to be in writing.

The second aspect to enforceability is the availability of contract defenses. In order to be enforced, a contract must be properly formed; however, not all properly formed contracts are enforced. There may be reasons to excuse a party from performance. The party may lack the legal capacity to enter into contracts because he or she is a minor or mentally incompetent. The statute of limitations may have run on the ability to enforce the contract. There may be defects in the formation of the contract, or something may arise after formation that excuses performance. These contract excuses or defenses include duress, fraud, mistake, changed circumstances, and unconscionability. There may be conflicting laws (such as bankruptcy laws) and public policy considerations that militate against enforcement. Contract enforceability then encompasses both proper contract form and formation and the absence of excusing or invalidating circumstances.

In the absence of a bargain or a promise, contractual obligations may be enforced because there was detrimental reliance or a transfer of rights, which are two alternative theories of enforcement. A distinction should thus be made between what a *contract is*, and *when performance obligations may be imposed*. Performance obligations may arise from the making of a bargained for express or implied promise, but they can also arise in the absence of a bargained for promise, because of the existence of circumstances that warrant the imposition of such obligations. Significantly, where performance obligations are imposed despite the absence of a bargained for promise, the nature of the obligation is *quasi-contractual*, meaning there is no real contract.

To understand what a contract is and what types of contracts get enforced does not answer the normative question of *why* courts enforce promises, which, as a topic to contemplate, is a perennial favorite issue among contract theorists. Many commentators have written about the lack of a complete theory of contracts.[6] The

---

[6] Alan Schwartz & Robert E. Scott, *Contract Theory and the Limits of Contract Law*, 113 YALE L. J. 541, 543 (2003); Daniel Markovits, *Contract and Collaboration*, 113 YALE L. J. 1417, 1419 (2004) (arguing that "individualistic theories do not capture or reflect the distinctive moral center of promise and contract."); Robert A. Hillman, *The Crisis in Modern Contract Theory*, 67 TEX. L. REV. 103 (1988). *See also* GRANT GILMORE, THE DEATH OF CONTRACT (The Ohio State University Press) (1974); P. S. ATIYAH, THE RISE AND FALL OF FREEDOM OF CONTRACT (Oxford University Press 1979).

proffered reasons for this are varied, including the broad range of contract types to be covered,[7] the confusion wrought by the sheer number of contract theories,[8] and the general disinterest of the courts in academic scholarship.[9] A promise is an agreement between two private actors. Why then should a court meddle in private affairs? What is the theory and justification underlying contract law? Stephen Smith divides normative theories into two broad categories: utilitarian theories and rights-based theories.[10] Utilitarian theories justify contract law on the basis that it promotes human well-being, including wealth, welfare and autonomy.[11] Rights-based theories justify contract law because it vindicates the rights of citizens.[12] Smith also considers a third category which he refers to as "mixed theories," which combine the two categories.[13] I offer my own very brief and very general version of the prevailing theories which, to a certain extent, reference Smith's categories. I divides normative theories into three broad categories: individualistic or deontic, utilitarian, and multivalue.

A. Individualistic/Deontic Theories

Many theories of contract law arise from the belief that humans are free and rational beings and that courts should facilitate the will of individuals to self-govern through contracting. Individual autonomy or "will theorists" emphasize self-determination and freedom of contract. The furtherance of individual autonomy is a laudable goal in a free society. According to individualist theories, parties should be free to engage in promissory exchanges with minimal government interference. Promises are expressions of individual will and the source of parties' obligations. Parties may promise anything that is not illegal, and are obligated only to perform what they have promised.

---

[7] Schwartz & Scott, *supra* note 6, at 543 ("Contract law has neither a complete descriptive theory, explaining what the law is, nor a complete normative theory, explaining what the law should be. These gaps are unsurprising given the traditional definition of contract as embracing all promises that the law will enforce."). *Id.*

[8] Jay Feinman, *The Significance of Contract Theory*, 58 U. CIN. L. REV. 1283, at 1283 (1990).

[9] E. Allan Farnsworth, *Essay: Developments in Contract Law During the 1980's: The Top Ten*, 41 CASE W. RES. L. REV. 203, 225 (1990) ("Viewed from the academe, the most significant non-event of the decade was the failure of contract theory to have a significant impact on practice."). *Id.* at 225.

[10] SMITH, *supra* note 1, at 106-107.

[11] *Id.* at 106.

[12] *Id.* at 107.

[13] *Id.*

Individualistic theories have important differences. Promise-based theorists like Charles Fried[14] and Seanna Shiffrin,[15] for example, argue that a contract is a moral obligation. The promise, according to this view, is the basis of the contract. Randy Barnett, however, argues that it is the manifestation of consent—and not a promise—which is the basis ofcontract.[16] While the differences among these theories are significant, what ties individualistic theories together is the belief that contractual obligations derive from actions taken by contracting parties; a promisor is bound because the promisor willed it, not because the promised act achieves a greater social good.[17]

B. Consequentialist Theories

In contrast to individualism, consequentialism focuses on the societal benefits of contracting. Law and economics or market efficiency theorists champion the utilitarian belief that contracts should be enforced because they maximize wealth.[18] One of the most influential proponents of this view, Richard Posner, explains that contracts are efficient vehicles for allocation of resources because parties would not agree to an exchange unless each party believed that she would be better off as a result.[19] Under this theory, contract law should reduce the costs of promissory exchanges by encouraging performance through the use of sanctions

---

[14] Charles Fried, Contract as Promise: A Theory of Contractual Obligations at 15 (Harvard University Press 1981) ("The moral force behind contract as promise is autonomy: the parties are bound to their contract because they have chosen to be.").

[15] Seanna Valentine Shiffrin, *The Divergence of Contract and Promise*, 120 HARV. L. REV. 708, 709 (2007).

[16] Randy Barnett, *Symposium: A Tribute to Professor Joseph M. Perillo: Consenting to Form Contracts*, 71 Fordham. L. Rev. 627, 634–35 (2002). ("Suppose that the enforcement of private agreements is not about promising but about manifesting consent to be legally bound. Suppose the reason why we enforce certain commitments, whether or not in the form of a promise, is because one party has manifested its consent to be legally bound to perform that commitment. According to this theory, the assent that is critical to the issue of formation or enforceability is not the assent to perform or refrain from performing a certain act—the promise—but the manifested assent to be legally bound to do so.") *See also* Randy E. Barnett, *A Consent Theory of Contract*, 86 COLUM. L. REV. 269 (1986); Randy E. Barnett, *Symposium, Some Problems with Contract as Promise*, 77 CORNELL L. REV. 1022 (1992).

[17] James Gordley, Contract Law in the Aristotelian Tradition, in The Theory of Contract Law 265, 267 (Peter Benson ed., Cambridge University Press 2001)

[18] *See* RICHARD POSNER, THE PROBLEMS OF JURISPRUDENCE at 356–57 (Harvard University Press 1990). *See also* A. MITCHELL POLINSKY, AN INTRODUCTION TO LAW AND ECONOMICS 10 (Aspen 1983) (discussing standard assumptions of economic analysis, including consumer sovereignty, exogenous preferences, and utility maximization).

[19] ANTHONY T. KRONMAN & RICHARD A. POSNER, THE ECONOMICS OF CONTRACT LAW 1–2 (Little, Brown & Co., 1979). Critics have argued that an individual may fail to maximize wealth due to cognitive errors or because she has other interests, such as fairness.

for breach. Not surprisingly, law and economics theorists tend to disfavor contract defenses based upon equitable principles, particularly those based on hardship and unfairness. Such defenses leave a contract vulnerable to judicial inquiry into the substance of the bargain, undermining the principle that contracting parties are in the best position to determine the value of a given good or service. Certain contract defenses, however, may provide a useful economic function. For example, fraud and duress defenses may be used to deter conduct that would otherwise diminish trust and reduce willingness to enter into contracts.[20] In general, however, law and economic theorists disapprove of contract defenses in all but a few, narrowly defined cases.[21]

Relationship or relational contract theorists, most notably Ian MacNeil[22] and Stewart Macaulay,[23] view contract law as governing relations rather than transactions; consequently, evaluation of contracts should take into account the relationship between the parties to that contract. Similarly, communitarian theorists, such as Daniel Markovits, view contracts as a way to encourage and protect important social relationships.[24] Coordination theorists view contracts as vehicles for coordinating and planning activities. According to Curtis Bridgeman a "planning theory" of contract law explains the fundamental doctrines "better than the presently available theories." Bridgeman believes that "viewing contracts as plans designed to solve a particular coordination problem better accounts for how we are able to make exchanges over time, even in situations where the parties involved might otherwise not be able to trust one another."[25]

Trust is a necessary component to contracts for utilitarian reasons. Erin O'Hara, for examples, describes the "safety net" function of contract law which fortifies the

---

[20] RICHARD A. POSNER, ECONOMIC ANALYSIS OF LAW, section 4.7 (Aspen 2011); Richard A. Epstein, *Unconscionability: A Critical Reappraisal*, 18 J.L. & ECON 293, 298 (1975) (fraudulent misrepresentation as a defense to a contract suit).

[21] *See* POSNER, *supra* note 20, section 4.7 at 104 ("Economic analysis reveals no ground other than fraud, incapacity and duress (the last narrowly defined) for allowing a party to repudiate the bargain . . .").

[22] Ian R. MacNeil, *Contracts: Adjustment of Long-Term Economic Relations under Classical, Neoclassical and Relational Contract Law*, 72 NW. U. L. REV. 854 (1978); Ian R. MacNeil, *Relational Contract Theory: Challenges and Queries*, 94 NW. U. L. REV. 877 (2000).

[23] Stewart Macaulay, *Non-Contractual Relations in Business—A Preliminary Study*, 28 AM. SOCIOLOGICAL REV. 1 (1963) (providing an empirical study of business practices governing transactions that emphasizes relationships and nonlegal norms).

[24] *See,* e.g. Markovits, *supra* note 6, 1417. Curtis Bridgeman describes communitarian theorists as focused "on the moral worth of the personal relationship between the promisor and promisee. Contract law is valued to the degree that it enhances the development of valuable, communal relationships or criticized to the degree that it inhibits such relationships." Curtis Bridgeman, *Contracts as Plans*, 2009 U. ILL. L. REV. 341, at 356.

[25] Bridgeman, *supra* note 24, 341.

trust that a party has in another, and increases the willingness to proceed with a transaction. The safety net function of contract law makes people "willing to contract with acquaintances and strangers—to take the leap of faith—at least for small-value transactions. By expanding the possible trading partners for each person, contract law makes us all wealthier because it provides greater possible gains from exchange."[26]

Distributive justice theories propose that the goal of contract law should be a just allocation of societal resources or the attainment of societal fairness.[27] While parties may not enter into contracts with the end goal of promoting fairness and/or equity, they expect to be treated fairly in the event of a contract dispute. As U.S. Supreme Court justice, Felix Frankfurter, in a dissenting opinion, wrote:

> Does any principle in our law have more universal application than the doctrine that courts will not enforce transactions in which the relative positions of the parties are such that one has unconscionably taken advantage of the necessities of the other?... Fraud and physical duress are not the only grounds upon which courts refuse to enforce contracts. The law is not so primitive that it sanctions every injustice except brute force and downright fraud. More specifically, the courts generally refuse to lend themselves to the enforcement of a 'bargain' in which one party has unjustly taken advantage of the economic necessities of the other.[28]

Another way in which contract law may distribute justice is in its gap-filler function, as the following quote from Morris Cohen explains:

> [W]e may look upon the law of contract as a number of rules according to which courts distribute gains and losses corresponding to the equities of such cases; and the pretense that the result follows exclusively from the agreement of the two parties is fictional.... If we view the law of contract as directed to strengthening the security of transactions by enabling men to rely more fully on promises, we see only one phase of its actual workings. The other phase is the determination of the rights of the contracting parties as to contingencies that they have not foreseen, and for which they have not provided. In this latter respect the law of contract is a way of enforcing some kind of distributive justice within the legal

---

[26] Erin O'Hara, *Choice of Law for Internet Transactions: The Uneasy Case for Online Consumer Protection*, 153 U. PA. L. REV. 1883, 1892, 1898–99 (2005).

[27] *See generally* Anthony Kronman, *Contract Law and Distributive Justice*, 89 YALE L. J. 472 (1980)(arguing that "rules of contract law should be used to implement distributional goals whenever alternative ways of doing so are likely to be more costly or intrusive.") *Id.* at 474.

[28] U.S. v. Bethlehem Steel Corp. 315 U.S. 289, 326 (1942)(Frankfurter, J., dissenting).

> system… In any case, the essential problem of the law of contract is the problem of distribution of risks. The other phase, namely the assurance that what the parties have actually agreed on will be fulfilled, is a limiting principle.[29]

Various doctrines are intended to protect individuals from contracts that are unfair or inequitable, even if the traditional elements of an enforceable contract, such as offer and acceptance, consideration, and specificity of terms, are present. Redistribution of wealth may be achieved, for example, through contract interpretation which is consistent with notions of substantive justice.[30] There are also doctrines such as promissory estoppel and implied contracts that, while not contractual in the strict sense of the term, enforce the terms to an extent that is equitable.

The notion of fairness becomes especially relevant when there are disparities in the information or resources available to the contracting parties.[31] Contract defenses relying upon the concept of fairness, such as unconscionability, permit a judge to rectify situations on an individual basis. Such judicial scrutiny, however, leaves the defendant vulnerable to questions regarding her competence in making important decisions. While such paternalism may be a lesser evil than enforcement of an oppressive agreement, it may have other, unintended effects such as the reinforcement of negative stereotypes.

C. Multivalue Theories of Contract Law

Multivalue theories of contract law explain that the justification for contract law derives from more than one societal value or objective. The leading multivalue theory is the "dynamic theory of contracts" proposed by Melvin Eisenberg, who explains that rather than establishing principles to support a given doctrine or theory, contract law should explain, establish, and uphold rules of behavior.[32] In other

---

[29] Morris R. Cohen, The Basis of Contract, 46 Harv. L. Rev. 553, 584-585 (1933).

[30] *See* William C. Whitford, *Symposium, The Role of the Jury (and the Fact/Law Distinction) in the Interpretation of Written Contracts*, 2001 Wisc. L. Rev. 931, 954 (2001) ("(O)ne way to counteract undue advantage gained through contract is simply to interpret contracts consistently with substantive justice, regardless of the words used in the writing. It is no news that there is a long history of such interpretations."). While wealth redistribution is not considered one of the objectives of contract law, it is often considered to be one of the goals of the law more generally. *See* Eric A. Posner, *Contract Law in the Welfare State: A Defense of the Unconscionability Doctrine, Usury Laws, and Related Limitations on the Freedom to Contract*, 24 J. Legal Stud. 283, 283-284 (1995).

[31] Whitford, *supra* note 30, at 953.

[32] As Melvin Eisenberg asserts, "Of course, doctrines have a role to play in substantive legal reasoning, but that is because of the social values that underlie doctrinal stability, not because doctrines are either self-evident

words, it should be adaptive, complex, substantive, and dynamic, rather than stringent, binary, formalistic, and static.[33] Eisenberg sets forth the principles of dynamic contract law[34] as follows:

> First, if but only if appropriate conditions are satisfied, and subject to appropriate constraints, contract law should effectuate the objectives of parties to a promissory transaction.
>
> Second, the rules that determine the conditions to, and the constraints on, the legal effectuation of the objectives of parties to promissory transactions, and the manner in which those objective are ascertained, should consist of the rules that would be made by a fully informed legislator who seeks to make the best possible rules of contract law by taking into account all relevant propositions of morality, policy, and experience (the Legislator). When more than one such proposition is relevant, the Legislator should exercise good judgment to give each proposition proper weight, and to either subordinate some propositions to others, or craft a rule that is the best vector of the propositions, considering their relative weights, and the extent to which an accommodation can be fashioned that reflects those relative weights to the fullest practicable extent.[35]

Thus, the theory of contract law is the theory of the "best content of contract law over the long run, not the theory of what contract law should be at any moment of time when institutional constraints are taken into account."[36] While dynamic contract law rejects single value theories of contracts, it considers values and ideas from differing schools of thought, even if those values conflict.[37] For example, while dynamic contract rejects the relational contract position that contract is not promise-based,[38] it supports the notion that contracts are relational. The intent and actions of the parties should therefore be viewed in the context of that relationship. Similarly, while furtherance of individual autonomy or providing economic

---

or established by deduction." Melvin Aron Eisenberg, *Symposium on Law in the Twentieth Century: The Emergence of Dynamic Contract Law*, 88 CAL. L. REV. 1743, 1753 (2000).

33 *Id.* at 1745.

34 In his article, *The Emergence of Dynamic Contract Law, supra* note 32, Eisenberg uses the term "basic contracts principle" to describe the principles that I refer to as "dynamic principles" in this chapter. I have used the term "dynamic" instead of "basic contract" to avoid confusing anyone not familiar with the discussion introduced in Eisenberg's article.

35 *Id.* at 1745.

36 *Id.* at 1747.

37 *Id.* at 1747.

38 *Id.* ("The basic contracts principle rejects the principle, most closely associated with relational contract theory, but also with the works of others, such as Atiyha, that contract law is not, or ought not be, promise based.").

incentives to contracting should not be the sole or primary objective of contract law, the values of individual autonomy and wealth maximization should be taken into account and examined in any given situation.

The dynamic contract theory proposed by Eisenberg comes closest to being a complete theory and best reflects contract law doctrine. The Restatement (Second), for example, reflects dynamic principles. Its objective is to set a normative standard, to state the "best rules," not necessarily the rules that most courts have followed.[39] It is individualized and subjective, rather than formalistic. It is dynamic because it looks at circumstances after contract formation rather than simply at the magical moment of acceptance.

The treatment of modifications illustrates the difference between classical contract law and dynamic contract law. Classical contract law held that a promise modifying a duty under a contract not fully performed lacked consideration.[40] The modern view, embodied by the Restatement (Second), states a different rule:

> A promise modifying a duty under a contract not fully performed on either side is binding
> (a) if the modification is **fair and equitable** [emphasis added] in view of circumstances not anticipated by the parties when the contract was made; or
> (b) to the extent provided by statute; or
> (c) to the extent justice requires enforcement in view of material change of position in reliance on the promise.[41]

Modern courts have increasingly adopted a view of contracts that is in accordance with dynamic principles.[42] Yet, this adoption by the courts has not been consistent or uniform in all jurisdictions.[43] Even where adoption of a particular dynamic principle is widespread, the rationale for such adoption varies.[44] Not surprisingly then, some

---

[39] Gregory E. Maggs, *Ipse Dixit: The Restatement (Second) of Contracts and the Modern Development of Contract Law*, 66 GEO. WASH. L. REV. 508, 510 (Mar. 1998).

[40] ARTHUR L. CORBIN, CORBIN ON CONTRACTS 265–66 (West 1952); 3 SAMUEL WILLISTON, THE LAW OF CONTRACTS, section 130 at 275–76 (Baker, Voorhis & Co. 1920).

[41] RESTATEMENT (SECOND) OF CONTRACTS § 89 (1981).

[42] Melvin Aron Eisenberg, *Symposium on Law in the Twentieth Century: The Emergence of Dynamic Contract Law*, 88 CAL. L. REV. 1743, 1745 (Dec. 2000). A recent survey of six sections of the Restatement that contradicted longstanding, traditional rules found that, despite the innovativeness of these sections, the majority of the courts surveyed accepted them. Maggs, *supra* note 39, at 511.

[43] "The American Law Institute's decision to include a rule in the Restatement (Second) does not mean that a majority of courts have adopted that rule. The Restatement (Second) strives to state the best rules, not necessarily the rules that most courts have followed." Maggs, *supra*, note 39, at 510.

[44] *Id.* at 527. ("First, a few courts appear to have followed the rules on grounds of precedent. Second, a few other courts appear to have followed the new rules for policy reasons. Third, several other courts adopted the

argue that the strength of a dynamic approach—its flexibility and adaptability—is also its weakness. They view the lack of predictability associated with dynamic theory as failing to provide courts with much guidance in decision making.

Such criticism of a dynamic or multivalue approach is misguided. It is not the role of theory to provide concrete guidelines in any given case; that is the province of doctrine. Theory provides the justification for doctrine, and doctrine should be justified by theory.

The problem with wrap contracts is that they fail on the level of doctrine; their existence, however, can be justified—at least to an extent—under a dynamic theory. Unfortunately, the early landmark wrap contract cases opened up a Pandora's box of doctrinal rules unmoored by theory. Remediating wrap contract doctrine and tying it back to dynamic theory is one of the objectives of chapter 11. The next chapter, chapter 3, provides the historical context in which wrap contracts developed and the policy justifications for contract enforcement. Although dynamic theory justifies the results in early, landmark wrap contract cases, it does not justify subsequent cases or the doctrine that developed in the wake of the early cases. The theory for wrap contracts exists, but the doctrine is in dire need of rehabilitation.

rules because statutes or case law require them to follow the Restatement (Second) absent contrary authority. Fourth, the remaining courts appear to have accepted the rules on grounds of convenience; rather than examine precedent or policy arguments, courts voluntarily deferred to the ALI's view of what the law should be.").

3 Contracts and Contract Law in Societal Context

THE VARIOUS THEORIES outlined in the preceding chapter illustrate the often competing objectives of contract law: to enforce the intent of the parties and to promote the security of transactions. The enforcement of promises promotes individual autonomy, yet the promotion of individual autonomy is not the sole basis for enforcement. The latter point is evident from the fact that not all promises, even if provable, are legally enforceable. Some promises simply don't rise to the level of "contract-worthiness." A promise to meet a friend for dinner, for example, is not an enforceable contract.

A contract, however, does not come into existence without a promise from at least one of the parties. A court will not extract property that is being neglected from the hands of its owner and place it in the hands of another who will better utilize it. Contracts are promises and planning tools and the objective of contract law is to both enforce the intent of the parties and ensure the security of transactions. These twin objectives of contracts are evident throughout the case law. Because contracts are not unitary in nature—and because the law itself recognizes their dual nature—both their promissory and their planning aspects must be recognized by any complete theory of contracts. Contract law involves both individual and societal interests and any given theory of contract should examine both rather than explain why one should always prevail over the other.

The duality of contracts is not surprising given their socio-political origin. As Friedrich Kessler stated:

> [O]ur legal lore of contracts reflects a proud spirit of individualism and of *laissez faire*.... Contract—the language of the cases tells us—is a private affair and not a social institution. The judicial system, therefore, provides only for their interpretation, but the courts cannot make contracts for the parties.[1]

Contract theories reflect the individual/state dichotomy, viewing the promissory exchange as rooted in individual rights or as a matter of policy, binding because the court determined it served social needs.[2] The overarching social need fulfilled by contracts is ensuring the security of transactions.

The security of transactions is considered to be of vital importance in a credit economy. The value of a credit economy is premised upon certain assumptions. The first assumption is that a promisee will rely upon the promise in some way. It also assumes that the transaction will be wealth maximizing for both parties. Finally, it assumes that the transaction will not be socially harmful or illegal. While fairness and distributive justice do not explain why we enforce contracts, they can be significant factors in determining whether a particular transaction or type of transaction is worth enforcing or "securing." In a classic law review article, Morris Cohen observed:

> A contract... between two or more individuals cannot be said to be generally devoid of all public interest. If it be of no interest, why enforce it? For note that in enforcing contracts, the government does not merely allow two individuals to do what they have found pleasant in their eyes. Enforcement, in fact, puts the machinery of the law in the service of one party against the other. When that is worthwhile and how that should be done are important questions of public policy.[3]

Given the fickle nature of human relationships and the complex nature of many commercial interactions, there is a social value in *not* enforcing every promise. As Lon Fuller explained, "There is a real need for a field of human intercourse freed from

---

[1] *See* Friedrich Kessler, *Contracts of Adhesion—Some Thoughts about Freedom of Contract*, 43 COLUM. L. REV. 629, at 630 (1943).

[2] Jay Feinman, *The Significance of Contract Theory*, 58 U. CIN. L. REV. 1283, 1286–87 (1990).

[3] Morris Cohen, *The Basis of Contract*, 46 HARV. L. REV. 553, 562 (1933).

legal restraints, for a field where men may without liability withdraw assurances they have once given. Every time a new type of promise is made enforceable, we reduce the area of this field."[4] Generally, transactions involving a trade of goods, services, and/or money are assumed to be worthy of judicial enforcement. Fuller describes as the "archetype" of an exchange one that involves a "business trade of economic values in the form of goods, services or money."[5] He adds that to "the degree that a particular case deviates from this archetype, the incentives to judicial intervention decrease, until a point is reached where relief will be denied altogether unless the attenuated element of exchange is reinforced, either on the formal side by some formal or informal satisfaction of the desiderata underlying the use of legal formalities, or on the substantive side by a showing of reliance or unjust enrichment, or of some special need for a regulation of the relations involved by private autonomy."[6]

There are nonlegal alternatives that provide many of the functions of contract and the threat of judicial intervention. For example, in nonarchetypical transactions there may be social relationships that reinforce the transaction so that there is less need for legal measures.[7] On a more abstract level, fairness is a relevant consideration in every area of the law, not just contract law, as it reflects upon the legitimacy of the courts as arbiters of justice. If, for example, the public were to perceive courts as rendering unfair decisions, this perception would undermine the legitimacy of the courts. Accordingly, the role of the *courts* is to render just and fair decisions, even if the role of *contracts* is not to promote fairness. The power of the courts should not be trumped by decisions made by private actors via a contract.

Contracts are necessary tools in a credit economy. As Morris Cohen wrote, the "development of contract is largely an incident of commercial and industrial enterprises that involve a greater anticipation of the future than is necessary in a simpler or more primitive economy."[8] In the absence of contract law, the integrity and reliability of a promise would depend upon the reputation of the promisor and nonjudicial methods of enforcement such as ostracizing promise breakers or vigilantism. The

---

[4] Lon L. Fuller, *Consideration and Form*, 41 Colum. L. Rev. 799, 813 (1941).

[5] *Id.* at 818.

[6] *Id.* at 818.

[7] Erin O'Hara explains the role of "internal," or personal, norms and social norms on behavior, including contracting behavior:

> Social norms are tied to rewards and sanctions that provide their own incentives for behavior. In contrast, internal norms of trustworthiness constrain an actor's willingness to behave opportunistically, even in the face of significant monetary or other temptations. Both social and internal norms (or their absence) thus work together to provide an "imputable reason" why it might be reasonable to predict that an actor will act in a trustworthy (or an untrustworthy) fashion. Erin Ann O'Hara, *Choice of Law for Internet Transactions: The Uneasy Case for Online Consumer Protection*, 153 U. Pa. L. Rev. 1883, 1891 (2004).

[8] Cohen, *supra* note 3, 553, at 555.

primary means of commercial exchange would be bartering goods and services. As a consequence, there would be fewer commercial transactions and no global credit economy. Without contract law, markets would remain local and contained.

Courts recognized the importance of contracts to planning and the need to ensure the security of transactions. The value of contracts to planning requires that contract law be predictable and certain. Granting the court too much discretion may discourage parties from contracting, and may reduce the reliability (and hence, value) of contracts. The familiar saying that "courts will not review the adequacy of the bargain" reflects the twin objectives of contract law to fulfill the intent of the parties and to ensure the security of transactions. Judges are reluctant to second guess the intent of the parties by revisiting the terms of the bargain. The assumption is that each party is in the best position to assess the value of the bargain to that party. The possibility of a judge remaking the parties' bargain also reduces the value of the bargain by increasing the risk of nonperformance or the risk of increased obligation.

A. Contract Law and Evolving Business Needs

Under the traditional model of contract law, parties to a contract are on roughly equal footing and can avoid oppressive contracts by shopping for terms and exercising their freedom of choice. Friedrich Kessler depicts traditional contract law as follows:

> Either party is supposed to look out for his own interests and his own protection. Oppressive bargains can be avoided by careful shopping around. Everyone has complete freedom of choice with regard to his partner in contract, and the privity-of-contract principle respects the exclusiveness of this choice. Since a contract is the result of the free bargaining of parties who are brought together by the play of the market and who meet each other on a footing of social and approximate economic equality, there is no danger that freedom of contract will be a threat to the social order as a whole.[9]

But as the business environment changed, this model of equality failed to reflect the reality of many contracting situations. As mass market sales became possible with industrialization, so did mass consumer form contracts.[10] Contracts, while important in clarifying the terms of transactions, also stall their progression. Simplifying

---

[9] Kessler, *supra* note 1, at 630.

[10] *Id.* at 631–32 (noting that mass production gave rise to the use of contracts of adhesion where the parties did not have equal bargaining power). Clayton P. Gillette notes, "Standard forms dominate both the consumer

the contracting process by discouraging or even preventing negotiations shortens the time from transaction inception to completion. Given the impracticability of negotiating, modifying, or even discussing contractual terms with each of their consumers, companies found it much more convenient and efficient to create standard terms for standard business transactions. These standard form contracts differed from traditional contracts because their terms were nonnegotiable and offered to the consumer on a "take it or leave it" basis.[11] These nonnegotiated forms became known as "contracts of adhesion" because the consumer was powerless to do anything other than adhere to their terms.[12]

Despite their shortcomings, courts and commentators generally recognized that standard form agreements were efficient and, to varying degrees, socially beneficial.[13] The Second Restatement of the Law Governing Contracts (Restatement (Second)) acknowledged that standardized agreements were essential to an economic system reliant upon mass production and distribution:

> Scarce and costly time and skill can be devoted to a class of transactions rather than to details of individual transactions.... Sales personnel and customers are freed from attention to numberless variations and can focus on meaningful choice among a limited number of significant features: transaction-type, style,

and the business environment so that only contracts that are sufficiently large, complicated, or idiosyncratic enough to justify negotiation over more than the basic terms of quantity, price, and delivery satisfy the meeting of the minds standard that underlies traditional notions of consent." Clayton P. Gillette, *Rolling Contracts as an Agency Problem*, 2004 WIS. L. REV. 679, 679.

11 Kessler, *supra* note 9 at 632.

12 Weaver v. Am. Oil Co., 276 N.E.2d 144, 147 (Ind. 1971) ("[I]n present-day commercial life the standardized mass contract has appeared. It is used primarily by enterprises with strong bargaining power and position. The weaker party, in need of the good or services, is frequently not in a position to shop around for better terms, either because the author of the standard contract has a monopoly (natural or artificial) or because all competitors use the same clauses."). The term "contracts of adhesion" at least in U.S. law, is credited to Edwin Patterson, who used it in the context of insurance policies. *See* Edwin W. Patterson, *The Delivery of a Life-Insurance Policy*, 33 HARV. L. REV. 198, at 222 (1919) ("Life insurance contracts are contracts of 'adhesion.' The contract is drawn up by the insurer and the insured, who merely 'adheres' to it, has little choice as to its terms.").

13 Kessler, *supra* note 1, at 632 ("In so far as the reduction of costs of production and distribution thus achieved is reflected in reduced prices, society as a whole ultimately benefits from the use of standard contracts."); E. ALLAN FARNSWORTH, CONTRACTS, § 4.26, at 283 (4th ed. Aspen Publishers 2004) ("Since standard forms can be tailored to fit office routines and mechanical equipment, they simplify operations and reduce costs."); Todd D. Rakoff, *Contracts of Adhesion: An Essay in Reconstruction*, 96 HARV. L. REV. 1173, 1222 (1983) ("Form documents promote efficiency within a complex organizational structure."); Robert A. Hillman, *Rolling Contracts*, Symposium: A Tribute to Professor Joseph M. Perillo, 71 FORDHAM L. REV. 743, 747 (2002) (While "[s]tandard-form exchanges obviously do not constitute the paradigm 'bargain' of classical contract law with the parties on equal footing and each term separately negotiated," they "benefit both sellers *and* consumers.").

quantity, price, or the like. Operations are simplified and costs reduced, to the advantage of all concerned.[14]

Marketplace changes brought about by the industrial revolution and the efficiency of standardized terms resulted in the proliferation of standard form contracts in consumer transactions.

There is another social benefit to contracts that has heavily influenced courts and it has less to do with transaction facilitation and more to do with development of a business and even the advancement of an entire industry. Contracts can be integral aspects of a business model and can be used to resolve a business need or address an industry-wide problem. The best early example of this may be the use of contracts to extend credit. Without contracts, we may never have heard of the Singer sewing machine or the Ford automobile.

Industrialization enabled the mass production of goods, but some of these goods were too expensive for the average consumer to purchase outright. Companies extended credit through installment payment plans to consumers, thereby enabling them to purchase items such as sewing machines and other expensive household items. Lendol Calder's engaging account of consumer credit in America, *Financing the American Dream: A Cultural History of Consumer Credit*, explains how the creation of certain costly consumer goods led to the widespread use of installment plans by the middle class, which is turn fueled the growth of industries producing those goods. Calder writes:

> While furniture dealers and building associations quietly introduced many people to the idea of installment terms, one household appliance in particular became synonymous with installment credit. This was the sewing machine. Led by the example of the I. M. Singer and Company, the sewing machine industry was largely responsible for popularizing the installment plan on a national scale. Sewing machines were the first durable, technologically complex household appliances to find a national market.[15]

Sewing machines were expensive but highly sought because they made consumers more efficient by freeing them from time and labor extensive tasks.[16] Companies implemented installment plans to enable consumers to purchase sewing machines

---

[14] Restatement (Second) of Contracts § 211 cmt. a (1981).

[15] Lendol Calder, Financing The American Dream: A Cultural History Of Consumer Credit at 162 (Princeton University Press 1999).

[16] *Id.* at 163.

on credit, which enabled consumers to use the goods while they were still paying for them. Companies had to find a way to protect their financial interests in these goods even while they relinquished physical control over them, and by standardizing terms they were able to do so in a cost-efficient and uniform manner. The growth in installment payment plans thus resulted in a concomitant increase in standard form contracts to set forth the terms of these credit-based transactions.

The popularization of installment plans fueled the growth of another industry—the automobile industry. Calder explains how the automobile greatly expanded installment credit as an integral part of a car company's business model:

> By 1924, almost three out of four new cars were bought "on time." Of the total volume of retail installment credit in that year, $670 million, or more than half, represented auto installment paper. No other consumer durable good accounted for nearly as much consumer debt. But if the automobile sold Americans on installment credit, it is also true that the installment plan sold most Americans their automobile. Without credit financing, the automobile would not so quickly have reached, and perhaps never have reached, a true mass market, and its impact on American life would have taken a very different course. Installment credit and the automobile were both cause and consequence of each other's success.[17]

Even more so than the sewing machine, the high cost of automobiles virtually guaranteed that the market for them would be small—and might disappear altogether without financing options. Contracts were used to help shape the market for automobiles. Without the ability to offer consumer financing, the automobile industry is unlikely to have developed to the extent that it has.

By enabling more consumers to purchase big-ticket items such as sewing machines and automobiles, contracts helped new industries to flourish and encouraged innovation. Extending credit to consumers on a mass scale made costly products accessible to more consumers and generated greater demand for these products, thus encouraging the further development of innovative products and the growth of new industries. The impact on society was significant. As Lendol Calder writes, "By augmenting consumer buying power, installment credit tremendously expanded the manufacturing and retail base of the national economy, to the point that today the sudden removal of credit buying from the economy would cause immediate economic collapse."[18]

---

[17] *Id.* at 184.

[18] *Id.* at 206.

The decision of a court to enforce, or invalidate, a contract thus may significantly impact whether a particular business model or industry flourishes or withers. Certain consumer goods improve efficiency and enhance the quality of life for consumers. The enforcement of contracts enabling the purchase of these goods thus provides a social benefit. Not surprisingly, contract law developed in conjunction with societal and economic changes in order to enforce executory promises that were essential to a credit-based free enterprise system.[19]

In addition, businesses may use contracts to encourage the development of a particular trade norm or practice. Legal historian Morton Horwitz writes that, until about 1830, parties could not enter into contracts to insure themselves from injuries arising out of their own negligence.[20] But after that time, courts began to allow private agreements to suspend long-standing customary duties.[21] Horwitz notes that the "foremost beneficiaries of the new legal doctrine were common carriers—mainly railroads and steamboat shippers—who sought to escape from the centuries old rule that carriers were strictly liable for the safe transit of goods."[22] It is not surprising that the shift toward permitting contractual limitations of liability for negligent acts occurred as the growth of the economy became more dependent upon fast and efficient shipping and transportation systems. One court, for example, found that to refuse to allow carriers to contract out of liability would be "an unwarrantable restriction upon trade and commerce."[23]

Mass consumer software licenses also developed out of a business concern.[24] When personal computers were first introduced in the consumer marketplace, software companies were uncertain about whether and to what extent copyright law

---

[19] Kessler, *supra* note 1, at 629 ("With the development of a free enterprise system based on an unheard of division of labor, capitalistic society needed a highly elastic legal institution to safeguard the exchange of goods and services on the market. Common law lawyers, responding to this social need, transformed 'contract' from the clumsy institution that it was in the sixteenth century into a tool of almost unlimited usefulness and pliability. Contract thus became the indispensable instrument of the enterpriser, enabling him to go about his affairs in a rational way.").

[20] Morton J. Horwitz, The Transformation of American Law, 1780–1860, at 202 (Harvard Univ. Press 1977).

[21] *Id.* at 204.

[22] *Id.* at 204.

[23] *Id.* at 206, citing Dorr v. N.J. Navig. Co., 6 N.Y. Super. Ct. Rep. (4 Sanf.) 136, 141–42 (Super Ct. N.Y. 1850).

[24] *See* Thomas M. S. Hemnes, *Restraints on Alienation, Equitable Servitudes, and the Feudal Nature of Computer Software Licensing*, 71 Denv. U. L. Rev. 577, 578 (1994) (discussing how, in the absence of protection under copyright and patent laws, "[l]awyers for software developers were therefore driven to the conclusion that trade secret law provided the only protection for their clients' programs"). Hemnes further explains that because a restriction on nondisclosure or resale on postsales copies of software may have constituted a restraint on alienation, "[t]o get around the conflict between the need for non-disclosure on the one hand, and the right of alienation on the other, lawyers invented the software license." *Id.* at 580. *See also* Mark A. Lemley, *Intellectual Property and Shrinkwrap Licenses*, 68 S. Cal. L. Rev. 1239, 1242–43 (1995) (explaining how the

protected software.[25] Even with copyright's protections, software producers were concerned about how to protect their products, which are easily reproducible and distributable.[26] The courts were sympathetic to these concerns, even if they did not always defer to them. For example, in a lengthy footnote, the court in *Step-Saver* explained the software industry's rationale for licensing, rather than selling, their product.[27] The Computer Software Rentals Amendment Act of 1990 addressed some of these concerns by prohibiting businesses from leasing software; it did not, however, prevent a consumer from selling his or her copy of a software program. With the growth of the online marketplace, consumers had greater ability to sell in the secondary marketplace after making copies for their own use. The licensing of software—rather than the selling of it—enabled software producers to bypass the first sale doctrine, which permits consumers to transfer possession of their copy of a software product.[28]

The first sale doctrine also gives software purchasers certain fair use rights under the Copyright Act, such as the right to make copies for purposes of interoperability.[29] By using a license, software companies could continue to control their product even after they relinquished physical possession of it. The licensing model, however, requires a contract. Software companies wanted the benefits of a contract without the transactional hassle of having the customer sign anything. Accordingly, they adopted the practice of bundling written terms with their products, encasing in plastic wrap both the paper containing the terms as well as the compact disc containing the software program. Thus the "shrinkwrap" license was born. While it is unclear

---

copyrightability of software remained uncertain until the 1980 amendments to the Copyright Act); Michael J. Madison, *Reconstructing the Software License*, 35 LOY. U. CHI. L.J. 275, 313–14 (2003) (noting that software developers needed a mechanism to protect their copyrights and proprietary interests while sharing their products with others); Maureen A. O'Rourke, *Defining the Boundary Between Copyright and Contract: Copyright Preemption of Software License Terms*, 45 DUKE L.J. 479, 488–90 (1995) (noting the differences between the "soft copy" and "hard copy" world and how they might compel licensing).

25 The U.S. Copyright Office permitted copyright registration on computer programs in 1964. Note, *Copyright Protection for Computer Programs*, 64 COLUM. L. REV. 1274, 1274 (1964). *See also* Robert L. Oakley, *Fairness in Electronic Contracting: Minimum Standards for Non-Negotiated Contracts*, 42 HOUS. L. REV. 1041, 1048–49 (2005) (noting the "considerable uncertainty… about the scope of copyright protection for software" which prompted software producers to use licenses to protect their interests).

26 Oakley, *supra* note 25, at 1048–49.

27 Step-Saver Data Systems, Inc. v. Wyse Technology, 939 F.2d 91, at 96, n. 7 (3rd Cir. 1991).

28 *See* Nancy S. Kim, *The Software Licensing Dilemma*, 2008 BYU L. Rev. 1103, 1111–12 (discussing the implications of the first sale doctrine on software).

29 *See id.*; Jessica Litman, *Copyright and Information Policy*, 55 LAW & CONTEMP. PROBS. 185, 197–98 (1992); David A. Rice, *Licensing the Use of Computer Program Copies and the Copyright Act First Sale Doctrine*, 30 JURIMETRICS J. 157, 163 (1990).

which company—or which company's lawyers—first invented the shrinkwrap license, its use by software companies was established by the early 1980s.[30]

B. Contracts of Adhesion

The introduction of the term "contracts of adhesion" into American jurisprudence is credited to Edwin Patterson when he described an insurance contract that an insured merely "adheres" to because he has little choice as to its terms.[31] Since then, many scholars have wrung their hands over the problem of contracts of adhesion. Friedrich Kessler described adhesion contracts as "standardized contracts" used by enterprises with stronger bargaining power:

> The weaker party, in need of the goods or services, is frequently not in a position to shop around for better terms, either because the author of the standard contract has a monopoly (natural or artificial) or because all competitors use the same clauses.... Thus, standardized contracts are frequently contracts of adhesion; they are *à prendre ou à laisser*.[32]

There is a vast academic literature on contracts of adhesion which I can scarcely do justice to in this section. One of the recurrent themes is that consent to form contracts is not voluntary; consequently, they are not expressions of individual autonomy and adhesion contracts should not be enforced. As every first year law student knows, one of the basic requirements for contract formation is mutual assent, meaning that each party agreed to the transaction. In actuality, if one did not know of a contract, or a particular contractual term, one could not have assented to it. Under the objective theory of contract law, however, the courts do not much concern themselves with whether the party had actual knowledge, and thus deliberately assented to the contractual term at issue. Instead, the courts have focused on the outward manifestations of the parties.[33] Morton Horwitz argues that the objective theory aided businesses and economic development, noting thatit was "another measure of

---

[30] Michael L. Rustad & Diane D'Angelo, *The Path of Internet Law: An Annotated Guide to Legal Landmarks*, 2011 DUKE L. & TECH. J., 12 at para. 33.

[31] Patterson, *Life-Insurance Policy*, 198, 222. In a later work, Patterson attributes the term "contracts of adhesion" to a French jurist, Raymond Saleilles. Edwin W. Patterson, *The Interpretation and Construction of Contracts*, 64 COLUM. L. REV. 833, 856 (1964).

[32] Kessler, *supra* note 1, at 632.

[33] "Agreement consists of mutual expressions; it does not consist of harmonious intentions of states of mind... we observe for judicial purpose... the conduct of the parties. We observe this conduct and we describe it as the expression of a state of mind. It is by the conduct of two parties, by their bodily manifestations, that we

the influence of commercial interests in the shaping of American law."[34] According to Horwitz, this "legal ideology of formalism, of which Williston was a leading exemplar" not only disguised "gross disparities of bargaining power under a façade of neutral and formal rules of contract law" it also enforced "commercial customs under the comforting technical rubric of 'contract interpretation.'"[35] But according to Joseph Perillo, "objective approaches have predominated in the common law of contracts since time immemorial"[36] and originate from "the legal profession's distrust of the testimony of parties."[37]

Contracts of adhesion pose a quandary for courts. A finding of lack of assent means that no contract was formed. Standard form contracts are efficient and facilitate the making of exchanges. Perhaps unsurprisingly, courts that wish to uphold a particular transaction or type of transaction have been more willing to find assent even in the absence of bargaining power. Assent in the context of adhesive contracts thus became construed to mean acquiescence rather than active agreement. While one of the objectives of contract law is universally acknowledged to be the promotion of individual autonomy, assent is often stripped of any requirement of volition or desire to enter into a contract. While such a passive notion of assent in cases involving adhesion contracts seems inconsistent with the very reason why we enforce contracts, in fact it reflects another of contract law's goals, which is to encourage and facilitate economic transactions. As previously discussed, contracts play an essential role in facilitating transactions because they increase trust, enhance reliability, and facilitate planning. The facilitation of transactions is socially beneficially because it maximizes economic gains for each of the contracting parties. Furthermore, contracts are often an essential part of a company's business model. A failure to recognize contracts of adhesion would mean slowing down and perhaps even stifling the growth of a valuable industry.[38]

---

must determine the existence of what is called agreement. This is what we meant by the anciently-honored term 'meeting of the minds.' This is what is meant by mutual assent." ARTHUR L. CORBIN, CORBIN ON CONTRACTS, § 9, p. 14 (one-volume ed., West Publishing 1952).

[34] HORWITZ, *supra* note 20, at 201.

[35] *Id.* at 201.

[36] Joseph M. Perillo, *The Origins of the Objective Theory of Contract Formation and Interpretation*, 69 FORDHAM L. REV. 427, 428 (2000).

[37] *Id.* at 477.

[38] According to Lendol Calder:

> "Before the sewing machine, sewing garments by hand was slow, tedious work. To make the average shirt required 20,620 stitches; at 35 stitches per minute, a competent seamstress completed one shirt in ten to fourteen hours of labor.[21] At home, where most clothing was made before the Civil War, the drudgery of hand-sewing was mitigated by the companionship of the sewing circle, but no remedy existed for the smarting eyes, tired back, and aching fingers brought on by hours of sewing—until sewing machine agents began selling their machines. A sewing machine operating at three thousand stitches per minute

The objective theory means that nondrafting parties have a "duty to read" the contract that they sign. The Farnsworth treatise states that a signatory to an agreement

> "is regarded as manifesting assent to it and may not later complain about not having read or understood it, even if the agreement is on the other party's standard form… . . And since the objective theory of contracts imposes no requirement that one intend or even understand the legal consequences of one's actions, one is not entitled to relief merely because one neither read the standard form nor considered the legal consequence of adhering to it."[39]

The Calamari and Perillo treatise notes that the duty to read "applies even without a signature if the acceptance of a document, which purports to be a contract implies assent to its terms."[40]

Another recurring theme in scholarship about adhesion contracts is that the benefits of such contracts are one-sided and that they often contain oppressive and unnecessary terms. Todd Rakoff, for example, observes that the unilateral drafting process may result in a document that is "unintelligible even to the normal businessman."[41]

Lucian Bebchuck and Richard Posner, however, provide the following justification for one-sided terms:

> [O]pportunistic buyers might try to use "balanced" terms to press for benefits and advantages beyond those that the terms were actually intended to provide. Slanting the terms of the contract in favor of the seller is… a way of redressing the balance. The existence of a one-sided contract does not imply that the *transaction* will be one-sided, but only that the seller will have discretion with respect to how to treat the consumer.[42]

---

could assemble a shirt in an hour or less, and with neater results. In fact, machine production of garments transformed the social meaning of clothing in the nineteenth century, making stylish, handsome clothing available to virtually everyone. It also fostered the organization of a large garment industry that could boast of fit and durability as well as style. Very quickly the production of clothing, especially men's apparel, was removed from the home and relocated to the factory and sweatshop. Thus were fulfilled the early predictions of Scientific American, that the sewing machine would create a "social revolution."" *Id. supra* note 15, at 163

39 Farnsworth, *supra* note 13, at § 4.26, p. 287.

40 Joseph M. Perillo, Calamari & Perillo on Contracts, § 9.41 at 342 (West 6th ed.2009).

41 Rakoff, *supra* note 13 at 1221–22.

42 Lucian A. Bebchuck & Richard A. Posner, *One-Sided Contracts in Competitive Consumer Markets*, 104 Mich. L. Rev. 827, 828 (2006).

Under this view, consumers (at least fair-minded ones) are not actually hurt by oppressive terms because businesses, at least in competitive consumer markets, will not enforce them without good reason.

But one-sided terms should raise concerns even if they are unlikely to be enforced. While most consumers do not read contracts prior to entering into standard transactions, many do so *afterward*. A contract may be used to deter litigation as much as it is used to win litigation. A consumer might read the contract after a problem with the transaction arises and believe that the egregious term is enforceable—and thus decline to have the grievance redressed. A consumer who does complain to the company may have a company representative direct the consumer's attention to the oppressive term in the relevant section of the contract. Many consumers will likely resign themselves at this point, believing that what the contract says is "the law." They may moan and complain, but many consumers won't sue. The cost of litigation is too high for most consumers and the expected benefits too low. The most likely plaintiff then may be an opportunistic one or one that is part of a class action lawsuit. Wrap contracts, however, often contain class action waivers or mandatory arbitration provisions so a court may not hear cases brought by fair-minded, good faith plaintiffs. Consequently, the cases that courts do end up hearing may very well be from opportunistic plaintiffs.

A court may be reluctant to find unconscionable a contract term that—while egregious on its face—is being used to stop an opportunistic plaintiff. Thus, the company's overreaching terms prevail, not because they are reasonable or fair, but because they prevent bad behavior on the part of the plaintiff. The decision in a case against a bad faith plaintiff then establishes a precedent that the substantive term is not "unconscionable" which can be used against good faith plaintiffs in subsequent cases.

A contract is created by the parties and not imposed by the state. The coercive power of the state in enforcing private agreements is justified because the courts are simply enforcing the parties' intent. Where contracts are entered into unwillingly or unwittingly, however, the coercive power of the state no longer seems justified; on the contrary, it is oppressive. Thus, contracts may contribute to a feeling of helplessness on the part of consumers who are deemed to have agreed to terms that are unilaterally imposed and of which they are often unaware.

Contracts are supposed to be economically efficient because the parties are in the best position to assess the value of a particular good or service—its "value." Parties are presumed to have entered into contracts after assessing the risks and benefits of a transaction. Their objective is to maximize the surplus that the deal can create. If, however, a party is unaware of the relevant information (for example, because it hidden or it is unduly burdensome to access), the decision to enter into the transaction is not an informed one. It neither reflects an accurate assessment of the value of the transaction nor the risks and benefits of the transaction to that party. The contract then is not the result of rational, utility-maximizing actors, but of impulsive or unwitting ones.

Some contracts scholars defend standard form contracts by stating that if the majority of consumers don't like certain terms, they will push back. But given the coordination problems associated with mobilizing individuals who are strangers to each other and dispersed across the globe, they may be unable to articulate a clear, unified message. More troubling, mass-scale dissatisfaction tends to gain momentum and publicity only after mass-scale societal harm has already occurred. The "market will respond" argument is a regressive argument, not a progressive, improving one.

C. Function, Fluidity, and Instructive Contracts

There are several assumptions made in contract law. The first is that enabling individuals to allocate their personal affairs—their "legal entitlements"—is good and valuable. A free society values individual liberty to make decisions more highly than it does the decision itself. In other words, it doesn't matter so much whether an individual makes the best, or even a good, deal—what matters is that the individual is free to make the deal. This value itself is based upon an assumption—that the decision is the result of an individual's free will. Inherent in the notion of free will is that of choice—the individual had the choice to accept or decline the agreement.

Another assumption made by contract law is that transactions or exchanges are beneficial for society. Transactions would not be encouraged nor their enforcement worth securing unless they were generally a net positive for society. Transactions are generally thought beneficial in a credit economy because resources can be optimally utilized, their value maximized. If, for example, I think your bicycle is worth at least $200 and you would rather have the $200 than the bike, we are each able to put our resources (my money and your bike) to a better use by agreeing to an exchange.

Furthermore, goods are less likely to sit idle. For example, if someone wants to open a home furnishing store, he can borrow the money rather than having to wait until he has the cash he needs. He is able to purchase lamps from a supplier and sell them to a customer. The lamps are put to use rather than sitting in the supplier's storeroom. In turn, the supplier can manufacture more lamps, keeping her workers employed. Her workers can continue to pay rent and buy food, and in this way the wheels of commerce keep spinning and the economy expands.

Securing transactions by enforcing contracts is essential in a credit economy. Legal channels for redress also discourage vigilantism. As previously discussed, contracts can even be used to promote business innovation by establishing limits and contours to new business models.

Contracts provide a channeling function and legitimize a transaction. A contract is a sign that the interaction should be taken seriously, that it is a legal matter, and that the parties have accepted it as such. Even though the customer may have no recollection of ever having agreed to the contract, the contract often provides a resolution should conflicts later arise. A quick reminder and reference to a relevant provision often serves to deter further action on the part of the consumer.

Closely related to this legitimizing function is what I refer to as the" instructive" function of contracts—the use of contracts as reference sources or manuals. In this capacity, the contract's function is to instruct or inform the non-drafting party.

Parties enter into agreements for a variety of reasons—to reallocate risks, restructure or define relationships, and change default rules that would otherwise apply to their relationships. Contracts can be transactional or relational; they can affect one isolated exchange or provide the terms for an ongoing relationship. They can also be used to avoid or minimize conflicts that may arise during the relationship or after the transaction. At the outset, it is important to clarify that contracts may, and typically do, serve more than one function. A long-term commercial lease between two sophisticated parties is a promise to fulfill certain obligations, a tool to plan future business-related activities, a set of instructions, and a way to legitimate and define a relationship. The essential nature of a contract, however, is typically understood as either interrelational or transaction-based.

The function of a contract is related to its form. The form of a contract captures and reflects its role in the interaction between the parties. My designation of a contract provision as "instructive" pertains to its function whereas a designation of a contract as "digital" or "paper," "adhesive" or "negotiated," pertains to form.

Purely instructive contracts are typically adhesive and often do not require a signature. Adhesive contracts, however, are not always purely instructive. Rather, adhesive contracts can be placed upon a spectrum. They are at their most legitimate when they are purely instructive, and they are least legitimate when they purport to impose affirmative obligations upon the adherent.

In their instructive capacity, adhesive contracts provide information about the product or services being sold and the obligations of each party, without imposing obligations unrelated to the use of the product or services. Adhesive contracts which are purely instructive may be referred to as policies, guidelines or codes of conduct. Significantly, the drafter may not even need the consent of the non-drafting party in order to impose and enforce those terms. The power of the drafting party to impose certain obligations arises from proprietary rights; they are not created via contract. The legitimacy of the obligations thus does not derive from the legitimacy of the assent. These purely instructive "contracts" are contractual only in that they seek the non-drafting party's acknowledgement to the existence of terms, not because the drafting party would be otherwise prevented from unilaterally imposing the terms.

A company's return policy is an example of a provision that does not require a consumer's consent, but to which a company may seek agreement. A company may have a thirty day return policy on regular priced items and a no return policy on sale items. It may seek a customer's agreement in advance to avoid later disputes and to set customer expectations. It does not, however, need the customer's consent to implement the policy (unless it is required by legislation).

Adhesive contracts differ from negotiated agreements because of how they affect and reflect the intent of the parties and their reasonable expectations. Negotiated agreements are usually tools to coordinate and plan activities; nonnegotiated contracts, however, are (or should be) primarily informational and provide instruction on how to use a product or service. The former requires the participation and input of both parties but the latter does not.

An adhesive contract is predominantly unidirectional, from the drafter to the nondrafting party. Because the adhering party is not even aware of their terms, there is no planning or promising function performed by these contracts, and often no channeling or even legitimating function. Given that there is a general understanding that the terms go unread, common sense dictates that one cannot actually promise to do anything without being aware of what that commitment is. Adhesive contracts nevertheless have been deemed to be legally binding commitments.

Adhesive contracts may be an integral part of a company's—indeed, an industry's—business model. While consumers may not read them prior to assenting to their terms, they may read them afterward, when a question or conflict arises. This enables companies to set expectations to avoid future conflict.[43]

For example, when a consumer buys an iPad, she is required to accept the terms of an online agreement. Given its length (over 15,000 words), and the circumstances under which she is presented with the contract (after she has waited an hour in a crowded Apple store to make her purchase, paid for the product, and now eagerly waits for the sales "Genius" to hand it over to her so that she can start playing with it), it is unlikely that she will read the agreement before accepting its terms. This doesn't mean, however, that she will *never* read the contract. In fact, she is likely to refer to it at some point after she has made her purchase, such as when a problem arises with the product. She may first refer to the contract when she is unable to get the product to function as expected or when she purchases a related item, such as a song on iTunes.

---

[43] Shmuel I. Becher & Esther Unger-Aviram, *Myth and Reality on Consumer Contracting Behavior*, *available at* http://papers.ssrn.com/sol3/papers.cfm?abstract_id=1443908. The study conducted by the authors indicated that "most potential consumers report a clear tendency to read [standard form contracts] as a first reaction once a legal dispute arises." *Id.* at 15.

She may, for instance, refer to the agreement when she accidentally downloads an entire album from the iTunes store when she only meant to sample one song. She may refer to the relevant provision in the contract, which states that all purchases are final. In the event that she contacts Apple Support rather than the contract, she may be told to refer to her contract. The directive to refer to the relevant contract provision lends authority to the company policy, buttressing the company's position.

Instead of contacting the company directly, she may decide to look for the answer elsewhere on the Apple website, such as on the "Communities" page. When she types "Accidental download" into the search box at the top of the page, she will find that there are many users who have had similar problems. She may feel comforted knowing that she is not the only one to have done this.

At this point, I should confess that I know she will do and feel these things because I was that user. So—could I get a refund? The answer appears to be completely at Apple's discretion. Based upon the Community responses, Apple will refund a request by someone who has never made a previous request. Many of the Community members referenced the contractual provision that states: "All sales are final."

An instructive contract leaves the company with room to maneuver. It typically contains terms that are maximally protective of the company but which are subject to discretionary and selective enforcement. Interestingly, a harsh contract term may actually benefit a company that chooses not to enforce it. For example, where a user had the experience of receiving a discretionary refund, the response on Apple's Community message board was extremely positive:

> Wow! They actually refunded me! Thank you so much Apple, for going against your terms of service policy![44]

Adhesive contracts are fluid; because their terms are unilaterally imposed, their nature shifts with the nondrafting party's awareness. They can be binding the way employment handbooks can be, depending upon their wording. They can be unilateral or bilateral contracts, depending on the obligations they contain and the intent of the parties.

For example, an agreement that outlines the scope of license may be interpreted as a unilateral contract, which the nondrafting party accepts by using the software with knowledge of the license. If, however, the agreement imposes certain obligations upon the licensee, such as the obligation to notify the licensor of bugs, it may be construed as a bilateral contract *provided that* the licensee intends to accept the agreement. In some cases, an instructive contract is not a contract at all, but a quasi-contract which

[44] Apple Support Communities Discussions, https://discussions.apple.com/message/1469432#1469432 (last visited Jan. 28, 2013).

is enforceable to prevent injustice. This would be the case where a reasonable person in the adherent's position would not have known of the terms. In that case, only the terms which are substantively justifiable should be enforced as equity requires. The right to establish the scope of the license terms arises from the licensor's proprietary rights, not from the contract. The right to impose additional obligations, however, depends upon the existence of consent and the intent of the parties.

Unfortunately, courts have failed to recognize the fluid nature of instructive contracts, typically ruling that they are bilateral contracts which are enforceable against all consumers or against none. Such a rigid perspective, however, is contrary to what courts are supposed to do in contract disputes—enforce the reasonable expectations of the parties. Corbin described a reasonable expectation as "one that most people would have; and the promise must be one that most people would perform."[45] The standard of reasonable expectations considers intent but tempers the problems of subjectivity with countervailing considerations. The "reasonableness" in "reasonable expectations" guards against falsehoods and typically assumes industry and social norms. The standard of reasonable expectations captures this careful balancing of intent with the need for ensuring the security of transactions. In some cases, the consumer may not be aware of the contract until after interacting with the website. In other cases, the consumer may knowingly enter into the contract. In yet other cases, the consumer may be completely unaware that a contract exists or refuse to reengage with the website after realizing that terms apply. While beneficial to businesses, to assume all adherents are in the same position as the most knowledgeable and consenting one betrays the objectives of contract law. To categorize all adhesive contracts as bilateral contracts ignores the complexities and realities of mass consumer contracting. Adhesive contracts may be valid as a contracting form—unilaterally imposed and nonnegotiated though they may be—but that should not mean that all adhesive standard forms are in fact contracts; nor does it mean that because some adherents have assented, it is reasonable or fair to assume that all others have done or will do the same.

---

[45] Corbin on Contracts, *supra* note 33, § 1, p. 2.

4 The Rise of Wrap Contracts
THE EARLY CASES

COURTS HAVE HANDLED doctrinal issues created by wrap forms by looking at each of the three primary types of wrap contracts: shrinkwraps, clickwraps, and browsewraps. Some commentators argue that the wrap terminology is needlessly confusing. Juliet Moringiello and William Reynolds, who have conducted several annual surveys of electronic contracting cases, find the distinction between clickwraps and browsewraps "meaningless," noting that courts have begun to reject the distinction between clickwraps and browsewraps in favor of an unconscionability-based approach.[1]

I employ the wrap terminology here for several reasons. The first is descriptive ease. To describe a particular type of agreement as a clickwrap or browsewrap explains—at least to a certain extent—how the terms were presented. The second reason is to emphasize that form matters. A browsewrap is perceived differently by

[1] Juliet M. Moringiello and William L. Reynolds, *From Lord Coke to Internet Privacy: The Past, Present and Future of Electronic Contracting*, 72 Md. L. Rev. 452, at 468 (2013).

a user than is a clickwrap—or a shrinkwrap, tapwrap, or ripwrap. In some cases, the difference in perception is of little or no consequence; in other cases, the form affects user cognition. Finally, the doctrinal issues associated with each wrap form differ. The courts often refer to the distinction between and among the various wrap forms, which has—for better or worse—affected the outcome of cases.

A. Shrinkwraps

A shrinkwrap refers to a contract that is wrapped in plastic with a compact disc containing a software program.[2] Does the tearing open of that plastic constitute assent? The first courts to address the issue indicated that it does not. In *Step-Saver Data Systems, Inc. v. Wyse Technology*, the Third Circuit held that a "box-top" license was invalid under the Uniform Commercial Code (U.C.C.).[3] The court stated that the contract for the sale of the software product was made when the product was purchased. Accordingly, section 2–207 of the U.C.C. governed. The court of appeals further stated:

> Under section 2–207, an additional term detailed in the box-top license will not be incorporated into the parties's contract if the term's addition to the contract would materially alter the parties's agreement.... Therefore, under UCC § 2–207(2)(b), the disclaimer of warranty and limitation of remedies terms of the box-top license did not become a part of the parties's agreement.... Because the warranty disclaimer and limitation of remedies terms would materially alter the parties's agreement, these terms did not become a part of the parties's agreement.[4]

In another case, *Vault Corp. v. Quaid Software, Ltd.*,[5] the plaintiff sought to enjoin the defendant from selling a program that unlocked the plaintiff's software program and thus permitted the making of copies. The defendant had created its program by purchasing the plaintiff's software and decompiling and reverse engineering the code. The plaintiff claimed that the defendant had violated a state statute, the Louisiana Software License Enforcement Act, and the terms of the plaintiff's shrinkwrap,

---

[2] A shrinkwrap license is an example of a "rolling contract." In a rolling contract situation, the customer orders and pays for the goods before having an opportunity to review the contract terms, which are included with the product. *See* Robert A. Hillman, *Rolling Contracts*, 71 FORDHAM L. REV. 743, 744 (2002).

[3] Step-Saver Data Sys., Inc. v. Wyse Tech., 939 F.2d 91 (3d Cir. 1991).

[4] *Id.* at 105–106.

[5] Vault Corp. v. Quaid Software, Ltd., 847 F.2d 255 (5th Cir. 1988).

which prohibited decompiling and reverse engineering. The district court held that Vault's license agreement was "a contract of adhesion which could only be enforceable if the Louisiana Software License Enforcement Act is a valid and enforceable statute [citations omitted]."[6] The court found that the statute was not enforceable because it was preempted by federal copyright law. The Fifth Circuit agreed with the district court that the Louisiana statute was preempted because it touched upon federal copyright law. It did not address the enforceability of the shrinkwrap agreement as a separate contract issue.

If early cases expressed doubt about the enforceability of shrinkwrap licenses, the landmark case of *ProCD, Inc. v. Zeidenberg*[7] paved the way for a slew of cases upholding them. The court in *ProCD* concluded that "[s]hrinkwrap licenses are enforceable unless their terms are objectionable on grounds applicable to contracts in general (for example, if they violate a rule of positive law, or if they are unconscionable)."[8] The plaintiff, ProCD, compiled information from more than 3,000 telephone directories into a computer database and sold its database to the general public for personal use at a significantly lower price than it did to manufacturers and retailers. Judge Easterbrook, writing the opinion for the Seventh Circuit, discussed the financial benefits to consumers of ProCD's price discrimination policy and noted that the outside of each box stated that the software was subject to enclosed license terms. The license limited use of the program to noncommercial purposes and was contained in the user's manual and appeared on the user's screen when the software was utilized. The defendant, Matthew Zeidenberg, formed a company to resell the information contained in ProCD's database product on the Internet, thereby undermining ProCD's business. Zeidenberg argued that ProCD made an offer by placing the software in stores, which he "accepted" by purchasing the software.[9] The Seventh Circuit disagreed, instead finding that

> ProCD proposed a contract that a buyer would accept by *using* the software after having an opportunity to read the license at leisure. This Zeidenberg did. He had no choice, because the software splashed the license on the screen and would not let him proceed without indicating acceptance.[10]

---

[6] Vault Corp. v. Quaid Software, Ltd., 655 F. Supp. 750 at 761 (1987) (E.D. La. 1987) *aff'd*, 847 F.2d 255, 270 (5th Cir. 1988)).

[7] ProCD, Inc. v. Zeidenberg, 86 F.3d 1447 (7th Cir. 1996).

[8] *Id.* at 1449.

[9] *Id.* at 1450.

[10] *Id.* at 1452.

The opinion continues that while "a contract can be, and often is, formed simply by paying the price and walking out of the store," U.C.C. section 2-204(1) permits contracts to be formed in a "different way" and "without protest Zeidenberg agreed."[11] U.C.C. section 2-204(1) states: "A contract for sale of goods may be made in any manner sufficient to show agreement, including conduct by both parties which recognizes the existence of such a contract." Yet, the referenced conduct occurred after the acts that would typically constitute a completed transaction—in other words, Zeidenberg's act of using the software and *not* returning it is one that, in the minds of a typical consumer, does not signal contract acceptance. It is to be expected that a consumer would use the software that he has just purchased. Yet, the court constructs a legal fiction that an unlikely-to-be-read notice posted outside of the box that indicates there are terms *inside* the box creates that state of affairs whereby the parties have tacitly agreed to a "different way" to form the contract.

Easterbrook also declined to apply section U.C.C .§ 2-207 and its rules governing offer and acceptance claiming that the section does not apply to single-form contracts. Yet, there is nothing in the section itself to lead to that conclusion, and at least one court has disagreed.[12]

Under the *ProCD* analysis, assent to the terms of a shrinkwrap license is presumed and the burden is placed upon the consumer to disaffirm assent. In other words, Judge Easterbrook's analysis places an affirmative obligation upon the consumer to establish nonconsent to the terms of the shrinkwrap agreement, even though under contract law silence or inaction typically does not constitute acceptance. For example, if I say to you, "I offer you my car for $20,000," and you don't reply, I can't claim that your silence was an acceptance of my offer. But in *ProCD*, the court construed Zeidenberg's failure to return the software as assent, even though a consumer might have failed to return the software because it was just too much trouble to drive back to the store.

Many scholars[13] have criticized the Seventh Circuit's analysis of contract formation doctrine in both *ProCD* and a follow-up case, *Hill v. Gateway 2000, Inc.*,[14] which extended the reasoning in a case clearly involving a sale of goods.[15] Despite

---

[11] *Id.*

[12] *See* Klocek v. Gateway, Inc., 104 F. Supp. 2d 1332, 1339 (D. Kan. 2000) (stating that "nothing" in the language of U.C.C. § 2-207 "precludes application in a case which involves only one form").

[13] A sample of these critiques include Jean Braucher, *Delayed Disclosure in Consumer E-Commerce as an Unfair and Deceptive Practice*, 46 WAYNE L. REV. 1805, 1823–1827 (2000); William Lawrence, *Rolling Contracts Rolling over Contract Law*, 41 SAN DIEGO L. REV. 1099, 1109 (2004); Stewart Macaulay, *Freedom from Contract: Solutions in Search of a Problem?*, 2004 WIS. L. REV. 777; and Deborah W. Post, *Dismantling Democracy: Common Sense and the Contract Jurisprudence of Frank Easterbrook*, 16 TOURO L. REV. 1205 (2000).

[14] Hill v. Gateway 2000, 105 F. 3d 1147 (7th Cir. 1997).

[15] In *Hill v. Gateway 2000*, Judge Easterbrook stated, "Plaintiffs ask us to limit *ProCD* to software, but where's the sense in that? *ProCD* is about the law of contract, not the law of software." *Id.* at 1149.

this criticism, only a minority of courts have rejected *ProCD*'s analysis,[16] while the majority of courts have adopted it and upheld the validity of shrinkwrap licenses. Shrinkwrap licenses, in turn, paved the way for other nontraditional standard form agreements, such as clickwraps and browsewraps.

B. Clickwraps

The agreement in *ProCD* accompanied the purchase of software contained in a box, but the case opened the door for another innovative contracting form, the "clickwrap" license. Clickwrap agreements do not permit a user to progress until and unless the user clicks on a box containing the words "I agree" or some similar expression of agreement. In some ways, clickwrap agreements are less problematic than shrinkwrap agreements for the simple reason that a user undertakes a physical act—pressing on the mouse to click on the "I agree" icon—which can be interpreted as a manifestation of consent.

One of the first cases to address the issue of clickwrap agreements, *CompuServe, Inc. v. Patterson*,[17] involved a forum selection clause. The defendant, Patterson, was a resident of Houston, Texas, who claimed never to have visited Ohio.[18] The plaintiff was CompuServe, a computer information service headquartered in Columbus, Ohio.[19] Patterson subscribed to CompuServe's computing and information services via the Internet and placed certain computer software products as "shareware" on the CompuServe system for others to use and purchase.[20] When Patterson became a shareware provider, he entered into a "Shareware Registration Agreement" (SRA) with CompuServe.[21] Pursuant to the SRA, CompuServe provided its subscribers access to the shareware that Patterson created as an independent contractor.[22] The SRA incorporated by reference two other documents, the CompuServe Service Agreement (Service Agreement) and the Rules of Operation. Both the SRA and the Service Agreement stated that they were entered into in Ohio.[23] The Service Agreement further provided that its terms were governed by and construed in

---

[16] *See* Klocek v. Gateway, Inc., 104 F. Supp. 2d 1332, 1340–41 (D. Kan. 2000); Wachter Mgmt. Co. v. Dexter & Chaney, Inc., 144 P.3d 747, 754 (Kan. 2006) (distinguishing *ProCD v. Zeidenberg* and *Hill v. Gateway 2000* because they were nonnegotiated contracts and not accepted until after consumers opened packaging).

[17] Compuserve, Inc. v. Patterson, 89 F.3d. 1257 (6th Cir. 1996).

[18] *Id.* at 1260.

[19] *Id.*

[20] *Id.*

[21] *Id.*

[22] *Id.*

[23] *Id.*

accordance with Ohio law.[24] The court noted that the SRA required Patterson to type "AGREE" at various points in the document "[i]n recognition of [his] online agreement to all the above terms and conditions."[25]

Patterson marketed his software for several years on CompuServe's system.[26] CompuServe later began to market a similar software product, which gave rise to Patterson's allegations of trademark infringement. CompuServe filed a declaratory judgment in the federal district court for the Southern District of Ohio, relying on the court's diversity subject matter jurisdiction.[27] Patterson filed a motion to dismiss on several grounds, including lack of personal jurisdiction.[28] The district court granted Patterson's motion to dismiss for lack of personal jurisdiction. On appeal, the Sixth Circuit addressed the issue of whether Patterson's contacts with Ohio were sufficient to support the district court's exercise of personal jurisdiction.[29] The Sixth Circuit referred to the Internet as representing "perhaps the latest and greatest manifestation of... historical globe-shrinking trends."[30] The court assumed the enforceability of the clickwrap agreement, noting that Patterson "entered into a written contract with CompuServe which provided for the application of Ohio law," and stated that he "then purposefully perpetuated the relationship with CompuServe via repeated communications with its system in Ohio."[31] The court emphasized that Patterson was "far more than a purchaser of services; he was a third-party provider of software who used CompuServe, which is located in Columbus, to market his wares in Ohio and elsewhere."[32] The court stated that while "merely entering into a contract with CompuServe would not, without more, establish that Patterson had minimum contacts with Ohio," that act *in conjunction* with Patterson's placement of his software product into the stream of commerce and other factors established sufficient contact to establish jurisdiction.[33] Patterson manifested actual assent to the SRA first at his computer in Texas, which was then transmitted to CompuServe in Ohio.[34]

---

24 *Id.*

25 *Id.* at 1260–61.

26 *Id.*at 1261.

27 *Id.* CompuServe sought a declaration that it had not infringed any common law trademarks of Patterson, or of Patterson's company, FlashPoint Development, and that it was not otherwise guilty of unfair or deceptive trade practice. *Id.*

28 *Id.*

29 *Id.*

30 *Id.* at 1262.

31 *Id.* at 1264.

32 *Id.*

33 *Id.* at 1265.

34 *Id.* at 1261.

In another early case, *Caspi v. Microsoft Network, LLC*,[35] the Superior Court of New Jersey upheld a forum selection clause in a clickwrap agreement. *Caspi* involved a class action complaint against Microsoft arising out of Microsoft's alleged practice of "unilateral negative option billing."[36] The named plaintiffs were residents of different states, and they purported to represent a nationwide class of 1.5 million MSN members. Microsoft moved to dismiss the complaint for lack of jurisdiction and improper venue by reason of a forum selection clause, which was in MSN's scrollable clickwrap membership agreement.[37] The forum selection/choice of law clause provided that the governing law was that of the state of Washington, and each member consents "to the exclusive jurisdiction and venue of courts in King County, Washington in all disputes arising out of or relating to your use of MSN or your MSN membership."[38]

Courts generally uphold clickwrap agreements, although many commentators find their "take-it-or-leave-it" nature troubling. Courts construe the act of clicking as a manifestation of consent. Browsewrap agreements, however, are a different story.

C. Browsewraps

Browsewrap agreements are terms and conditions that are posted on a website or web page (or other means by which terms are digitally accessible to the user). On most websites, they are indicated as a hyperlink at the top or bottom of the page, with words such as "Legal Terms," "Terms of Use," or "Conditions of Use." Browsewraps do not require users to affirmatively manifest consent. In most cases, the browsewrap includes a statement that the user's continued use of the website or the downloaded software manifests assent to those terms. The user is deemed to have manifested consent if she continues on the website after having had notice of the terms. Notice can be either actual or constructive.

In *Pollstar v. Gigmania, Ltd.*,[39] the court refused to enforce the terms of an online license agreement because the link to it was hard to read and unidentifiable as a hyperlink. The court agreed with the defendant that "many visitors to the site may not be aware of the license agreement. Notice of the license agreement is provided by small gray text on a gray background."[40] Notably, that court did not rule that the

---

35 Caspi v. Microsoft Network, 732 A.2d 528 (N.J. Super. Ct. App. Div. 1999).

36 Under this practice, Microsoft without notice or permission from MSN members, unilaterally increased membership fees attributing the increase to changes in the service plans. *Id.* at 529.

37 *Id.* at 529.

38 *Id.*

39 Pollstar v. Gigmania, 170 F. Supp. 2d 974 (E.D. Cal. 2000).

40 *Id.* at 980-981.

browsewrap form was unenforceable, only that it was unenforceable the way it was presented in this particular case—in small gray text on a gray background, without underlining, and with other colored text that was not hyperlinked and which "may confuse visitors who may then think that all colored small text, regardless of color, do not link the homepage to a different web page."[41] The court stated that it "hesitates to declare the invalidity and unenforceability of the browse wrap license agreement at this time."[42] It referred to the Seventh Circuit's decision in *ProCD* and stated that as "people sometimes enter into a contract by using a service without first seeing the terms—the browser wrap license agreement may be arguably valid and enforceable."[43]

In another early case, *Specht v. Netscape Communications Corp.*,[44] the Second Circuit refused to enforce an arbitration clause in a browsewrap agreement because users were able to download the free software without indicating assent or acknowledging the license agreement. Furthermore, in order to view the license terms, the users were required to scroll down *past* the software download button and then access the agreement by clicking on a hyperlink. The court held that "a reasonably prudent offeree" would not have known of the existence of the license agreement as the offer did not carry an "immediately visible notice of the existence of license terms or require unambiguous manifestation of assent to those terms."[45] Thus, the court tied the manifestation of consent to notice of the terms, finding that the act of downloading software could not be construed as manifesting assent if the terms were not immediately visible.

The case that may have had the most influence in persuading subsequent courts to enforce the browsewrap form was *Register.com v. Verio, Inc.*[46] In that case, the Second Circuit found that Verio's continued use of Register.com's WHOIS database constituted consent to Verio's terms of use, expressly rejecting Verio's argument that they were not enforceable because the user had not clicked an "I agree" icon. The defendant Verio sold a variety of website design, development, and operation services which competed with the plaintiff Register.com's website development business. Verio obtained daily updates of information from Register.com's computers relating to newly registered domain names via an automated software program. Verio's practice of e-mail solicitations to those registered names was inconsistent with the

---

[41] *Id.* at 981.
[42] *Id.* at 982.
[43] *Id.*
[44] Specht v. Netscape Communs. Corp., 306 F.3d 17 (2d Cir. 2002).
[45] *Id.* at 31.
[46] Register.com, Inc. v. Verio, Inc., 356 F.3d 393 (2d Cir. 2004).

terms of the restrictive legend Register.com attached to its responses to Verio's queries. Some of the recipients of Verio's solicitations believed they were coming from Register.com (or an affiliate), and were sent in violation of the registrant's election not to receive solicitations from Register.com.[47] When Register.com sent Verio a cease-and-desist letter, Verio refused to comply. Verio claimed that it never became contractually bound to the conditions imposed by Register.com's restrictive legend because, in the case of each query Verio made, the legend did not appear until after Verio had submitted the query and received the WHOIS data.[48] Verio contended that it did not receive legally enforceable notice of the conditions Register.com intended to impose and, therefore, should not be deemed to have taken WHOIS data from Register.com's systems subject to Register.com's conditions. The court rejected Verio's argument, stating that

> Verio's argument might well be persuasive if its queries addressed to Register's computers had been sporadic and infrequent. If Verio had submitted only one query, or even if it had submitted only a few sporadic queries, that would give considerable force to its contention that it obtained the WHOIS data without being conscious that Register intended to impose conditions, and without being deemed to have accepted Register's conditions. But Verio was daily submitting numerous queries, each of which resulted in its receiving notice of the terms Register exacted. Furthermore, Verio admits that it knew perfectly well what terms Register demanded. Verio's argument fails.[49]

In other words, even if Verio was not aware of Register.com's terms of use at the time it entered into the transaction, it subsequently became aware of the terms. While Verio did not have an opportunity to read the terms prior to each transaction, because it engaged in multiple transactions, it had actual notice of such terms at the time Register.com contacted it.

Subsequent cases have enforced browsewrap agreements, provided that there is notice of the terms.

---

[47] *Id.* at 396–97.
[48] *Id.* at 401.
[49] *Id.*

5 Contract Terms as Sword, Shield, and Crook

THE VALIDATION OF the shrinkwrap license paved the way for the acceptance of the "clickwrap" and "browsewrap" forms for online transactions. While courts that seek to enforce digital contracts often cite to cases enforcing shrinkwraps, the digital agreements (clickwraps and browsewraps) are in fact quite different from shrinkwraps in terms of the *type* of terms they contain. This chapter examines the substantive terms contained in wrap contracts and how they have evolved with changes in form.

A. Contract as Shield

Some provisions in standard form contracts limit the liability of the contract drafter for the product or service it offers to the other party. An example of this type of provision is a limited warranty or a warranty disclaimer. Companies need to assess the risks of entering into a particular type of business, producing a particular type of product, or entering into a particular type of transaction, especially given the uncertainty generated by tort and product liability law. Contract law enables parties to establish the rules of the transactions. The drafter of a form contract uses the contract as a shield to protect itself from claims by the other party and to contain or limit the responsibility it would have for the product or service it introduces into the marketplace.

The Uniform Commercial Code ("U.C.C.") imposes an implied warranty of merchantability upon goods offered for sale.[1] Sellers, however, are able to disclaim this warranty using specific, expressly disclaiming, conspicuous language.[2] The U.C.C, recognizing a company's need to assess and contain risks, also permits businesses to limit their liability.[3] An unintended consequence of this ability to limit risks, however, may be that it further perpetuates the use of standard form contracts to govern commercial transactions.

The introduction of digital products on a mass consumer level brought with it a somewhat different shield function. The digital product owner uses a contract (e.g., a shrinkwrap license) to draw boundaries of use around its product. In *ProCD, Inc. v. Zeidenberg*, for example, one of the relevant provisions in the shrinkwrap license stated:

> The listings on this product are licensed for authorized users only. The user agreement provides that copying of the software and the data may be done only for individual or personal use and that distribution, sublicense or lease of the software or the data is prohibited. The agreement provides expressly that:
>
> [Y]ou will not make the Software or the Listings in whole or in part available to any other user in any networked or time-shared environment, or transfer the Listings in whole or in part to any computer other than the computer used to access the Listings.[4]

---

[1] U.C.C. § 2-314 (2003) ("[A] warranty that the goods shall be merchantable is implied in a contract for their sale if the seller is a merchant with respect to goods of that kind.").

[2] *Id.* at § 2-316(2).

[3] *Id.* at § 2-719(1)(a) ("[T]he agreement may provide for remedies... in substitution for those provided in this Article and may limit or alter the measure of damages recoverable...."); *id.* at § 2-719(3) ("Consequential damages may be limited or excluded unless the limitation or exclusion is unconscionable."). An exclusive remedy, however, should not "fail of its essential purpose." *Id.* at § 2-719(2).

The federal consumer protection law, the Magnuson-Moss Warranty Act, does not permit disclaimers of implied warranties if the product is accompanied by a written warranty but does not require any warranty whatsoever. 15 U.S.C. § 2302(b)(2) (2006) ("Nothing in this title... shall be deemed... to require that a consumer product or any of its components be warranted."); 15 U.S.C. § 2308(a) (2006) ("No supplier may disclaim or modify... any implied warranty to a consumer with respect to such consumer product if... such supplier makes any written warranty to the consumer with respect to such consumer product ...."). The Magnuson-Moss Act does, however, permit limitations of liability provided there is a "repair, replace or refund" remedy. *See* 15 U.S.C. § 2304(a)(3) (2006).

[4] ProCD, Inc. v. Zeidenberg, 908 F. Supp. 640, 645 (W.D. Wis. 1996), *rev'd*, 86 F.3d 1447 (7th Cir. 1996).

This contract provision was used to set limitations around the consumer's use of the product, thus "shielding" the software producer's business model from unfair business practices. The software producer, as the copyright holder, sold the license to use the software to the consumer. The scope of that license was contained in the shrinkwrap. Given the susceptibility of digital products to unauthorized copying and distribution, the Seventh Circuit upheld the shrinkwrap as a valid contracting form.[5] Judge Easterbrook's opinion in *ProCD* exemplifies judicial prioritization of business needs over doctrinal fidelity. In addition to noting that ProCD's database product could probably not be copyrighted, leaving ProCD vulnerable to Zeidenberg's unfair business practices, Judge Easterbrook stressed the importance of price discrimination, citing it as a cornerstone of ProCD's business model and an advantage to consumers.[6]

The court strayed from formalistic notions of offer and acceptance to prevent what would happen if it adhered to them too rigidly:

> On Zeidenberg's arguments, these unboxed sales are unfettered by terms—so the seller has made a broad warranty and must pay consequential damages for any shortfalls in performance, two "promises" that if taken seriously would drive prices through the ceiling or return transactions to the horse-and-buggy age.[7]

The *ProCD* court deferred to the needs of the software industry, favoring commercial interests over doctrinal requirements. This interest in accommodating business needs is, in the court's decision, aligned with the interests of the average consumer, rather than opposed to it. Throughout the opinion, the court highlights the benefits of shrinkwraps and rolling contracts to consumers. Shrinkwraps streamline transactions and permit price discrimination, which save time and money that benefit *both* parties. Zeidenberg was not the typical consumer, and most consumers would not be disadvantaged by the "non-commercial use" terms at issue before the court; on the contrary, most consumers would presumably benefit from it.

Unlike the "non-commercial use" only provision, the warranty disclaimer or limitations of liability are terms that, if enforced, disfavor consumers. Yet, a failure to enforce such terms would detrimentally affect the development of the fledgling software industry. Software is fickle and susceptible to viruses and bugs that may prevent a particular program or a single copy of a program from working properly. A business may be stymied or its operations interrupted by a failure in its software

---

[5] ProCD, Inc. v. Zeidenberg, 86 F.3d 1447, 1449 (7th Cir. 1996).
[6] *Id.* at 1449–50.
[7] *Id.* at 1452.

operating system, resulting in a costly loss of productivity. It was (and is) unclear what it means for software to be merchantable. The result is that a software company could face a potentially ruinous judgment without the ability to disclaim warranties and limit liabilities, which would have stifled the burgeoning industry.

The alternatives to shrinkwraps were unappealing for software companies: either have consumers sign agreements prior to purchase, or wait for companies to create "bug-free" programs—which means that I'd probably be tapping this book out on a typewriter. Courts recognized that businesses needed to contain their potential risk exposure and recognized the shrinkwrap as a valid contracting form.

Like software companies, companies with web-based businesses had unique challenges arising from the digital environment. Owners of physical stores can usually deter customers from leaving the store with unpaid items through a variety of measures. They can place sensors in merchandise and sensor detectors by doors. They can install security cameras and hire personnel to monitor customers. In addition, they can require that customers check-in their bags or subject them to bag searches. Finally, they can eject customers from their stores or, in some cases, detain suspected shoplifters and call the police. By contrast, website operators initially had little ability to monitor or control the actions of their visitors (this ability has dramatically improved over time). The content that websites made available to users could be easily copied and widely distributed, thereby diminishing its value. Stopping wrongdoers was difficult and complicated. Not only were they difficult to identify, there were few laws addressing online activity. Legislation lagged far behind technology. Quite often, the boundaries of fair play and fair use were unclear. Rather than leaving uncertain fates for a court to decide, companies decided to draw those boundaries themselves. Not surprisingly, the early cases testing the validity of the wrap contract form involved situations that challenged the very existence of web-based businesses and typically involved an arguably bad faith contract challenger. For example, in *ProCD v. Zeidenberg*, the defendant Zeidenberg was fully aware that he should not make copies of the software program and resell them. Furthermore, allowing him to do so might have stifled the growth of companies selling digital information.

Practices such as "deep linking" "web scraping," or "web crawling" were the subject of several influential early wrap contract cases.[8] Deep linking is the creation of a hyperlink that directs the user to an interior web page, instead of a website's home page. Web scraping and web crawling are practices involving the searching and/or copying of data on a website using an automatic software program. Mark Lemley has

[8] *See* Pollstar v. Gigmania, 170 F. Supp. 2d 974 (E.D. Cal. 2000), Cairo, Inc. v. Crossmedia Services, Inc., 2005 WL 756610 (N.D. Cal.), Register.com v. Verio, 356 F.3d 393 (2d Cir. 2004).

observed that "almost all of the Internet cases to enforce a browsewrap come up in the property/trespass context."[9]

But shrinkwraps often contained more than just those terms intended to shield a company from unfair practices. Due to the nature of blanket assent, these terms were typically enforceable if the contracting form was enforceable. Karl Llewellyn noted that assent to boilerplate clauses means assent to "the few dickered terms,... the broad type of the transaction, and... a blanket assent (not a specific assent) to any not unreasonable or indecent terms... which do not alter or eviscerate the reasonable meaning of the dickered terms."[10] As the court in *Caspi v. Microsoft Network, LLC* noted, to conclude that a particular provision was not enforceable "would be equivalent to holding that they were bound by no other clause either, since all provisions were identically presented."[11] In other words, the blanket nature of contractual assent typically means that acceptance of the shielding provisions requires acceptance of the provisions that serve functions other than shielding.

B. Contract as Sword

A contract provision may serve a function other than simply shielding the drafter from liability for unfair or unauthorized business practices; it may affect and terminate rights held by the other party. One might argue that a limitation of liability or a warranty disclaimer also terminates a party's rights by prohibiting recovery for damages that would otherwise be available under contract law. Yet, the U.C.C. expressly permits a party to do just that. Regardless of whether software transactions are "sales" under the purview of the U.C.C.,[12] the U.C.C. can provide guidance regarding what are generally accepted fair and reasonable commercial practices. The limitation of liability and warranty disclaimers are directly tied to the liability attached to the use of the product and reflect the drafter's attempt to calculate the risk of doing business, the risk of producing a particular product, or both. They are part of the product offering and thus, for purposes of this discussion, considered to be shielding provisions.

---

9 Mark A. Lemley, *Terms of Use*, 91 MINN. L. REV. 459, 470 (2006).

10 *See* KARL N. LLEWELLYN, THE COMMON LAW TRADITION: DECIDING APPEALS 370 (1960).

11 Caspi v. Microsoft Network, LLC, 732 A.2d 528, at 532 (N.J. Super. App. Div, 1999).

12 For a discussion of whether software transactions are "licenses" or "sales," see Nancy S. Kim, *The Software Licensing Dilemma*, 2008 B.Y.U. L. Rev. 1103 (2008). *See also* Richard A. Epstein, ProCD v. Zeidenberg*: Do Doctrine and Function Mix?*, *in* CONTRACTS STORIES 94, 100–04 (Douglas G. Baird ed., 2007) (discussing the implications of categorizing a software transaction as a license or a sale, including the applicability of the U.C.C. provisions governing contract formation).

Similarly, the license grant is a shielding provision and part of what the seller/drafter is offering to the buyer/licensee. Essentially, the license is permission to use and a concomitant promise by the seller/drafter not to sue, provided the buyer adheres to the scope of the license. The promise not to sue applies only to the authorized use. Any use beyond that which is expressly authorized is subject to the licensor's proprietary rights. The "assent" of the buyer/licensee then is not essential to the license grant, warranty disclaimer, or limitation of liability provisions (provided that those disclaimers and limitations meet the conspicuousness and other requirements of commercial law).

By contrast, contract provisions which serve a sword function destroy the other party's rights or entitlements[13] that are independent of or unrelated to the use of the product. Exclusive jurisdiction or mandatory arbitration clauses, for example, aim to destroy the nondrafting party's ability to bring a lawsuit in civil court or in a state that would otherwise have jurisdiction over the disputed matter. To illustrate, the following provision from the Groupon terms of use serves a sword function because the user must submit to binding arbitration, the arbitrator must apply Illinois law, and the user must essentially waive classwide arbitration even though these matters pertain to ancillary issues of dispute resolution and not to the use of Groupon's service:

> We will make every reasonable effort to resolve any disagreements that you have with Groupon. If those efforts fail, by using this Site you agree that any claim, dispute, or controversy you may have against Groupon arising out of, relating to, or connected in any way with this Agreement this Site or the purchase or sale of any voucher(s), shall be resolved exclusively by final and binding arbitration administered by the American Arbitration Association ("AAA") and conducted before a single arbitrator pursuant to the applicable Rules and Procedures established by AAA ("Rules and Procedures"). You agree further that: (a) the arbitration shall be held at a location determined by AAA pursuant to the Rules and Procedures (provided that such location is reasonably convenient for you), or at such other location as may be mutually agreed upon by you and Groupon; (b) the arbitrator shall apply Illinois law consistent with the Federal Arbitration Act and applicable statutes of limitations, and shall honor claims of privilege recognized at law; (c) there shall be no authority for any claims to be arbitrated on a class or representative basis; arbitration can decide only your and/or Groupon's individual claims; and the arbitrator may

---

[13] I use the term "rights" in a broad way to encompass Hohfeld's notion of "privileges." *See* Wesley Newcomb Hohfeld, *Some Fundamental Legal Conceptions as Applied in Judicial Reasoning*, 23 YALE L.J. 16 (1913).

> not consolidate or join the claims of other persons or parties who may be similarly situated...[14]

In some cases, the contract will restrict rights that the user has under other laws such as the Copyright Act pertaining to the use of the product or service. For example, in *Davidson & Associates v. Jung*,[15] the Court of Appeals for the Eighth Circuit upheld a clickwrap agreement that prohibited reverse engineering. In that case, the appellee, Blizzard, created and sold software games and provided a gaming service available exclusively to purchasers of its games.[16] Because it was concerned about piracy, Blizzard restricted access to its service and required agreement to a clickwrap that prohibited reverse engineering.

Appellants, by reverse engineering, were able to create an online gaming system as an alternative to Blizzard's system. The appellants' system contained operational differences from Blizzard's system and enabled users to play pirated versions of appellee's games.[17] The court stated that the appellants had expressly relinquished their right to reverse engineer by agreeing to the terms of the license agreement.[18]

As troubling as sword provisions may be, their purpose, like those of shield provisions, is to enable the drafting party to assess the benefits and minimize the risks of doing business by reducing costs and uncertainty. In other words, the ultimate function of sword provisions is risk management. In most cases, the company would not have agreed to enter into the transaction without the protection afforded by both the sword and shield provisions. Unfortunately, both sword and shield provisions have paved the way for contract provisions that do more than simply reduce business risk.

C. Contract as Crook

In this section, the metaphor of a "crook" is used to describe a company's stealthy appropriation (via a nonnegotiated agreement) of benefits ancillary or unrelated to the consideration that is the subject of the transaction. Prior to the advent of wrap contracts, standard form agreements generally performed sword and shield functions. Even if their limitations of liabilities and warranty disclaimers and exclusions reduced the value of the bargain for the consumer, contracts of adhesion typically did not seek to extract additional benefits from consumers that were not part of the

---

14 Groupon, Terms, http://www.groupon.com/terms (last visited Dec. 11, 2012).

15 Davidson & Associates v. Jung, 422 F.3d 630 (8th Cir. 2005).

16 *Id.* at 633.

17 *Id.* at 636

18 *Id.* at 639.

primary transaction without the consumer's actual, specific assent. For example, a hotel that charged an additional fee for late checkouts would have its customers separately initial the rate and the late checkout fee.

The physical constraints of paper agreements acted as a natural rein on companies' contracting behavior. Companies were generally reluctant to repel potential customers with multipage contracts that required a signature. Even though shrinkwrap agreements did not require a signature, they too were typically limited in size due to the impracticability, cost, and general undesirability of enclosing a bulky contract with a software product. With judicial validation of the clickwrap and browsewrap forms, however, companies further expanded the reach of their contractual clauses. They began to use contracts to extract from consumers additional benefits that were unrelated to the transaction.

Given that digital terms are weightless, reproduction and distribution costs nonexistent, and consumers highly unlikely to read online agreements, companies could add additional terms with no concomitant financial or reputational cost. Companies thus began using their online agreements to do more than contain costs and assess the risks of doing business. For example, the browsewrap of the professional social networking site, LinkedIn, requires that users grant the company "a nonexclusive, irrevocable, worldwide, perpetual, unlimited, assignable, sublicenseable, fully paid up and royalty-free right" to

> "copy, prepare derivative works of, improve, distribute, publish, remove, retain, add, process, analyze, use and commercialize, in any way now known or in the future discovered, any information you provide, directly or indirectly to LinkedIn, including, but not limited to, any user generated content, ideas, concepts, techniques or data to the services, you submit to LinkedIn, without any further consent, notice and/or compensation to you or to any third parties."[19]

While LinkedIn needs a license to post user content, the license that it requires users to give it is much broader than is required to protect itself from liability. Most users are likely unaware of the rights granted via these crook provisions since most people fail to read online agreements.[20]

---

[19] LinkedIn, User Agreement, http://www.linkedin.com/static?key=user_agreement&trk=hb_ft_useragHttp://www.linkedin.com/static?key=user_agreement&trk=hb_ft_userag (last visited Dec. 11, 2012).

[20] *See, e.g.*, Yannis Bakos, Florencia Marotta-Wurgler, & David R. Trossen, *Does Anyone Read the Fine Print? Testing a Law and Economics Approach to Standard Form Contracts*, 3 (N.Y. Univ. Sch. of Law, Ctr. for Law, Econ. & Org., Working Paper No. 09-40, 2009), *available at* http://ssrn.com/abstract=1443256 (finding that "only about one or two in one thousand shoppers" of software access a product's end-user license agreement

More troubling, at least some contract adherents would have declined the primary transaction if they had known about the additional benefits being extracted via the crook provisions. For example, Facebook users threatened to defect in droves when they discovered that the company, via a crook provision, intended to retain a perpetual license to user-generated content.[21] Facebook eventually backed down and changed the terms of the contract. Curiously, the perpetual contract provision had been in place for several years. It attracted member ire only because Facebook tried to clarify the language. Few online companies, however, are subject to as much scrutiny as Facebook and changes to the terms of use of other websites may go unnoticed.

Companies may also use crook provisions to resell and share customer personal information. For example, the clothing company J. Crew states that it "may share your information, including, without limitation, email addresses (but not your credit card information), with unaffiliated third parties whose products or services may be of interest to you and who have their own privacy policy in place."[22] The social networking site Twitter states that it "may share or disclose your non-private, aggregated or otherwise non-personal information, such as your public user profile information, public Tweets, the people you follow or that follow you, or the number of users who clicked on a particular link (even if only one did)."[23]

The crook is a more apt metaphor than the sword because the customer's use of the information or extraction of the entitlement is stealthily appropriated rather than destroyed. Furthermore, unlike sword or shield provisions, a crook provision is not designed to protect a company's business model or assess its risks. When a company uses a sword or shield provision, the purpose is defensive; the company anticipates an undesired use or an offensive move by the consumer, such as a lawsuit, and the company seeks to curtail that use or block that move. By contrast, a crook provision anticipates no such offensive action by the consumer and has no direct relationship with the product or services offered by the company. It is simply an attempt to sneak an entitlement from the user without payment, either in terms of money or goodwill.

(EULA) for at least one second). Recently, a computer game retailer included a clause in its online contract that gave it a right to the "souls" of 7,500 of its online customers. *7,500 Online Shoppers Unknowingly Sold Their Souls*, FoxNews.com, Apr. 15, 2010, http://www.foxnews.com/tech/2010/04/15/online-shoppers-unknowingly-sold-souls/. The customers had the option of nullifying the soul-claiming clause but very few did so. *Id.*

21 Brad Stone & Brian Stelter, *Facebook Withdraws Changes in Data Use*, N.Y. Times, Feb. 18, 2009, http://www.nytimes.com/2009/02/19/technology/internet/19facebook.html.

22 J. Crew, Our Privacy Policy, Http://www.jcrew.com/help/privacy_policy.jsp (last visited Oct. 8, 2012).

23 Twitter, Twitter Privacy Policy, Http://twitter.com/privacy (last visited Oct. 8, 2012).

6 Problems of Form

WRAP CONTRACTS ARE similar to other contracts of adhesion in many ways.[1] They contain standard terms, are typically nonnegotiated, and are unread by the adhering party. Wrap contracts differ from other contracts of adhesion in their form and manner of presentment. But does this difference in form justify calling them by a different name? Given their similarities, is there any reason to distinguish wrap contracts from other contracts of adhesion?

A. Is a Wrap Contract Just Another Contract of Adhesion?

Todd Rakoff identified a "model contract of adhesion" as follows:

1. The document whose legal validity is at issue is a printed form that contains many terms and clearly purports to be a contract.

[1] Leon Trakman states that "it remain debatable whether mass consumers in wrap contracting are fundamentally different from mass consumers generally were a century ago." Leon E. Trakman, *The Boundaries of Contract Law in Cyberspace*, 38 PUB. CONT. L.J. 187, 235 (2008).

2. The form has been drafted by, or on behalf of, one party to the transactions.
3. The drafting party participates in numerous transactions of the type represented by the form and enters into these transactions as a matter of routine.
4. The form is presented to the adhering party with the representation that, except perhaps for a few identified items (such as the price term), the drafting party will enter into the transaction only on the terms contained in the document. This representation may be explicit or may be implicit in the situation, but it is understood by the adherent.
5. After the parties have dickered over whatever terms are open to bargaining, the document is signed by the adherent.
6. The adhering party enters into few transactions of the type represented by the form—few, at least, in comparison with the drafting party.
7. The principal obligation of the adhering party in the transaction considered as a whole is the payment of money.[2]

A wrap contract shares many of these characteristics except for those set forth in 5 through 7. Wrap contracts are not signed. Furthermore, the adhering party enters into the transactions on a daily basis, often multiple times a day, and with different companies. Finally, the adhering party's principal obligation in the wrap contract is typically not the payment of money.

The differences between wrap and other contracts of adhesion have significant ramifications regarding the way wrap contracts are perceived—or rather, *not* perceived. Friedrich Kessler said of standard form contracts that they enable companies to "legislate in a substantially authoritarian manner without using the appearance of authoritarian forms."[3] What Kessler said applies with greater force to online agreements which contain numerous terms and are presented unobtrusively. Many commentators have written about the failure of consumers to read standard form contracts. There are many reasons for this failure to read, including the inability to negotiate and the failure to understand legalese. But online, the problem is even worse than the consumer not reading the contract—the consumer is often not even aware there is a contract.

A contract that can appear anywhere and which is presented in any medium and manner deceives the nondrafting party who is conditioned to think of a legal undertaking as one requiring more ceremony and formality. A wrap contract does not

---

[2] Todd D. Rakoff, *Contracts of Adhesion: An Essay in Reconstruction*, 96 HARV. L. REV. 1173, 1177 (1983).

[3] Friedrich Kessler, *Contracts of Adhesion—Some Thoughts About Freedom of Contract,* 43 Colum. L. Rev. 629, 640 (1943).

usually require the adherent to pay money, which can mislead the adherent into believing that no price at all is paid.

Lon Fuller identified the functions of formalities, such as consideration and the statute of frauds, as evidentiary, cautionary, and channeling.[4] In other words, the purpose of formalities in contract law is to enhance the reliability of testimony in cases of contract dispute, encourage deliberation before entering into contracts, and signify an intent to enter into a transaction that is legally binding.[5] Online contracts greatly diminish and often undermine all three of these functions. As Juliet Moringiello cautions, "[t]he importance of signals in law and the adaptation of the law to new forms of transacting cannot be ignored in the Internet age."[6]

People automatically click to accept terms of online agreements, if they are asked to click on anything at all. A person may simply be browsing a website without intent to be legally bound and have no idea that terms even exist. Given that many websites state that they have the ability to modify their contractual terms at any time—without individually notifying their users of such change—wrap agreements may fail to satisfy even the evidentiary function.[7] While signatories of paper contracts of adhesion may feel powerless and resentful, they at least realize what they are doing. The ubiquity of wrap contracts and the lack of signaling associated with them means that adherents to these contracts are typically oblivious to what they have done.

The ways in which wrap contracts are different from other contracts of adhesion can be explained by the differences in *form*. A model wrap contract would be characterized as follows:

1. to 4, in accordance with Rakoff's model.
5. The terms are presented in a "nontraditional" format, meaning in a way other than on paper requiring a signature. Most wrap contract terms are presented in digital form, but they can also be presented in tangible form.

The broad definition of wrap contracts reveals much about the problems with them. The generous nature of the definition of wrap contracts is not the product of some immutable fact or characteristic—it is a conclusion rendered by courts. Businesses proposed that the imposition of terms in nontraditional formats be

[4] Lon L. Fuller, *Consideration and Form*, 41 COLUM. L. REV. 799, 800–801 (1941).

[5] *Id.* at 799.

[6] Juliet M. Moringiello, *Signals, Assent and Internet Contracting*, 57 RUTGERS L. REV. 1307, at 1316 (2005).

[7] Cheryl B. Preston & Eli W. McCann, *Unwrapping Shrinkwraps, Clickwraps, and Browsewraps: How the Law Went Wrong from Horse Traders to the Law of the Horse*, 26 BYU J. PUB. LAW 1, 23 (2011) (noting unilateral modifications as a common provision in browsewraps).

called contracts, and courts endorsed this position by enforcing these formats as valid contracting forms. Wrap contracts are only contracts because courts recognize them as such.

Aside from descriptive ease, there is another very important reason to retain "wrap" in front of the word "contract." What we call something matters.[8] To retain the word "wrap" underscores that this type of contract differs from others in its form and manner of presentment.

Courts and commentators have tended to deny the difference that presentment makes, insisting that new contracting environments have not, and should not, fundamentally change the principles of contract. For example, the Second Circuit in *Register.com v. Verio* stated that while Internet commerce has "exposed courts to many new situations, it has not fundamentally changed the principles of contract."[9] Yet, in the case before it, the Second Circuit had to make a decision regarding *which* principle to apply. Recall in that case, the applicable "contract" was a legend delivered with query results from the drafting party restricting the use of those results. The court stated that it is "standard contract doctrine that when a benefit is offered subject to stated conditions, and the offeree makes a decision to take the benefit with knowledge of the terms of the offer, the taking constitutes acceptance of the terms, which accordingly becomes binding on the offeree."[10] But in the case before it, there was no "offer"—the legend arrived with the results. The transaction was completed. The benefit had already been received. There are situations where a party may seek compensation for a benefit previously rendered to another party, but that is a remedy based upon equitable principles. It is a *quasi contract*, not a contract.

The judicial treatment of wrap contracts contrasts with the way courts tackled traditional adhesive contracts. Recognizing that standard form contracts were different from negotiated agreements, courts adopted legal controls to keep abusive or socially harmful contracting practices at bay. Courts developed the unconscionability doctrine and interpretation rules that recognized the limitations of standard form

---

[8] As Arthur Leff stated in his article, *Contracts as Thing*,

> To call a thing a contract is to make a legal classification. It is to carry out that most basic step in what is sometimes called legal reasoning (and what is confused, often, with legal logic). It is to make a move in the mind game which, to coarsen a lot of distinctions, goes something like this: given that I cannot efficiently treat this thing as *sui generis*, with what other thing or group of things can I best associate it for less-than-individual treatment.

Arthur Allen Leff, *Contract as Thing*, 19 Am. U. L. Rev. 131, 132 (1970). Leff objected to the classification of contracts of adhesion as contracts and proposed a new way of thinking of them as part of the product.

[9] Register.com v. Verio, 356 F.3d 393, 403 (2d Cir. 2004) (also cited in *Cairo Inc. v. Crossmedia Services*, 2005 WL 756610 at 4 (N.D. Cal.)).

[10] *Id.*

contracts.[11] For example, they applied the rule of *contra proferentem*, which requires that ambiguous contract terms be constructed against the drafter.[12] With respect to insurance contracts, courts adopted the "reasonable expectations" rule set forth in section 211(3) of the Restatement (Second) and held that if one party has reason to believe that the other party would not have entered into the agreement "if he knew that the writing contained a particular term, the term is not part of the agreement."[13] Legislatures, too, responded to the fine print in insurance contracts by prohibiting certain provisions and requiring others.[14] These requirements or prohibitions might include minimum font size or specified type.[15]

To label a contract as a wrap contract is to recognize the unique problems that form creates. Many commentators have written about the failure of consumers to read standard form contracts. There are many reasons for this failure to read, including underestimating the risk of harmful terms, the inability to negotiate, and the failure to understand legalese. While the adherents of contracts of adhesion tend not to read contract terms, the form of wrap contracts encourage this tendency.

For example, shrinkwraps are bundled with a product and accessible to the consumer only after the product has been purchased and physical possession transferred. The consumer is then expected to unwrap the product and the shrinkwrapped license. Only then does the consumer have the ability to read the terms. If the consumer does not like them, she may reject them by putting the product back in its packaging, driving back to the store, and seeking a refund. Given the high hassle

---

11 E. Allan Farnsworth,, CONTRACTS, §4.26, .at 287 (4th ed. Aspen Publishers 2004) (noting that courts have developed "several techniques" to avoid harsh results in hard cases). *See also* Moringiello, *supra* note 6, 1333–40 (discussing a half century of cases in which courts have found a duty to explain terms where terms were delivered mechanically or where the contractual nature of the document was unclear).

12 *See* Florence Nightingale Nursing Serv., v. Blue Cross/Blue Shield, 41 F.3d 1476, 1481 (11th Cir. 1995) ("If the claimant has established a reasonable interpretation, then under *contra proferentem*, which requires ambiguities to be construed against the drafter of a document, the claimant's interpretation is taken as correct."); HPI/GSA-3C, LLC v. Perry, 364 F.3d 1327, 1334 (Fed. Cir. 2004) (applying the rule of *contra proferentem* where contract had latent ambiguity); Kunin v. Benefit Trust Life Ins. Co., 910 F.2d 534, 538–39 (9th Cir. 1990) ("According to the law of California and, indeed, every other state as well as the District of Columbia, ambiguities in insurance contracts must be construed against the insurer.").

13 Restatement (Second) of Contracts § 211(3) (1981); *see also* Chicago & N. W. Transp. Co. v. Emmet Fertilizer & Grain Co., 852 F.2d 358, 360 (8th Cir. 1988) (declining to give drafting party the benefit of ambiguous language where "it relies on an undeclared interpretation of the license terms which it should have known would have been unacceptable to [the nondrafting party] at the time of negotiation"); Lancaster v. United States Shoe Corp., 934 F. Supp. 1137, 1140 (N.D. Cal. 1996) (holding that denial of benefits was improper under the reasonable expectations doctrine).

14 *See* Note, *Contract Clauses in Fine Print*, 63 Harv. L. Rev. 494, 497–99 (1950) (noting that the statutory requirements "makes the question of the insured's assent irrelevant as to the clauses thus regulated, by declaring in effect a status relationship between the parties in which the policy serves as to these provisions only as a means of information to the insured."). *Id.* at 498.

15 *Id.* at 499.

factor of rejecting terms, it's not surprising that few customers bother reading the terms. Furthermore, many retailers have a store policy of not accepting returns of any digital product that has been opened, thus making it pointless to attempt to reject terms.

The form of a contract affects the way it is perceived by the consumer. It also affects the volume and nature of legal terms capable of being compressed into the form. One major reason for the magnitude of online terms is the absence of marginal cost associated with digital contracts. Each additional page of a paper contract extracts some type of cost. The company incurs the financial costs of printing and reproducing each additional page. Thicker paper contracts occupy more space in a cabinet or drawer. There are other problems associated with lengthy paper contracts. Pages tend to rip and may get lost. Their delivery becomes more cumbersome. Digital terms, on the other hand, are weightless and adding additional terms does not affect the marginal cost of an agreement. It costs the company the same to reproduce a single page electronic document as it does one that has forty pages.

There is another type of cost associated with lengthy paper contracts, and that is the cost to the company in terms of customer goodwill. The length of a contract signals the importance of a transaction to a customer. Even if consumers generally don't read their contracts, they may view with suspicion a thick contract handed to them to complete a simple transaction. Even if a customer is unable to negotiate, she will likely flip through the pages and skim the terms. An unusually hefty document for a minor transaction is likely to arouse the customer's suspicion.

Given the low cost of digital contracting, many websites engage in "contracting mania," where they stuff their online contracts with many pages of terms, typically without suffering a corresponding loss of customer goodwill since the customer is unlikely to read any of it. Often digital contracts link to other digital contracts, or they may simply reference the applicability of third-party agreements. The use of hyperlinks—the digital version of "incorporation by reference"—means that there are more contracts, more terms in those contracts, and terms that are more difficult to detect than for similar offline transactions. Due to the frequent updating of terms and the myriad terms that are cross-referenced, even the companies themselves have a hard time keeping track of which terms apply to a given transaction with a particular user.

When you rent a car, you are typically asked to sign one contract; you are not asked to sign four others that belong to "affiliates," nor are you asked to fetch the agreements yourself from different filing cabinets. The agreement is typically short, not forty pages long. Even if you are not inclined to read the contract, its length signals the significance of the transaction and the burden which you are accepting as part of that transaction.

Contracts are much more ubiquitous online than in the physical world. Practically every website professes to be governed by a browsewrap and/or clickwrap, and customers typically encounter several wrap agreements each time they go online. Unlike in the physical world, in the online environment, customers are asked to enter into wrap contracts for even trivial or minor transactions. As Mark Lemley notes, most offline consumer transactions do not require a written contract, whereas "many of those same retail outlets impose standard form contracts on their online users, probably because it is easier to get someone to click 'I agree' as part of an online transaction than it is to have a clerk obtain a signature on a written form."[16] In the physical world, customers are typically asked to sign lengthy, multipage contracts only for significant transactions, such as the purchase of a house, or for transactions where the drafting party has a continuing property interest, such as a car rental agreement or a lease agreement. Online, a customer may be deemed to have assented to a thirty-page document simply by visiting a website. An analogy would be stopping to browse at a shop and being asked to sign a lengthy agreement prior to entering. (A more precise analogy to browsewraps would be one where you walk into the store and are deemed to have agreed to that agreement simply by setting foot in the door and not immediately exiting.)

Due to the ubiquitous nature of wrap agreements, consumers may become habituated to them and take less notice or care of their terms. Clickwraps, browsewraps, and now tapwraps are as commonplace as computer screens and mobile devices. The ways to engineer a contracting form multiplies with advances in technology, and companies use consumer habituation to their advantage.[17] The proliferation of contracts on computer screens and other devices makes it difficult for consumers to discern their legal significance and easier for them to ignore. Not surprisingly, consumers may manifest assent without being aware of what they are doing.

The online contracting environment is devoid of formalities, making it even less likely that a consumer will read the terms. There is no clerk asking for a signature, no scribbling with a pen, no duplicate copy to crumple in a pocket. As Juliet Moringiello observes, "a written signature provides the traditional evidence of assent because when we are asked to sign something, we are conditioned to think that we are doing

---

[16] Mark A. Lemley, *Terms of Use*, 91 MINN. L. REV. 459, 466 (2006).

[17] The *Wall Street Journal* recently reported a story on the way Facebook app developers exploit consumer habituation to their advantage: "Apps are required to ask people's permission to access their Facebook data. But the way they ask plays on a fundamental human tendency—namely, that people who see frequent warnings come to disregard them." Julia Angwin & Jeremy Singer-Vine, *Selling You on Facebook*, WALL ST. J., Apr. 7, 2012, http://online.wsj.com/article/SB10001424052702303302504577327744009046230.html.

something important."[18] She notes that even "clicking" may not fulfill the cautionary function of a signature.[19] A study conducted by Rainer Böhme and Stefan Köpsell found that users tended to blindly accept terms whose presentation resembled an end-user license agreement, probably because the ubiquity of such agreements have trained users to "accept" their terms without reading them.[20]

Furthermore, all digital agreements are not created equally. It is a mistake to treat the assent issue the same way simply because a click of a mouse is involved. While some clickwraps display all their provisions on a single computer page, others appear in small text boxes that require constant scrolling in order to review their terms. "I agree" buttons may be placed alongside the text box rather than contained within it. By making the review of the terms cumbersome and the physical act of assent easy, some types of clickwrap agreements discourage reading of terms more than others.

With digital contracts, consumers typically are not able to assess at a glance whether the contract contains multiple pages or just a couple. Although unlikely to read contracts, consumers handed a multipage document may be more likely to scan the pages and catch an unsavory term. The terms of online contracts are not immediately visible. Because they typically require a click on a hyperlink or scrolling in order to read their terms, the likelihood of a chance encounter with an unusual or objectionable term is reduced.

The ease with which terms may be disseminated and copied makes them contagious. In the past, it was relatively difficult to access another company's standard contract without being a customer. Now, however, a company can simply log on to another company's website to locate standard terms for many types of transactions. Rather than competing to offer better terms, companies may seek out competitors' contract terms simply to free ride, thereby saving legal fees and time. They can also reassure themselves that nobody else is offering *better* terms. Because the terms of online contracts tend to be contagious, shopping for more favorable terms becomes an exercise in futility and negotiating for different terms is generally unrealistic. The rapid standardization of terms, combined with their use in newer industries and by smaller companies (which may have, in the past, been willing to negotiate terms), may establish norms and expectations which unfairly disadvantage consumers. Mark Lemley and David McGowan have referred to adoption of standardized terms by industry players as a "'network effect' of a sort—those who draft contracts of adhesion with one-sided terms benefit if their competitors adopt the same

---

[18] Moringiello, *supra* note 6, 1307, 1316.

[19] *Id.* at 1331.

[20] Rainer Böhme & Stefan Köpsell, 2010 ACM Conference on Human Factors in Computing Sys., Trained to Accept? A Field Experiment on Consent Dialogs 2403 (2010), *available at* http://www1.inf.tu-dresden.de/~rb21/publications/BK2010_Trained_To_Accept_CHI.pdf.

one-sided terms."[21] The network effect of terms helps establish industry norms more quickly—which in turn may make a court less likely to find these norms surprising or unconscionable.

Consumers themselves may be different online than they are offline. While an offline user may be subject to certain external time pressures (such as other customers or an unfriendly company representative), the online user may be subject to internal time pressures. Time plays tricks online, as anyone knows who has ever waited an eternity for software to download yet looked up in surprise at how the hours have passed while playing an online game.

The Internet seems uniquely suited to impulsivity and impatience. Robert Hillman observes that the online environment may be less conducive to informed contracting than the offline one as users may not assign the "same significance to a mouse click as a signature on a paper form," may "expect speed and instant gratification," and may be "overeager, even 'click-happy.'"[22] Rather than luxuriating in a leisurely shopping experience, many online shoppers turn to websites rather than physical stores primarily because it is more convenient and they are in a hurry.[23] There is a feeling of unreality or "online disinhibition," which is a term sociologists and psychologists use to mean that users disassociate their online personas from their offline selves.[24] Online disinhibition is what makes users more likely to post outrageous comments on online forums than to make those same comments in face-to-face communications; it may also make them more likely to enter into lengthy legal contracts without reading. While customers may have no ability to negotiate paper contracts of adhesion, it's a rare customer who will sign a twenty-page document with nary a glance at any of the pages; even rarer still, is a customer who would sign a lengthy document for the mere privilege of entering a store. Digital contracts are difficult to

---

21 Mark A. Lemley & David McGowan, *Legal Implications of Network Economic Effects*, 86 CALIF. L. REV. 479, 589 (1998).

22 *See* Robert A. Hillman, *Online Consumer Standard Form Contracting Practices: A Survey and Discussion of Legal Implications, in* CONSUMER PROTECTION IN THE AGE OF THE "INFORMATION ECONOMY" 285 (Jane K. Winn, ed., 2006). He notes that the "Internet likely promotes impulsive purchasing" (citing Dennis W. Rook & Robert J. Fisher, *Normative Influences on Impulsive Buying Behavior*, 22 J. OF CONSUMER RES. 305–13 (1995)); Xiaoni Shang, Victor R. Prybutok, & Chang E. Koh, *The Role of Impulsiveness in a TAM-Based Online Purchasing Behavior Model, in* INNOVATIVE TECHNOLOGIES FOR INFORMATION RESOURCE MANAGEMENT 334, 335 (Mehdi Khosrow-Pour ed., 2008).

23 *See* Kuan-Pin Chiang & Ruby Roy Dholakia, *Factors Driving Consumer Intention to Shop Online: An Empirical Investigation*, 13 J. CONSUMER PSYCH 177, 178 (2003) (summarizing studies that indicate that the "distinct characteristic of online shopping is its convenience" and finding that convenience is a "major motive for consumers to shop electronically").

24 *See* John Suler, *The Online Disinhibition Effect*, The Psychology of Cyberspace, http://www-usr.rider.edu/~suler/psycyber/disinhibit.html; *see also* John M. Grohol, *Teens, Sex and Technology*, PSYCHCENTRAL, Jan. 6, 2009, http://psychcentral.com/blog/archives/2009/01/06/teens-sex-and-technology.

skim and easy to skip, and our online selves are more shortsighted and less careful than our offline selves. In short, the Internet is a less than ideal setting for realizing the promise of classical contracts.

In the online context, boring legalistic text must compete with arresting visual images and even animation. Who can blame a website visitor for clicking "I agree" without reading terms when they are primed for viewing funny YouTube clips or images of cute cats? The online experience is a visually oriented one. Fine print and static text just can't compete. Companies take advantage of the online environment and exploit consumers' online tendencies in the ways they present their contract terms.[25] They burrow multiple pages of terms several hyperlinked pages deep. They provide technical notice of terms but make finding the actual terms very difficult. They lead consumers through an image-filled landscape of enticing things to buy but use easily ignored fine-print terms to communicate legal obligations. They present contract terms alongside more interesting or relevant information rather than sequentially, which results in a disjointed, distracting process.[26] For example, a consumer may be presented with notice of terms accessible only via a hyperlink while filling out an online form to join a website. In order for the consumer to read the terms, she would have to toggle from the form to the terms. It makes more sense to have the terms presented first—in their entirety—and then present the form fields. The technical requirement of "notice," which ignores contracting realities, does nothing to alleviate the problem of unobtrusive or ineffective presentment.

The differences in form and the manner of presentment between digital wrap contracts and other contracts of adhesion have led us to the current state of contracting mania. And like rabbits, wrap contracts keep multiplying.

B. Sadistic Contracts

Much of the problems associated with wrap contracts—indeed, with any standard form contract—can be traced to the bastardized version of blanket assent. The notion of blanket assent was not outrageous in its original physical world context. Someone signing a form agreement has indicated by his or her signature that he or

[25] Ty Tasker & Daryn Pakcyk, *Cyber-Surfing on the High Seas of Legalese: Law and Technology of Internet Agreements*, 18 ALB. L.J. SCI & TECH. 79 (2008) (noting that certain computer effects intended to attract user attention "might draw a reader's attention away from contract terms. Imagine the difficulty of trying to concentrate on noticing or reading a contract while rapidly moving animation dances before one's eyes, or while a sound effect or a catchy tune are playing."). *Id.* at 106.

[26] *Id.* (noting that one "can easily envision a web site containing fast-moving animation that invites computer users to navigate into another topical area, thereby causing them to be distracted away from contractual provisions.").

she has read and agreed to its terms. When Karl Llewellyn referred to assent in the context of standard form contracts, he understood that there was no specific assent to any particular provision. Rather, there was actual assent to the negotiated terms and the type of transaction and blanket assent to those terms that were not unreasonable or indecent. Llewellyn hadn't foreseen wrap contracts.

Wrap contract doctrine replaces deliberate acts of contracting with manifestations of consent and awareness of terms with reasonable notice. Reasonable notice can be either actual or constructive notice, meaning that the nondrafting party actually knew there was a contract or that a reasonable person in that party's position would have known that a contract governed the transaction. While subsequent courts could have interpreted *Specht v. Netscape Communications Corp.* to mean that contract terms must be immediately visible, they have generally declined to do so, instead finding that reasonable notice does not mean that all the terms must be visible as long as the user was aware that additional terms existed.

For example, several cases have enforced terms in scrollable text boxes. In *Forrest v. Verizon Communications, Inc.*,[27] the court found assent where the user had clicked on the acceptance icon even though the terms, contained in the scrollable box, were thirteen pages long. In *Caspi v. Microsoft Network, LLC*,[28] the court found reasonable notice where the user clicked "I agree" to the terms of a scrollable text box even though the relevant provision was in the last paragraph. In yet another case, *Feldman v. Google, Inc.*, the court found that a "reasonably prudent internet user" would have had notice of the "existence of the terms" in a seven-paragraph scrollable box.[29]

Companies have pushed the boundaries of notice with hyperlinks, and courts have been willing to follow. In *Hubbert v. Dell Corp.*, for example, the court found reasonable notice where a hyperlink indicated the existence of terms and conditions, even though none of the terms were actually visible on that web page.[30]

In another case, the plaintiff clicked a box to indicate acceptance, even though the actual terms of the agreement were visible only by clicking on a separate link directly above the box.[31] The court stated that the plaintiff had an "opportunity to review the terms" by clicking on the hyperlink and that the plaintiff's claim that he did not read the contract is "irrelevant" as a "failure to read a contract is not a get out of jail free card."[32] The use of multiple wrap forms—"multiwrapping"—fulfills the mechanical requirement of assent but actually makes it harder for the consumer

---

[27] Forrest v. Verizon Communications, Inc., 805 A.2d 1007, 1010–11 (D.C. 2002).

[28] Caspi v. Microsoft Network LLC, 732 A.2d 528, 532 (1999).

[29] Feldman v. Google, Inc., 513 F. Supp. 2d 229, 237–38 (E.D. Pa. 2007).

[30] Hubbert v. Dell Corp., 835 N.E. 2d. 113, at 121 (Ill. App. 5 Dist. 2005) *app. denied*, 844 N.E.2d 965 (Ill. 2006).

[31] DeJohn v. The TV Corporation International, 245 F. Supp. 2d 913, 915–916, 919 (C.D. Ill. 2003).

[32] *Id.* at 919.

to access the terms than does a stand-alone clickwrap because the user is asked to perform two competing actions, clicking on the "accept" icon and clicking on the terms hyperlink.

For example, in *Swift v. Zynga Game Networks, Inc.*, putative class action plaintiffs alleged that defendant Zynga violated various consumer protection laws by working with and profiting from deceptive and fraudulent third-party advertisers.[33] There were actually two agreements at issue in the case. The first terms of service (first TOS) were accessible via a hyperlink when the user first decided to start playing a Zynga game through a platform such as Facebook.[34] The user was presented with a screen stating, "Allow Access? Allowing YoVille access will let it pull profile information, photos, your friends' info, and other content that it requires to work."[35] Underneath the request were a large "allow" icon and a smaller "cancel" icon, and smaller gray font which stated, "By proceeding you are allowing YoVille to access your information and you are agreeing to the Facebook Terms of Service in your use of YoVille. By using YoVille, you also agree to the YoVille Terms of Service." Both the words "Facebook Terms of Service" and "YoVille Terms of Service" were highlighted in blue to indicate they were hyperlinks.[36] Zynga did not track whether users clicked on the hyperlink and there was no evidence that "Plaintiff or anyone else ever clicked on the blue hyperlinked YoVille Terms of Service."[37]

The first TOS included a mandatory arbitration clause and a modification at will clause, which stated that Zynga had the right to change the terms at any time, that changes took effect after notice, that notice was effected by posting the changes on the service "or by any other method of notice Zynga deems appropriate," and that users accept changes by using the service after notice.[38] The first TOS was superseded by a second terms of service ("second TOS"), which prohibited arbitration on a class basis.[39]

Zynga filed a motion to compel arbitration of the plaintiff's claims on an individual basis pursuant to the terms of the first and second TOS.[40] The plaintiff argued that because the first TOS was not visible on the page, but accessible via a hyperlink, this "modified clickwrap" did not constitute sufficient notice.[41] The court rejected

---

[33] Complaint at 19, Swift v. Zynga Game Networks, Inc., 2009 WL 4237049 (N.D. Cal) (No. CV 09 5443 EDL).
[34] Swift v. Zynga Game Networks, Inc., 805 F. Supp. 2d 904, 907–908 (2011).
[35] *Id.* at 908.
[36] *Id.*
[37] *Id.*
[38] *Id.* at 907–08.
[39] *Id.* at 908.
[40] *Id.* at 910.
[41] *Id.*

this argument finding there was notice because the plaintiff was required to click on an "Accept" button "directly above a statement that clicking on the button served as assent to the YoVille terms of service along with a blue hyperlink directly to the terms of service."[42] (The court did not discuss the validity of the "modification at will" provision. As discussed below, courts are split on whether such provisions render an agreement illusory and unenforceable.)[43]

Recently, a federal district court found that the use of a window on a website was adequate to constitute notice even though the relevant information was not contained in the window. In *Lebowitz v. Dow Jones & Co.*,[44] the box on the website stated only: "IMPORTANT NOTICE TO READERS,"[45] but the customer had to click on the box in order to learn that the relevant information concerned a change in subscription fees.

Notice triggers the duty to read. The duty to read is onerous when the terms are convoluted and voluminous. It is frustrating when there is no ability to negotiate for different terms. It is troubling when the duty is triggered by notice that terms exist rather than by the terms themselves. But it is unrealistic and maybe even sadistic given the burdensome nature of some standard wrap contract terms. There are two kinds of provisions that are particularly mean-spirited. The first is the "now you see it, now you don't," or unilateral modification, provisions. The second is the "casting net," or incorporation by reference, provisions.

1. *"Now you see it, now you don't": Unilateral modification clauses*

Modification at will, or unilateral modification clauses, typically state that the website can modify the agreement at any time, and the consumer assents by using the site after such modification. Some courts have found that these provisions are illusory and unenforceable but others have enforced them. Cheryl Preston and Eli McCann analogize these provisions as "akin to using one wish to wish for infinite additional wishes."[46]

---

[42] *Id.* at 911.

[43] *See,* Vernon v. Qwest Communications International, Inc., 857 F. Supp. 2d 1135, 1153–56 (D. Colo. 2012) (upholding modification at will provision); *but see* Harris v. Blockbuster, Inc., 622 F. Supp. 2d 396, 399 (N.D. Tex. 2009) (striking down modification at will provision at illusory); *In re* Zappos.com, Inc., Customer Data Security Breach Litigation, 2012 WL 4466660 at 5 (D. Nev.) ("Most federal courts that have considered this issue have held that if a party retains the unilateral, unrestricted right to terminate the arbitration agreement, it is illusory and unenforceable, especially where there is no obligation to receive consent from, or even notify the other parties to the contract.").

[44] Lebowitz v. Dow Jones & Co. Inc., 847 F. Supp. 2d 599 (S.D.N.Y. 2012).

[45] *Id.* at 603.

[46] Preston & McCann, *supra* note 7, 1, at 23.

A quick visit to a few randomly selected sites reveals that these "now you see it, now you don't" provisions are common. For example:

> (From Wells Fargo Bank's Terms of Service)
>
> Wells Fargo reserves the right to modify these Terms of Use at any time without notice, but the most current version of the Terms of Use will always be available to you by clicking on the link at the bottom of the Site. If you find the Terms of Use unacceptable at any time, you may discontinue your use of the Services. By continuing to use the Services after the date of any change to these Terms of Use, including accessing the Site, you agree to be bound by the rules contained in the most recent version of this Agreement.[47]
>
> (From Google's Terms of Service)
>
> We may modify these terms or any additional terms that apply to a Service to, for example, reflect changes to the law or changes to our Services. You should look at the terms regularly. We'll post notice of modifications to these terms on this page. We'll post notice of modified additional terms in the applicable Service. Changes will not apply retroactively and will become effective no sooner than fourteen days after they are posted. However, changes addressing new functions for a Service or changes made for legal reasons will be effective immediately. If you do not agree to the modified terms for a Service, you should discontinue your use of that Service. If there is a conflict between these terms and the additional terms, the additional terms will control for that conflict.[48]
>
> (From Amazon.com)
>
> Please review our other policies, such as our pricing policy, posted on this site. These policies also govern your visit to Amazon.com. We reserve the right to make changes to our site, policies, and these Conditions of Use at any time. If any of these conditions shall be deemed invalid, void, or for any reason unenforceable, that condition shall be deemed severable and shall not affect the validity and enforceability of any remaining condition.[49]

---

[47] Wells Fargo, General Terms of Use, Https://www.wellsfargo.com/privacy_security/terms (last visited Dec. 12, 2012).

[48] Google, Google Terms of Service, Http://www.google.com/intl/en/policies/terms/ (last visited Feb. 12, 2013).

[49] Amazon.com, Conditions of Use, Http://www.amazon.com/gp/help/customer/display.html/ref=footer_cou/186-9776335-7971638?ie=UTF8&nodeId=508088 (last visited Dec. 12, 2012).

Courts are split on whether modification at will provisions are enforceable. In *Harris v. Blockbuster*,[50] plaintiffs sued Blockbuster under the Video Privacy Protection Act for entering into an agreement with Facebook whereby Blockbuster's customers' movie rental selections were distributed to their Facebook friends.[51] Blockbuster sought to enforce an arbitration provision in its online agreement. The court found that because Blockbuster reserved the right to modify the agreement "at its sole discretion" and "at any time" the modification was illusory and unenforceable.[52] On the other hand, in *Vernon v. Qwest Communications International, Inc.*,[53] the district court upheld a provision that allowed Qwest to "at any time, effective upon posting… or any written notice to you, including e-mail: (1) stop offering the Service and/or rental Equipment, (ii) modify the Services and/or any of the terms and conditions of this Agreement."[54]

2. *"Casting net" provisions: Incorporation by reference*

The second type of mean-spirited contract provision casts a wide net that captures other contracts, leaving the consumer with the daunting task of reconciling possibly conflicting terms. These contracts are typically referenced through a mélange of wrap contracts. There may, for example, be a clickwrap that incorporates several hyperlinks to browsewraps on different pages. In addition, an agreement may contain hyperlinks or references to agreements of affiliated sites which are incorporated by reference and deemed to be part of the agreement between the drafting party and the consumer. Here are a few examples of "casting net" provisions:

> (From Amazon.com)
>
> We offer a wide range of Amazon Services, and sometimes additional terms may apply. When you use an Amazon Service (for example, Your Profile, Gift Cards, Amazon Instant Video, Your Media Library, or Amazon applications for mobile) you also will be subject to the guidelines, terms and agreements applicable to that Amazon Service ("Service Terms"). If these Conditions of Use are inconsistent with the Service Terms, those Service Terms will control.[55]
>
> (And elsewhere in the agreement)

---

[50] Harris v. Blockbuster, 622 F. Supp. 2d 396 (N.D. Tex. 2009).

[51] *Id.*

[52] *Id.* at 398-400.

[53] *Vernon v. Qwest Communications International, Inc.*, 857 F. Supp. 2d 1135 (D.Colo. 2012)).

[54] *Id.* at 1153-1154.

[55] Amazon.com, Conditions of Use, Http://www.amazon.com/gp/help/customer/display.html/ref=footer_cou/187-0283978-2240650?ie=UTF8&nodeId=508088 (last visited Dec. 12, 2012).

Please review our Privacy Notice, which also governs your use of Amazon Services, to understand our practices.[56]

(From YouTube)

By using or visiting the YouTube website or any YouTube products, software, data feeds, and services provided to you on, from, or through the YouTube website (collectively the "Service") you signify your agreement to (1) these terms and conditions (the "Terms of Service"), (2) Google's Privacy Policy, found at http://www.google.com/intl/en/policies/privacy/ and incorporated herein by reference, and (3) YouTube's Community Guidelines, found at www.youtube.com/t/community_guidelines and also incorporated herein by reference.[57]

Another "casting net" type provision is one that references agreements in different formats. For example, in *Vernon v. Qwest Communications International, Inc.*,[58] defendant Qwest sent letters to its subscribers which informed them that they were subject to the terms of their online Subscriber Agreement.[59] The Subscriber Agreement itself referenced other agreements and stated that the subscriber agrees to "OTHER TERMS AND CONDITIONS QUOTED TO YOU DURING THE ORDERING PROCESS AND ON www.qwest.com/legal/highspeedinternetsubscribersagreement/ and www.qwest.com/legal, ALL OF WHICH ARE INCORPORATED BY REFERENCE."

The combination of unilateral modification and incorporation by reference clauses is particularly cruel as it requires the consumer to read all the relevant policies each time she visits the website. The following is an example of such a clause.

(From Wells Fargo Bank's Terms of Service)

If you are enrolled in *Wells Fargo Online®*, or *Wells Fargo Business Online®*:

- your use of the Services is governed by our Online Access Agreement, which incorporates these Terms of Use by reference, and
- if there is a conflict between these Terms of Use and the Online Access Agreement, the Online Access Agreement controls.

---

56 Amazon.com, Conditions of Use, Http://www.amazon.com/gp/help/customer/display.html/ref=footer_cou/186-9776335-7971638?ie=UTF8&nodeId=508088 (last visited Dec. 12, 2012).

57 YouTube, Terms of Service, Http://www.youtube.com/t/terms (last visited Dec. 12, 2012).

58 *Vernon v. Qwest Communications International, Inc.*, 857 F.Supp.2d 1135 (D. Colo 2012).

59 *Id.* at 1144.

> Wells Fargo reserves the right to modify or terminate the Services and the Site or to terminate your access to the Services and Site, in whole or in part, at any time. These Terms of Use constitute a contract between you and Wells Fargo governed by the laws of the South Dakota, with the exception of its conflicts of laws provisions.[60]

While courts claim that wrap contracts are no different from other contracts, companies have exploited differences in form to their benefit. As Chapter 7 explains, wrap contract forms manage to extract unwitting assent from users while obscuring important terms, leading to significant changes in the marketplace.

[60] Wells Fargo, General Terms of Use, Https://www.wellsfargo.com/privacy_security/terms (last visited Dec. 12, 2012).

7 Problems of Substance

PERHAPS THE MOST significant difference between digital and paper contracts is that the nature of the terms contained in digital agreements are often much more aggressive. Unlike contracts of adhesion in the physical world, wrap contracts include sword and crook terms dealing with matters ancillary to or independent of the primary transaction. These terms may significantly affect the rights and expectations of the adherents. For example, a purchase of books on Amazon.com also includes an "agreement" to allow the company to track customer's online movements and share (or sell) their information with third parties.

The rapaciousness of terms in the unchartered digital environment makes consumer obliviousness of terms more consequential. While a consumer signing a car rental agreement has no ability to negotiate terms, she is cognizant that there are limits to her authorization to drive the vehicle and that she will be responsible for damage to it under certain circumstances. The consumer is aware of this even if she fails to read the car rental agreement. She understands that she will pay money for the use of the car and is certain to ask about the price (and, if she's smart, any hidden fees). Furthermore, the contract language and practices of car rental agencies are established so she should have a general idea of what to expect (including fees for late return or failing to return the vehicle with a full gas tank, for example).

The business practices of companies on the Internet are less well established and unknown to the general public. This chapter explains how companies strategically use wrap contracts to acquire rights without bargaining and to stealthily establish and embed practices before users, and regulators, realize what has happened.

A. Wrap Contracts and Norm Shifting

There are some terms that, although not expressly stated, are understood by the parties to be part of the contract. These are terms that are implied by law or social norms. For example, a user of a social networking website knows that he or she may not post video clips that depict sexually explicit content even without reading that website's terms of use. Users understand that social norms and laws apply to online conduct, even if they may not always abide by them. Wrap agreements, however, often do more than ensure adherence to social norms or laws. They create their own laws that are contrary to what a reasonable user expects. Furthermore, they may alter social norms or laws that would otherwise be applicable so that the expectation the consumer has about their applicability to a transaction is inaccurate.

In addition to limiting the drafter's obligations and liabilities, wrap contracts, via crook provisions, may sneak entitlements from their users to an extent unprecedented in paper contracts. Consumers may not realize, for example, that some sites claim a perpetual license to user-generated content. Some websites may do even more than that—they may claim ownership to any creative works that the user then posts to the website, which means that they can change the content of the work by, for example, drawing a moustache on the photo you posted of your dear deceased grandmother. Similarly, the user of a shopping website may type in personal information for the purpose of having merchandise delivered to her home. She may not realize that the website, as stated in its terms of use, also claims a right to the customer's data and will sell it to third-party marketers.

Some may protest that this is much ado about nothing. Given the hundreds of millions of users that a company like Facebook or Google has, how likely is it that a company will enforce a contract provision against *you*? The "likelihood of the harm" argument does not refute the concerns raised by wrap contracts; rather it refers to the somewhat aleatory nature of contracts in general. The likelihood of *any* contract being breached or its provisions enforced in a lawsuit is typically low. This rationale would justify doing away with insurance companies—and lawyers. One of the purposes of entering into contracts is to minimize the risks of entering into a transaction. It is, in fact, the reason businesses have standard form contracts—to protect against unlikely events and to manage risks. To justify the contracting of everything by arguing that wrap contracts are unlikely to be enforced against any one consumer is a nonresponse and does not justify their use.

In any event, the sentiment is simply inaccurate. Wrap contracts are being utilized against users every day. Companies may not be suing their users on the basis of breach of contract (although they occasionally do), but they *are* relying upon contracts to shape the online business landscape in their favor and to subtly change the meaning of legal standards, such as reasonableness and unconscionability.

In order to determine whether a contract is unenforceable on the grounds of unconscionability,[1] the terms of a contract are considered "in the light of the general commercial background and the commercial needs of the particular trade or case."[2] Modern contract law and the Uniform Commercial Code (U.C.C.) state that contractual terms that reflect trade usage or industry standards should be interpreted as part of the contract.[3] Corbin suggests that the test should be whether the terms are "so extreme as to appear unconscionable according to the mores and business practices of the time and place."[4] But where there is a pronounced unevenness in the bargaining power within an industry, industry standards or norms may be established that reflect the interests of only one side.[5] Using industry standards as a guideline where contracts of adhesion[6] are involved merely reinforces overreaching by the

[1] For a discussion and analysis of unconscionability, see Arthur Allen Leff, *Unconscionability and the Code—The Emperor's New Clause*, 115 U. PA. L. REV. 485 (1967). Leff sets forth a framework for analyzing claims of unconscionability that entails both the manner in which the contract was entered into (i.e., whether there was "procedural" unconscionability) and whether the terms were fair (i.e., whether there was "substantive" unconscionability). *Id.* at 486–88.

[2] U.C.C. § 2-302 cmt. (2003); *see also* Williams v. Walker-Thomas Furniture Co., 350 F.2d 445 (D.C. Cir. 1965).

[3] *See* U.C.C. § 1-303(d) (2006) ("[U]sage of trade... is relevant in ascertaining the meaning of the parties' agreement, may give particular meaning to specific terms of the agreement, and may supplement or qualify the terms of the agreement."); RESTATEMENT (SECOND) OF CONTRACTS § 222 (1979) ("Unless otherwise agreed, a usage of trade in the vocation or trade in which the parties are engaged or a usage of trade of which they know or have reason to know gives meaning to or supplements or qualifies their agreement.").

[4] 1 ARTHUR LINTON CORBIN, CORBIN ON CONTRACTS, section 128, at 551 (West 3d ed. 1963).

[5] *See* Robert L. Oakley, *Fairness in Electronic Contracting: Minimum Standards for Non-Negotiated Contracts*, 42 HOUS. L. REV. 1041 (2005) (stating that the U.S. standard of unconscionability is too high a bar to provide reasonable consumer protection and proposing minimum contract standards for nonnegotiated contracts).

[6] The introduction of the term "contracts of adhesion" into American jurisprudence is credited to Edwin Patterson when he described an insurance contract that an insured merely "adheres" to because he has little choice as to its terms. Edwin W. Patterson, *The Delivery of a Life-Insurance Policy*, 33 HARV. L. REV. 198, 222 (1919). In a later work, Patterson attributes the term "contracts of adhesion" to a French jurist, Raymond Saleilles. Saleilles stated:

> Eventually the law must ... yield to the shading and differences that have emerged from social relations. There are pretended contracts that have only the name.... For these ... the rules of individual

party with greater market power.[7] Given the lack of transparency, this is especially true when it comes to online business practices.

Businesses can use wrap contracts to accomplish significant changes in commercial and business practices, which they could not do in a more obvious manner. As Douglas Phillips notes, "[c]ontracts in general involve a kind of private law-making, because they create obligations for the parties that the law otherwise does not impose."[8] This is especially true where the privately made law involves new business models and practices.

The boundaries of acceptable practices are undefined when it comes to new marketplace innovations. Contracts serve a dual purpose in this context in that not only do they set forth the legal obligations of the parties, they legitimate new practices. A new business practice that is socially and legally questionable, but not yet regulated, gains legitimacy through the notion that the practice has been consented to via contract.

A classic example is the licensing, rather than the sale, of software. Michael Rustad and Diane D'Angelo state that the "greatest story never told about Internet-related copyright developments is how information age companies use license agreements to protect intangible assets such as software and website content."[9] Currently all software, including so-called "free" software, is licensed but it did not need to be that way—that was a business decision. There was a strategic reason for licensing rather than selling software, and that was to deprive a purchaser of certain rights granted under the Copyright Act. As Jean Braucher writes:

> The main reason for licensing is to try to limit the rights that customers get under intellectual property law when they are deemed owners of copies. Under the Copyright Act, copy owners get first sale rights to sell their copies. Also, copy owners of computer programs get rights to make another copy "as an

---

> interpretation should undergo important modifications, if only that one might call them, for lack of a better term, contracts of adhesion, those in which a single will is exclusively predominant, acting as a unilateral will which dictates its law, no longer to an individual, but to an indeterminate collectivity....

Edwin W. Patterson, *The Interpretation and Construction of Contracts*, 64 Colum. L. Rev. 833, 856 (1964).

7 *But see* Richard A. Epstein, *Contract, Not Regulation: UCITA and High-Tech Consumers Meet Their Consumer Protection Critics*, *in* Consumer Protection in the Age of the 'Information Economy' 205, 208–14 (Jane K. Winn ed., 2006 (stating that a "convergence in terms across competitors," should not be treated as collusion but as "evidence only of the imitation that allows successful practices to succeed while others fail").

8 Douglas Phillips, The Software License Unveiled: How Legislation by License Controls Software Access at xii (Oxford University Press 2009).

9 Michael L. Rustad & Diane D'Angelo, *The Path of Internet Law: An Annotated Guide to Legal Landmarks*, 2011 Duke L. & Tech. J. 12, at 33.

essential step in the utilization of the computer program in conjunction with a machine... or... for archival purposes."[10]

The licensing of software thus created two related business practices that quickly became industry norms—contractual prohibitions on reverse engineering and prohibitions on transfers to third parties. Richard Warner notes, "[b]oth terms restrict the intellectual property rights buyers would otherwise typically acquire when purchasing the software."[11]

Another norm created by wrap contracts is that of online data collection.[12] Consumers consent because they have no choice if they wish to do business online. A recent study of the top 100 websites conducted by the Berkeley Center for Law and Technology at U.C. Berkeley found that *all* of them employed cookies, which are text files stored on a user's computer to track user online activity.[13]

But the problem with norms created by wrap contracts is more complicated than the issue of bargaining power. Many consumers were not even aware that their online movements were being tracked until after online tracking became an entrenched business practice. Even today, most consumers are unaware of how they are being tracked, or to what extent, or how different technologies or data collection policies may interact. Users don't always understand how the information they relinquish can be used as illustrated by a controversial iPhone app called "Girls Around Me." The app used publicly available information from Facebook and Foursquare, a location-based social network, to enable men to locate women who were in the vicinity. These men could then access personal data of these women from their Facebook profiles.[14] This would allow someone to, for example, approach a woman in a bar and manipulate her into thinking they had shared interests and common friends. Many users were surprised that their Facebook and Foursquare information could be combined in this way.

---

[10] Jean Braucher, Symposium*: Contracting Out of the Uniform Commercial Code: Contracting Out of Article 2 Using a "License" Label: A Strategy that Should Not Work for Software Products*, 40 Loy. L.A. L. Rev. 261, 271 (2006). Braucher argues that "[w]hether a customer acquires ownership of a copy for copyright purposes should be resolved under federal law in light of federal policies."

[11] As Richard Warner observes, "the widespread, intense criticism of the norm" shows that it is not value justified. Richard Warner, *Turned on Its Head? Norms, Freedom, and Acceptable Terms in Internet Contracting*, 14 J. Internet L. 18, at 25 (Nov. 2010).

[12] *Id.* at 29.

[13] Web Privacy Census, *available at* http://www.law.berkeley.edu/privacycensus.htm"; *see also* Natasha Singer, *More Companies Are Tracking Online Data, Study Finds*, N.Y. Times, Nov. 12, 2012, *available at* http://bits.blogs.nytimes.com/2012/11/12/more-companies-are-tracking-online-data/.

[14] Julie Angwin & Jeremy Singer Vine, *Selling You on Facebook*, Wall St. J., Apr. 7, 2012, *available at* http://online.wsj.com/article/SB10001424052702303302504577327744009046230.html. The authors cite a U.C. Berkeley study that indicated that most Facebook users were not aware of what was happening with their data or what type of data was collected by an app.

As technology develops, more intrusive ways of online monitoring will also develop. Consumers who have granted companies broad licenses through wrap agreements may be powerless to do anything to stop these companies from exploiting their information in objectionable ways.

Judicial accommodation of a particular business need or environment (i.e., the brave new cut-and-paste world online) may be applied to other environments (i.e., the physical world offline) with potentially disastrous and unanticipated consequences. Wrap contracts create their own laws, and these laws may create online norms that migrate offline. The most glaring current example of this is online data collection. The norm of tracking and collecting user movements and information threatens to move offline so that a consumer's movements may be tracked and recorded while she is in a store—and even after she leaves. Facebook reportedly entered into an agreement with Datalogix, a company that obtains information from retailers about what customers are buying.[15] This agreement would enable Facebook to match its users with those in the Datalogix databases and prepare reports for its advertisers, who can then determine whether ads on Facebook resulted in offline purchases. This has the potential to greatly expand the personal information that Facebook already has about its users regarding what they buy, how much, for how much, and where. (Facebook currently has an opt-out feature, but it is not easy to find, and the company can always remove it.) By claiming that a user has assented to its online terms, a company such as Facebook may shield its invasive practices from governmental scrutiny or regulation even when these tracking and collection practices involve users' offline movements and purchases.

Facebook is not the only company engaging in offline/online data collection. The marketing industry giant, Acxiom, is integrating information culled from online, offline, and mobile sources to create detailed consumer profiles which industry insiders refer to as a "360-degree view" of users.[16] Contractual assent supplies the veneer of legitimacy for these murky practices.

As market pressures bear down upon newly public companies, they may be tempted to test existing limits. Tom Simonite, an editor at *Technology Review*, writes that now that Facebook has gone public, "the pressure to develop new sources of profit... is likely to force it to do more with its hoard of information. That stash of data looms like an oversize shadow over what today is a modest online advertising business,

---

15 Rebecca Greenfield, *Facebook Now Knows What You're Buying at Drug Stores,* The Atlantic Wire, Sept. 24, 2012, *available at* http://www.theatlanticwire.com/technology/2012/09/facebook-tracking-you-drug-store-now-too/57183/.

16 Natasha Singer, *You for Sale: Mapping and Sharing, the Consumer Genome,* N.Y. Times, June 16, 2012, *available at* http://www.nytimes.com/2012/06/17/technology/acxiom-the-quiet-giant-of-consumer-database-marketing.html?pagewanted=all&_r=0.

worrying privacy-conscious Web users... and rivals such as Google."[17] Companies who strive to maintain standards favoring consumers may find themselves forced to lower them in order to keep pace with less scrupulous competitors—or else they may find themselves pushed out of the market altogether.

B. Getting Something for Nothing: The Old Bait and Switch

Skeptics may respond, if consumers don't like how companies operate, they shouldn't use their services. Nobody was ever forced to join Facebook or Google Plus, right? And isn't that what freedom of contract is all about? Isn't that what the free market is all about?

About that word "free"...

The very notion of "contract" is premised upon free will. While there is disagreement among academics and philosophers about the contours of free will, all would agree that at the very least, free will needs to be voluntary and not the product of coercion.

Free will also requires knowledge or at least awareness. An act is an expression of free will if the actor intends it, and then only if the actor can choose not to undertake that action. Without awareness of what an act means, the meaning imputed to it does not reflect volition—free will—but a reflex, a response. The action may not be coerced, but it is devoid of will. This is why contract law cares about intent.

The free market is premised upon rational decision making on the part of both parties, and rational decision making presupposes, at a minimum, that the parties are acting of their own free will. Accordingly, a free market economy functions optimally only if there is transparency regarding the circumstances surrounding transactions. Where transactions are shrouded in mystery or where there are information asymmetries, the parties are not making accurate cost-benefit analyses.

Wrap contracts contribute to market failure when businesses use them to legitimate practices lacking in transparency and courts enforce them by constructing assent which is divorced from the intent of the parties. To put it plainly, users are being deceived by businesses, and courts are giving them the green light. Rather than making informed decisions, users are acting in ignorance. Their ignorance leads to suboptimal conditions resulting in market dominance by companies that don't necessarily reflect consumer preferences. Let me explain.

---

[17] Tom Simonite, *What Facebook Knows*, TECHNOLOGY REVIEW, Aug. 2012, at 44, *available at* http://www.technologyreview.com/featuredstory/428150/what-facebook-knows/.

In the early days of the Internet, there were two primary ways for companies to generate revenue. They could sell merchandise, or they could sell advertising. Those who sold advertising did so by attracting users or "eyeballs" to their site with content. Advertisers would pay for access to those eyeballs. Consumers were initially distrustful of online commerce and activity, fearing that their credit card information would be stolen by hackers or that a virtual retailer would charge for merchandise that was never delivered. Eventually, however, consumers became more comfortable with using the Internet for their everyday needs.

Companies soon sought additional sources of revenue. Technology evolved and developed so that it became easier to track customers' online movements and to track them more intrusively. The information that could be gleaned from online tracking could be used to engage in more effective online campaigns, known in industry parlance as "targeted" or "behavioral" advertising. The information could also be sold or traded to third parties. Marketers were eager to pay for consumer information. But was it legal to do so?

The area surrounding online tracking and the buying and selling of customer information was unregulated. Technology outpaces the political process. One way for companies to hold off regulators was to get customer permission. But customers, who were just getting comfortable with online activity would undoubtedly balk. Companies were unwilling to frighten them away and hesitated to make their intrusive tracking practices transparent. They wanted, in other words, to have it both ways—consent, but without the customer backlash that transparency would certainly bring. One solution was using wrap contracts, thereby getting consumers to consent to data collection without being aware that they were doing so.

For the most part, courts went along. The collection of data in accordance with a conspicuous privacy policy is generally viewed as legally permissible.[18] (Interestingly, when users seek to enforce a privacy policy against a website, courts have generally found they were not enforceable as contracts.)[19] As Woodrow Hartzog notes, "[m]ost privacy

---

[18] *See* discussion chapter 10, section B; *see also In re* JetBlue Airways Corp. Privacy Litig., 379 F. Supp. 2d 299; *In re* Nw. Airlines Privacy Litig., 2004 WL 1278459 (D. Minn. 2004). *See also* Richard Raysman & Peter Brown, *Contractual Nature of Online Policies Remains Unsettled*, N.Y. L.J. (Aug. 10, 2010); Allyson W. Haynes, *Online Privacy Policies: Contracting Away Control Over Personal Information?*, 111 PENN. ST. L. REV. 587, 588 (2007) ("[I]f the website complies with its own promises, there is little else to prevent the site from doing with the information whatever it wants ... besides the website company's own interest in attracting and maintaining customers.").

[19] *See In re* Nw. Airlines Privacy Litig., 2004 WL 1278459 (D. Minn. June 6, 2004) at 6 (finding that Northwest Airlines privacy policy found on its website did not constitute a unilateral contract); Dyer v. Northwest Airlines Corporation, 334 F. Supp. 2d 1196, 1200 (D.N.D. 2004) (finding that Northwest Airlines' privacy policy was unenforceable as a contract because it was too indefinite, and that plaintiffs did not allege that they read or relied upon it and did not allege any contractual damages arising out of the alleged breach.) *Id.* at 1200.

disputes involving online agreements look to the 'consensual' aspect of the agreement. Judges have struggled to support the privacy interests of individuals when those individuals have consented to surveillance, collection, or use of their information."[20]

In *People v. Direct Revenue LLC*,[21] for example, the court dismissed a petition brought by the attorney general of the state of New York alleging deceptive and unfair practices against a company that installed pop-up advertising software on consumer computers. The court found that the consumers had consented to the installation of the software by clicking on a "Yes" dialog box that indicated consent to the terms of a hyperlinked agreement. The court stated that "[t]his conduct created a binding 'click-wrap' agreement which bars any claim for deceptive or unlawful conduct. Under New York law, such contracts are enforced so long as the consumer is given a sufficient opportunity to read the EULA, and assents thereto after being provided with an unambiguous method of accepting or declining the offer."[22]

Wayne Barnes states that the "primary method" to obtain user consent to "spyware" or software that monitors user's online movement, is disclosure in an end-user license agreement (EULA), and that consent is "at the heart of the spyware debate."[23] Spyware is not simply innocuous software that serves tailored ads; it can strain a computer's processing power, which leads to crashes and loss of data. Barnes notes that spyware "represents a significant privacy threat to Internet user." He explains that such software

> is capable of monitoring consumers' visits to financial, medical, political, and religious sites and even individual chat rooms where private conversations take place... The amount of personal private information transmitted to marketing companies that distribute spyware is extensive and can be contrary to expectations of the consumers who download bundled applications. In short, spyware can allow hackers and marketing companies to monitor all of a consumer's online activity.... These bits of personal information are stored indefinitely because the cost of memory has become cheaper and cheaper....[24]

By the time the general public became aware of what they had constructively consented to, they were already ensnared. They had grown dependent on the Internet for their shopping, for keeping in touch with friends, for banking. If they had known

---

[20] Woodrow Hartzog, *Website Design as Contract*, 60 Am. U. L. Rev. 1635, at 1648 (2011).

[21] 19 Misc.3d 1124(A) (Mar. 12, 2008), 2009 WL 1849855 (N.Y. Sup.)

[22] *Id.* at 4.

[23] Wayne R. Barnes, *Rethinking Spyware: Questioning the Propriety of Contractual Consent to Online Surveillance*, 39 UC Davis L. Rev. 1545, 1553–54 (2006).

[24] *Id.* at 1561.

from the beginning where this would lead, they might have stayed offline. But now, unplugging is not a viable option. That doesn't mean consumers are happy with the current state of affairs.

A recent poll of 1,500 random registered voters showed that even in high-tech-friendly California, the vast majority of respondents (82 percent) were "somewhat concerned" or "very concerned" about the data collected by Internet and smartphone companies.[25] Seventy-eight percent also believed that collection of personal information online is an invasion of privacy.[26] Even among younger voters, who reportedly share everything online, 71 percent of those between the ages of 18 and 29 believed such collection was an invasion of privacy.[27]

Trust in Internet-based companies is also eroding. According to that same poll, on a scale of zero to ten, with ten being the most trustworthy and zero being not trustworthy at all with their personal information, participants gave Twitter a shameful 2.4, Facebook barely better at 2.7, Google an anemic 3.8, and Apple the highest at a measly 4.6.[28]

So, you might ask, if these users are so unhappy with these companies, why don't they just shut down their Facebook, Google, and Twitter accounts? For the same reason that bank customers don't shut down their checking accounts when they are unhappy with fees. It's what researchers refer to as "behavioral lock-in." William Barnes, Myles Gartland, and Martin Stack state that behavioral lock-in "occurs when the behavior of the agent (consumer or producer) is 'stuck' in some sort of inefficiency or sub-optimality due to habit, organizational learning, or culture."[29]

Many factors contribute to consumer behavioral lock-in. Consumers are myopic or "present-biased"[30] in that they are focused on the present or short term rather than the future or long term.[31] Facebook users, for example, may be more interested

---

[25] Press Release, USC Dornsife/Los Angeles Times Poll, Voters Across the Political Spectrum Concerned about Tech Companies Invading Their Privacy (Mar. 31, 2012), *available at* http://dornsife.usc.edu/usc-lat-poll-privacy-march-2012/. *See also* David Sarno, *Tech Firms' Data Gathering Worries Most Californians, Poll Finds*, L.A. TIMES, Apr. 1, 2012 (citing to USC Dornsife/Times poll), *available at* http://articles.latimes.com/2012/mar/31/business/la-fi-privacy-poll-20120331.

[26] *Id.*

[27] *Id.*

[28] Sarno, *supra* note 25.

[29] William Barnes, Myles Gartland, & Martin Stack, *Old Habits Die Hard: Path Dependency and Behavioral Lock-In*, 38 J. OF ECONOMIC ISSUES 371–77, at 372 (no. 2, June 2004).

[30] Ted O'Donoghue and Matthew Rabin, Doing it Now or Later, 89 AMER. ECON. REV. 103-124, at 103 (March 1999).

[31] As Oren Bar-Gill writes, "Myopic consumers care more about the present and not enough about the future....Myopia is common. People are impatient, preferring immediate benefits even at the expense of future costs." OREN BAR-GILL, SEDUCTION BY CONTRACTS: LAW, ECONOMICS AND PSYCHOLOGY IN CONSUMER MARKETS at 21-22 (2012).

in the immediate satisfaction of using the service than the potential long-term harm to their future selves of doing so.

In addition, there are, as economists like to say, "switching" costs when you have all of your contacts and content in one account. Members of a site may have invested significant time and energy into a site by uploading content and storing communications. There may be path dependence as users are familiar with certain sites and how they work. Familiarity breeds inertia. As economist Harvey Liebenstein wrote, if "new information does not increase the utility gain of a change in effort position sufficiently to overcome the 'inertial cost' of altering one's ways of doing things, then the individual will remain in his inert area and not take advantage of additional information."[32] While Liebenstein was referring to behavior in organizations, this notion also helps to explain consumer behavior in the face of new information regarding distasteful business practices.

But there are reasons for lock-in other than myopia, inertia or laziness. There is also a market inefficiency problem, where the data collection practices have become the industry norm. In other words, even if you were willing to take your content and go somewhere else—there would be nowhere else to go.

In a speech to the American Bar Association, Senator Al Franken expressed the complexities involved in switching:

> If people don't like what's happening to the personal information that's collected when they use a service, they'll switch to a competing service with a better privacy policy—and thus, the market will pressure companies to protect privacy. At least, that's the idea. But what if the market fails to do so—what if a company is able to establish a dominant market share and insulate itself from that pressure? What we're seeing is that, just like Americans' pocketbooks and access to information, their right to privacy can be a casualty of anti-competitive practices. Here's an example: Google's recent changes to its privacy policy. Now, Google isn't just Google, the search engine. There's Gmail, Google Maps, and YouTube. And Google has always tracked your use of these services. That was the basic deal. You got to use these amazing, innovative, helpful services—and, unless you knew where to find that opt-out link, Google got to use your use of these services to better target ads to you. Over time, though, the deal changed. In September 2010, Google told people it might use

[32] Harvey Leibenstein, *X-Efficiency, Technical Efficiency, and Incomplete Information Use: A Comment*, 25 Economic Development and Cultural Change 311–16, at 316 (no. 2, Jan. 1977). *See also* Harvey Leibenstein, *Allocative Efficiency vs. "X-Efficiency,"* 56 The American Economic Review 392–415 (June 1966).

> data from the content of your Gmail messages to better target the ads you'd see on other Google sites.... When a company is able to establish a dominant market position, consumers lose meaningful choices. You might not like that Facebook shares your political opinions with Politico, but are you really going to delete all the photos, all the posts, all the connections—the presence you've spent years establishing on the world's dominant social network? The more dominant these companies become over the sectors in which they operate, the less incentive they have to respect your privacy.... And so when companies become so dominant that they can violate their users' privacy without worrying about market pressure, all that's left is the incentive to get more and more information about you.... And shouldn't we be concerned that, as these companies that trade in your personal information keep getting bigger and bigger, they become less and less accountable?[33]

Wrap contracts were instrumental in creating norms that led to this market failure in online privacy. At a time when the legality of tracking practices was uncertain, contracts gave them legitimacy by allowing companies to claim customers consented. They reframed the discussion, so that instead of one that focused on whether these practices *should* be permitted, it became one replete with the rhetoric of free will and choice. The claim that users had consented kept claims of privacy invasion at bay, at least for a while. Companies, under cover of contract and emboldened by court decisions finding assent in the unlikeliest of places, swapped their old terms for ever more intrusive ones.

Eventually, the discourse did turn to the practices themselves, as they might have sooner were it not for the legitimating work done by contracts. The Federal Trade Commission finally called for the development of a "do not track" system that would allow consumers to opt out of having their online movements tracked. The Commission's call to action aims to provide guidance to lawmakers in their legislative efforts. Unfortunately, many of the proposals circulating around Congress enable companies to continue their practices with customer "consent." Worse, this consent often takes the form of an "opt-out" rather than an "opt-in" provision.[34]

---

[33] Al Franken, *How Privacy Has Become an Anti-Trust Issue*, Huffington Post, Mar. 30, 2012, http://www.huffingtonpost.com/al-franken/how-privacy-has-become-an_b_1392580.html.

[34] For example, draft legislation, released by Representatives Rick Boucher (D-VA) and Cliff Stearns (R-FL) and circulated for comment, attempts to offer comprehensive consumer privacy protection but has been criticized by both consumer privacy advocates and by marketers. Chloe Albanesius, *Boucher's Privacy Bill Scolded by Consumer Groups*, PC Mag, May 4, 2010, http://www.pcmag.com/article2/0,2817,2363404,00.asp. Another bill introduced by Representative Bobby Rush (D-IL) has also received mixed reception. Declan McCullagh, *New Bill Renews Internet Privacy Fight*, CNET, July 20, 2010, *available at* http://news.cnet.com/8301-31921_3-20011016-281.html. In both proposed bills, consent is defined as passive, a failure to opt-out.

Accordingly, a failure to act on the part of the consumer would constitute consent to a website's information collection practices.

Opponents of privacy legislation argue that limiting data collection and behavioral advertising would change the nature of the Internet and reduce access to free content.[35] This argument distorts the current state of affairs. Access to information is currently not free; it is paid for by consumers with their privacy. This payment, however, is not transparent; the consumer is not aware of what type of information is being used, how it is being used, and who has access to it. The cost is uncertain, but the information absolutely has value as evidenced by the size of the multibillion dollar online advertising industry.[36] The argument espoused by the advertisers assumes that the consumer places no value on privacy or that access to any content is equivalent to whatever price the consumer may place upon privacy.

Because the process of information collection lacks transparency, the marketplace is inefficient. The seemingly cost-free nature of certain websites distorts behavior and, consequently, may reward the wrong players, and punish or fail to adequately reward the right players. A user may visit a website only because it is free and readily accessible and not because the user highly values the content on this site—we can call this the "free sample" response. A shopper at Costco on a busy Saturday morning may take a sample or five from the many food purveyors offering them not because she is hungry or interested in buying the food product but simply because it is offered—and is, as far as the user knows, free.[37]

On the other hand, there are other websites that the user may value more even if she visits them less frequently. The user may even be willing to pay for the information on these sites. But because online advertising prices are usually dictated by user activity on a website, websites are rewarded for more user activity rather than for providing more *valuable* user activity. Websites that offer valuable content but

---

35 Dan Jaffe, the executive vice president of the Association of National Advertisers, complained that proposed legislation to regulate web tracking "basically attacks the financing model of the Internet" and "will cut down on the amount of free information that consumers have on the Internet, create incentives for online companies to erect pay walls, and lead to more shotgun forms of advertising." Kevin J. O'Brien, *Privacy Advocates and Advertisers at Odds over Web Tracking*, N.Y. TIMES, Oct. 4, 2012, *available at* http://www.nytimes.com/2012/10/05/technology/privacy-advocates-and-advertisers-at-odds-over-web-tracking.html?pagewanted=all&_r=0.

36 A recent report issued by the Interactive Advertising Bureau and PricewaterhouseCoopers reported that in the first half of 2012, online advertising revenues reached $17 billion. Press Release, Interactive Advertising Bureau, Internet Ad Revenues Rise to Historic $17 Billion in First Half 2012, Up 14% Over Half-Year 2011, According to IAB (Oct. 11, 2012), *available at* http://www.iab.net/about_the_iab/recent_press_releases/press_release_archive/press_release/pr-101112.

37 Of course, some samplers may be converted into customers by the quality of the product or the oppressiveness of their guilt.

do not elicit or encourage repeat activity are undervalued in the marketplace even though users may actually value them more.

For example, a user may visit Facebook several times a day, not because she obtains valuable information from the site but simply because she is procrastinating and because it costs her nothing (as far as she can tell) to do so. On the other hand, she may visit the WebMD website only once in a while. The information she receives from the site, however, is valuable to her. She may actually value the WebMD website more than Facebook even though she visits it much less frequently. The economics of the Internet, however, do not reflect this preference.

The lack of transparency may result in market failure if advertisers decide to move their business from one site to another with greater activity. Because the activity is based on the "free" nature of the content and not the value the user places upon the content, the market rewards players based upon the wrong criteria. Companies like WebMD may be driven out of business while those like Facebook flourish, even though the consumer may actually value WebMD more highly than Facebook. Furthermore, if the user actually understood what was happening with her data, she might visit Facebook much less frequently or not at all.

Finally, the seemingly free nature of online services may result in social welfare-reducing productivity loss. The ready accessibility of Facebook, for example, means the user may be spending time on the site without making an accurate cost-benefit analysis of the time spent doing so. The user is unable to make an informed decision regarding whether to visit Facebook (or any other site) because she doesn't know what the website does with her information. She does not have to engage in a trade-off analysis because she is not aware that any trade-off exists.

Even if she did read the privacy policy of a particular website, she likely still doesn't understand what the data use and collection practices of that website are given the complexity of most privacy policies. One study found that of 35 of 64 privacy policies examined (54 percent) required the equivalent of more than fourteen years of education in order to understand their content; 13 percent of the policies were only understandable by people with a postgraduate education.[38] Oren Bar-Gil writes that complexity in agreements "hides the true cost of the product from the imperfectly rational consumer.... The imperfectly rational consumer deals with complexity by ignoring it."[39]

---

[38] Carlos Jensen & Colin Potts, *Privacy Policies as Decision-Making Tools: An Evaluation of Online Privacy Notices*, paper presented to the Conference on Human Factors in Computing Systems, Apr. 24–29, 2004, Vienna, Austria.

[39] Oren Bar-Gill, Seduction by Contract: Law, Economics, and Psychology in Consumer Markets (Oxford University Press 2012).

A user who read the privacy policy upon signing up with a website service might have mistaken or outdated understandings of that website's practices since privacy policies are constantly evolving. As technology improves, data collection practices keep changing, gradually becoming more intrusive and burdensome. Like predatory pricing strategies, these practices ensnare consumers by offering amazing services with seemingly benign consequences. They grow in power and eventually kill off the competition. (Myspace and Friendster, anyone?) After they dominate the marketplace, they no longer fear enraging their users because those users effectively have nowhere else to go.

The wrap contract is instrumental in implementing these unsavory practices because they provide the mechanism by which the consumer ostensibly and constructively provides consent. The Electronic Frontier Foundation (EFF) constructed a timeline of Facebook's "eroding" privacy policies, illustrating how over the past few years the company has made changes that have diminished user control over personal information.[40] EFF observes:

> the successive policies tell a clear story. Facebook originally earned its core base of users by offering them simple and powerful controls over their personal information. As Facebook grew larger and became more important, it could have chosen to maintain or improve those controls. Instead, it's slowly but surely helped itself—and its advertising and business partners—to more and more of its users' information, while limiting the users' options to control their own information.[41]

But, you may object, the updated policies might apply to their new members but not you. You signed up eons ago, when Sheryl Sandberg was still at Google and Myspace was still a contender. Unfortunately, many wrap contracts contain unilateral modification clauses which give the websites the right to change the terms at any time with "notice." Notice often constitutes posting a change to the website. Given the low probability of users' actually reading the posted notice, most contract changes go unnoticed despite the legally sufficient notice.

When changes do attract user attention, it is usually too late. By the time companies are big enough to attract watchdog scrutiny, their users are hooked. Because these companies dominate the marketplace, their users have nowhere else to go. Even if competitors exist, they have likely adopted the same terms as the market giants.

---

[40] Kurt Opsahl, *Facebook's Eroding Privacy Policy: A Timeline,* April 28, 2010, https://www.eff.org/deeplinks/2010/04/facebook-timeline (last visited Oct. 8, 2012).

[41] *Id.*

The dominance of players has another effect on users—it may lead them to a false sense of security. It's generally accepted that familiar brands reassure consumers that their products are better than products from unfamiliar companies.[42] Accordingly, consumers may pay more for branded products even when generics are readily available at a lower price. Similarly, consumers may feel that Amazon.com is a "safer" site than a smaller online retailer even if their data collection practices are actually much more intrusive.

There are other cognitive biases involved where dominant players are involved. The sheer number of other users may cause consumers to rationalize and convince themselves that there is safety in numbers. The same herd mentality or bandwagon effect[43] that got users to join Facebook in the first place makes it difficult for its users to act when the rules of the game start to gradually change. Or they may rationalize that if the change in terms were as bad as it looks, there would be more of a backlash and discount their own intuition or bad feeling about what the change means. This is similar to what psychologists refer to as the "bystander effect." Researchers Bibb Latané and John M. Darley conducted a series of experiments and found that a failure to intervene in emergency situations stems, not from apathy, but from situational factors, especially the social environment and the relationship among the bystanders.[44] In particular, they found that "[p]eople were less likely to take a socially responsible action if other people are present than if they are alone."[45] They concluded that an individual may "through a process of social influence, be led to interpret the situation as less serious than he would if he were alone, and consequently be less likely to take action."[46] The result is a state of "pluralistic ignorance," where each bystander is led "by the *apparent* lack of concern of the others to interpret the situation as being less serious than he would if alone."[47]

Another cognitive tendency that may deter users from reacting to egregious wrap contract terms may be optimism. Optimism bias makes users overestimate their

---

[42] *See generally* Leo Bogart & Charles Lehman, *What Makes a Brand Name Familiar?*, 10 JOURNAL OF MARKETING RESEARCH 17 (Feb. 1973) (noting that "a great deal of advertising is designed to reinforce the public's sense of brand familiarity on the assumption that familiarity is translated into acceptance and preference when the brand is juxtaposed with less familiar ones at the point of sale.") *Id.* at 17.

[43] The bandwagon effect is used to describe a phenomenon whereby individuals adopt a trend or opinion influenced by the number of others who have done so. *See, for example*, Walter M. Pierce, *Climbing the Bandwagon*, 4 THE PUBLIC OPINION QUARTERLY 241–43 (1940) (noting that public opinion polls may cause voters to "climb onto the bandwagon" and that such polls "greatly increase the bandwagon vote.") *Id.* at 241.

[44] Bibb Latane & John M. Darley, *Bystander "Apathy,"* 57 AMERICAN SCIENTIST 244, 268 (Summer 1969).

[45] *Id.* at 259.

[46] *Id.*

[47] *Id.* at 265.

abilities and underestimate the risks involved with activities they undertake.[48] Daniel Kahneman notes that "optimistic bias plays a role—sometimes the dominant role—whenever individuals or institutions voluntarily take on significant risks. More often than not, risk takers underestimate the odds they face."[49] It may also convince them that a company would never enforce bad contract clauses against *them*, that nothing will go wrong, that even if others get into trouble with the site, they won't. The optimism, bandwagon, and bystander effect phenomena converge as consumers get the sense that there is safety in numbers and feel no obligation to object to egregious terms. A billion users couldn't have agreed to something that was so bad—surely someone else would bring an egregious term to the attention of the rest of the herd? Surely someone is looking out for their interests?

Sometimes somebody is. Several years ago, Facebook angered some of its members by changing its terms of service.[50] (The only reason anyone noticed was because it is such a high-profile company and was on the verge of going public.) Facebook backpedaled, but it was a younger company then.[51] Since that time, it has grown in size and market power, with pressures to respond to investor demands. Not surprisingly, it has recently made several changes to its terms of service, securing for itself more rights to member information and posted content. Even when consumers are able to score a win, it is only temporary. Despite the help of social networking tools (such as Facebook), the coordination problems are just too great.

Facebook is not much concerned that dissatisfaction and frustration with privacy intrusions will make users leave *en masse*. They know it is not easy for users to move their Facebook community and content elsewhere—where would a billion users go? Instead, the company likely hopes that Facebook users will resign themselves to whatever new forms of data collection the company can conjure, so that what is distasteful today becomes the new normal—in the same way that Facebook has made oversharing the new normal.

Some might argue that it is part of the bargain consumers make with a company. The consumer can make the choice whether to use Facebook's services to connect with old friends or Google's search engine in exchange for giving up some privacy. But that argument ignores that the practices are opaque and consumers often are not

---

[48] *See* Daniel Kahneman & Amos Tversky, *Conflict Resolution: A Cognitive Perspective*, *in* CHOICES, VALUES AND FRAMES (Daniel Kahneman & Amos Tversky eds., Cambridge University Press 2000) (defining "optimistic overconfidence" as the "common tendency of people to overestimate their ability to predict and control future outcomes") *Id.* at 473.

[49] DANIEL KAHNEMAN, THINKING, FAST AND SLOW at 256 (Farrar, Straus and Giroux 2011).

[50] Brad Stone & Brian Stelter, *Facebook Withdraws Changes in Data Use*, N.Y. TIMES, Feb. 18, 2009, *available at* http://www.nytimes.com/2009/02/19/technology/internet/19facebook.html.

[51] *Id.*

aware of the terms of the bargain. The services are advertised as being free—in fact, Facebook's slogan is: "It's free, and always will be."[52] If the bargain were clear and the practices transparent, consumers might have made other choices. For example, they might have stuck with using Myspace if they had known how Facebook was going to treat them. They might have continued to pay a couple of bucks more for their books at Borders than order online from Amazon.com. Consumers might have been perfectly happy with Google's original privacy policy (assuming they even read and understood it) but less so with the latest one. If only they had known what would happen, they might have stuck with the Excite search engine!

This leads to another, less discussed problem with changing privacy policies and norm shifting, which has to do with competition and consumer choice. When companies expand their intrusive practices *after* they have already dominated the marketplace, they effectively trap the consumer into accepting the new, unilaterally imposed norm. It is extremely difficult for a new company with a less intrusive privacy policy to compete against Google given the latter company's vast resources. (This is especially true with respect to Google since it controls search results. The Federal Trade Commission recently concluded an antitrust investigation focusing on whether Google manipulates search results to favor its own products and submerge competitor's results. The Commission ultimately concluded that Google did not violate antitrust law.)[53] Of course, any new company that does manage to make it big in the online marketplace could eventually shift gears to itself become a bait-and-switcher since it likely has reserved the right to do so in its terms of use.

C. The Limits of Unconscionability and the Problem of Other Laws

Contract law has a mechanism for dealing with unfair or deceptive contracts—unconscionability. But there are several problems with relying upon the doctrine of unconscionability to prevent enforcement of nonnegotiated agreements. Outcomes are unpredictable and subjective, more so than in other doctrinal areas. As Leon Trakman observed, "[n]o consistent jurisprudence has emerged over the limits of substantive unconscionability in wrap contracting."[54]

Furthermore, unconscionability is a defense to contract enforcement, meaning that a contract must have already been formed. In some cases, it makes a difference

[52] Facebook home page, http://www.facebook.com/ (last visitedJanuary 7, 2013).

[53] Edward Wyatt, *A Victory for Google as FTC Takes No Formal Steps,* N.Y. TIMES (Jan. 3, 2012) *available at* http://www.nytimes.com/2013/01/04/technology/google-agrees-to-changes-in-search-ending-us-antitrust-inquiry.html?_r=0.

[54] Leon E. Trakman, *The Boundaries of Contract Law in Cyberspace*, 38 PUB. CONT. L.J. 187, at 232–33 (2008).

whether a plaintiff contests formation or enforcement because it affects whether a contract is "void" or "voidable." It may, for example, affect the burden of proof.[55] The doctrine of unconscionability looks to industry norms to determine whether a term is enforceable, which may be problematic where the norms are set by an industry player with greater bargaining power. In addition, courts have generally been reluctant to strike down agreements on the basis of unconscionability, provided that there was notice and an opportunity to read the contract terms.[56] The party seeking to avoid the contract on the grounds of unconscionability has a "heavy burden" and often requires proving that the agreement was both procedurally and substantively unconscionable.[57] This burden is even greater if the party seeking avoidance is another business entity even though the employees clicking "I accept" are just as oblivious to what they are doing as consumers. For example, in *Margae v. Clear Link Technologies, LLC*,[58] the parties were both Internet marketing companies who had a dispute about work being performed by the plaintiff. The plaintiff sued, claiming that the defendant was using its proprietary materials without compensation or acknowledgment.[59] The court found that the plaintiff had agreed to the terms of the defendant's online agreement, which permitted the defendant to modify the agreement at any time by notifying the plaintiff or by posting a new agreement on the website.[60] The agreement also included a venue clause.[61] The defendant later amended the agreement to include an arbitration clause.[62] The plaintiff argued that it did not assent to the amended agreement, but

---

[55] JOSEPH M. PERILLO, CALAMARI & PERILLO ON CONTRACTS, § 9.22 (WEST 6TH ED., 2009) ("The void-voidable dichotomy also has an effect on the burden of proof. The defrauded party normally has the burden of proof on matters of avoidance; the party seeking to enforce the contract has the burden of establishing the existence of the contract.").

[56] *See* Blake Morant, *The Quest for Bargains in an Age of Contractual Formalism: Strategic Initiatives for Small Businesses*, 7 J. SMALL & EMERGING BUS. L. 233, 261–66 (2003); Amy J. Schmitz, *Embracing Unconscionability's Safety Net Function*, 58 ALA L. REV. 73, 91 (2006) (stating that courts have become more formulaic in their application of the doctrine, thereby undermining the doctrine's "safety net" function); *see also* Larry A. DiMatteo & Bruce Louis Rich, *A Consent Theory of Unconscionability: An Empirical Study of Law in Action*, 33 FLA. ST. U. L. REV. 1067 (2006) (conducting an empirical study of cases tending to show that claims of unconscionability are difficult, although not impossible, to win). Elsewhere, I have discussed the limitations of the unconscionability doctrine, including a high standard of unfairness, review of events limited to events existing at the time of contract formation, doctrinal vagueness, and judicial discretion. *See* Nancy S. Kim, *Evolving Business and Social Norms and Interpretation Rules: The Need for a Dynamic Approach to Contract Disputes*, 84 Neb. L. Rev. 506, 550–53 (2005).

[57] *See* Margae, Inc. v. Clear Link Technologies, 2008 WL 2465450 (D. Utah June 16, 2008).

[58] *Id.*

[59] *Id.* at 1–3.

[60] *Id.* at 4.

[61] *Id.*

[62] *Id.* at 5.

the court rejected this argument, finding that the defendant "should have monitored to determine whether any amendments had been posted."[63] The court further found that the agreements were not unconscionable, noting that the plaintiff was a "sophisticated corporation" and that the modification at will provision was not substantively unconscionable.[64]

Finally, there is the question of truth and unintended consequences. As previously noted, courts have been less sympathetic to unconscionability claims made by businesses than they have been to claims made by consumers. If a click is indeed as valid as a signature on a page, then a wrap contract can effectively modify or replace the terms of a paper one. A business may be unpleasantly surprised if a court finds that the terms of a negotiated paper agreement are superseded by the terms of a wrap contract. For example, a company could spend months negotiating the terms of a multimillion dollar software and services agreement with another company. Upon installation of the software, however, an employee of the purchasing company may be required to accept the terms of a clickwrap. The employee would likely do so out of habit and without awareness. Consequently, the terms of that clickwrap could supersede the terms of the negotiated agreement under wrap contract doctrine.

Contracts should capture the parties' intent; at a minimum, a party should be cognizant of what she is agreeing to do, even if she does not desire the contract and feels she has no choice but to agree to its terms. Wrap contract doctrine, however, recognizes as enforceable unilaterally imposed terms that are hidden, convoluted, and overly long. These terms are often oppressive, but the argument against them is not based solely, or even primarily, upon their substance—it is based upon their form.

Contract law is not the only law that may apply to an interaction. The greater the distance between contract law's standards and the standards of these other laws, the greater the risk that a company may run afoul of those other laws. Companies relying upon wrap contract case precedent do so at their peril. A contract that is validly formed and enforceable by contract law's flaccid standards may fail to pass muster under other regulatory regimes, to the chagrin of the drafting company. Most notably, the Federal Trade Commission Act (FTCA) prohibits "unfair or deceptive acts or practices," including online advertising claims, sales practices, and marketing activities.[65] The Federal Trade Commission (FTC) requires that "clear and conspicuous" disclosures be used to prevent misleading or deceptive statements. The

---

[63] *Id.*

[64] *Id.* at 6.

[65] *Id.* at 3.

FTC's Consumer Protection Bureau's guidelines for meeting the standard of "clear and conspicuous" offer the "Four P's": prominence, presentation, placement, and proximity. These four P's stand in marked contrast with the requirements for notice under contract law. For example, the test for prominence is not whether the text is readable, but whether it is *read*. The guidelines also suggest that companies clearly label hyperlinks in a way that signals their importance, noting that labels like "Legal" or "Disclosure" are insufficient.

Companies would be ill-advised to rely upon wrap contract doctrine to satisfy the FTC's requirements for disclosure. In May 2000, the FTC published a staff working paper which discussed the applicability of FTC rules and guides to online activities, including disclosures.[66] The FTC guidelines are refreshing in their common sense approach, especially when compared to the obscene lengths to which courts have twisted the meaning of "reasonable notice." The FTC adopts a contextual approach which recognizes that some disclosures are "quite short, while others are more detailed. Some ads use only text, while others use graphics, video and audio."[67] Therefore, in evaluating whether a particular disclosure is "clear and conspicuous," the FTC recommends consideration of the "placement of the disclosure in an advertisement and its proximity to the claim it is qualifying," the "prominence of the disclosure," whether other parts of the advertisement "distract attention from the disclosure," whether the advertisement is so lengthy that the disclosure should be repeated, and whether the language is "understandable to the intended audience."[68] It also notes that disclosures in audio messages should be presented in "adequate volume and cadence" and that "visual disclosures appear for a sufficient duration."[69] The paper notes that "[o]n a Web page, the disclosure is more likely to be effective if consumers view the claim and disclosure together on the same screen." The FTC specifically states that disclosures that are an "integral part of a claim or inseparable from it.... should be placed on the same page and immediately next to the claim."[70] Courts, by contrast, have found reasonable notice where the notice was not on the same page as the hyperlinked terms. Furthermore, the FTC states that if scrolling is necessary, "advertisers should ask

[66] Federal Trade Commission, "Dot Com Disclosures: Information about Online Advertising" (2000) at 8, *available at* http://www.business.ftc.gov/sites/default/files/pdf/bus41-dot-com-disclosures-information-about-online-advertising.pdf. Rules specifically prohibit specific practices that the Commission has found to be unfair or deceptive and guides provide guidance to businesses on how to avoid unfair or deceptive practices. *Id.*

[67] *Id.* at 5.

[68] *Id.* at 5–6.

[69] *Id.* at 6.

[70] *Id.* at 7.

whether consumers are likely to do it."[71] The paper also suggests text or visual cues to encourage consumers to scroll and that such prompts "should be tied to the disclosure that it refers to," meaning that there should be some indication about the subject matter or importance of the information.[72]

The FTC filed a complaint against the Sears Holdings Corporation (SHC) alleging that it failed to adequately disclose the extent to which a downloadable software application would monitor users' online activity. The SHC *did* make that disclosure, but it was in a lengthy user license agreement. The FTC and Sears settled the matter, with Sears agreeing to make the relevant disclosures, clearly and prominently, "and prior to the display of, and on a separate screen from, any final 'end user license agreement,' 'privacy policy,' 'terms of use' page, or similar document."[73] As the FTC stated in a letter to one of the commenters, "there are occasions when disclosure in a EULA alone may not be sufficient to correct a misleading impression created elsewhere."[74] One commentator has noted that, given the recent FTC enforcement action against the SHC, it "may not be enough to present consumers with online contracts.... if the material terms have not been presented clearly, prominently, and in a meaningful manner."[75]

The standard for what constitutes consent under wrap contract doctrine has fallen much too low. Companies that believe they are providing sufficient notice because they meet the minimal standards imposed by contract law may be surprised to find that they fall short of the FTC requirements for clear and conspicuous disclosures.

Finally, given the global nature of electronic commerce, companies should realize that other countries provide much greater protection to consumers than does the United States—and that wrap doctrine simply does not translate. The European Union (EU), for example, has issued the Unfair Contract Terms Directive of 1994.[76] As Jane Winn and Mark Webber note, "it is not sufficient for businesses to simply deploy U.S. versions of their online terms and conditions in their European operations."[77] They note that the EU regulation of unfair contract terms "establishes a much lower threshold for intervention by courts and regulators than

---

[71] *Id.* at 6.

[72] *Id.* at 7.

[73] Sears Holdings Management Corporation, FTC Matter No. 0823099, Docket No. C-4264.

[74] *Id.*, Letter from Donald S. Clark, Secretary, FTC, to Alan Charles Raul, Sidley Austin, LLP (Aug. 31, 2009), *available at* http://www.ftc.gov/os/caselist/0823099/090909searsletteraustin.pdf.

[75] Susan Gindin, *Nobody Reads Your Privacy Policy or Online Contract? Lessons Learned and Questions Raised by the FTC's Action against Sears*, 8 Nw. J. Tech. & Intell. Prop. 1, at 5.

[76] Council Directive 93/13, 1993 O.J. (L. 95) 29 (EEC), *available at* http://eur-lex.europa.eu/LexUriServ/LexUriServ.do?uri=CELEX:31993L0013:EN:HTML. The Directive is implemented by each member state.

[77] Jane K. Winn & Mark Webber, *The Impact of EU Unfair Contract Terms Law on U.S. Business-to-Consumer Internet Merchants*, 62 Bus. Law. 1, at 2 (Nov. 2006).

unconscionability under U.S. contract law or federal and state regulation of unfair and deceptive trade practices."[78] They caution that "U.S. Internet businesses that target consumers in Europe need to be aware that standard form contracts that work well in the U.S. may be unenforceable in the EU."[79] The EU is not alone in the world. Its regulatory approach is closer to that of other countries, including Canada, Australia, New Zealand, and Japan than is the U.S. approach.[80]

---

78 *Id.* at 9

79 *Id.* 1, at 20.

80 *Id.* at 4.

8 The Sense and Nonsense of Wrap Contract Doctrine

THE CONCLUSION THAT shrinkwraps, clickwraps, and browsewraps were valid contracting forms—that they were contracts at all—was not foreordained or obvious. Rather, it required certain doctrinal adjustments to traditional contract law. The range of cases makes it difficult to predict what may constitute adequate notice in any given case or what level of action constitutes a manifestation of consent. A particularly vexing issue is the increasing prevalence of multiwrapping, a term I employ to refer to the use of more than one type of wrap contract. Although wrap terminology is helpful in describing the form of the agreement, it is typically less useful in understanding the outcome in a particular case. The next section attempts to provide a coherent framework for understanding the existing case law in this area.

A. Notice and Wrap Contract Formation

After the initial uncertainty about enforceability of browsewraps, courts in the past ten years have generally focused on whether the presentation of terms was sufficient to constitute "notice."[1] As discussed in chapter 4, the issue of notice is complex, and early cases often involved use of a website's services that the nondrafting party knew was clearly prohibited.

Cairo v. CrossMedia Services, Inc.[2] was one such case. Cairo and CrossMedia Services (CMS) operated websites that allowed users to search for local retailer sales. As part of its business, CMS hosted its customers' promotional materials on more than 250 websites that it operated. Every web page that CMS operated contained the following notice: "By continuing past this page and/or using this site, you agree to abide by the *Terms of Use* for this site, which prohibit commercial use of any information in this site."[3] The terms of use were accessible by clicking on the hyperlink. The first paragraph on the new page stated, "These terms of use constitute a binding legal agreement (the "Agreement") between the user and CrossMedia Services, Inc. ("CrossMedia"), the owner and operator of the Website. If you do not accept the terms stated here, do not use the Website." The words clearly indicated that there was an agreement—but they were not visible until the user clicked on the hyperlink. The terms of use allowed users to "view and download a single copy of content... solely for lawful, non-commercial and personal use to users, and other authorized users as expressly permitted by and subject to the restrictions" of the agreement.[4] They prohibited users from "deep linking" to CMS's websites and from accessing their sites with "any robot, spider, or other automatic device or process to monitor or copy any portion" of a site.[5]

Cairo's business involved collecting information from retailers' websites by means of computer programs referred to as "robots" or "spiders" that "automatically visit retailers' websites, record the relevant sales information from the retailers' weekly circular web pages, and then return that information to a database maintained by Cairo."[6] CMS discovered that Cairo's web-scraping program was copying materials from CMS's websites and posting them on Cairo's site.[7] Users searching Cairo's website for products viewed thumbnails of the materials that were copied from CMS's pages.[8] If the user then clicked on one of the thumbnails, the user was connected to a CMS web page via a deep link that permitted it to bypass CMS's home page.[9]

---

[1] Juliet M. Moringiello & William L. Reynolds, *Survey of the Law of Cyberspace Electronic Contracting Cases 2007–2008*, 64 BUS. LAW. 199, 200 (Nov. 2008) (noting that "courts were not paying much attention to the once much-mooted distinction between browsewrap and clickwrap" and focused on whether the seller provided enough information "so that the buyer could know for what, if anything, it was contracting").

[2] Cairo v. CrossMedia Services, Inc., C 04-04825 JW, 2005 WL 756610 (N.D. Cal., April 1, 2005).

[3] *Id.* at 2..

[4] *Id.*

[5] *Id.*

[6] *Id.* at 3.

[7] *Id.*

[8] *Id.*

[9] *Id.*

CMS sent Cairo a letter claiming, among other things, that its conduct constituted a breach of the terms of use.[10] Cairo, in turn, filed an action for declaratory relief in the U.S. district court in California. CMS filed a Motion to Dismiss, claiming that the terms of use required Cairo to file lawsuits in a court in Chicago.[11] Cairo claimed that no one at Cairo was aware of the terms of use until immediately prior to receiving CMS's letter.[12] Cairo also argued that it had not assented to CMS's terms of use or forum-selection clause, and that there was no agreement between it and CMS.[13] Although ruling solely on the issue of venue, the court stated that "Cairo's repeated and automated use of CMS' web pages can form the basis of imputing knowledge to Cairo of the terms on which CMS's services were offered... Thus, even accepting Cairo's allegation that it did not explicitly agree to CMS's Terms of Use, the Court finds that Cairo's use of CMS's web site under circumstances in which Cairo had actual or imputed knowledge of CMS's terms effectively binds Cairo to CMS's Terms of Use and the forum selection clause therein."[14]

In *Southwest Airlines v. BoardFirst, LLC*,[15] the court stated that "the validity of a browsewrap license turns on whether a website user has actual or constructive knowledge of a site's terms and conditions prior to using the site."[16] In that case, Southwest Airlines claimed that BoardFirst's use of the airline company's website violated its terms of use. BoardFirst accessed Southwest Airlines' website in order to check in passengers early and obtain for them early boarding times. On Southwest Airlines' home page, in "small black print at the bottom of the page," were words indicating that "[u]se of the Southwest websites... constitutes acceptance of our Terms and Conditions."[17] The "Terms and Conditions" were hyperlinked to the actual terms and conditions page and limited the use of the website to "personal, non-commercial purposes." Southwest Airlines later added language that "third parties may not use Southwest web sites for the purpose of checking Customers in online or attempting to obtain for them a boarding pass in any certain boarding group."[18] Rather than determining that BoardFirst noticed the hyperlink to the terms of use at the time it used the website, the court found that it had notice of the terms *at the time plaintiff sought to enforce them*. The court found the notice requirements were met because the "evidence shows that

---

[10] *Id.*

[11] *Id.*

[12] *Id.*

[13] *Id.*

[14] *Id.* at 5.

[15] Sw. Airlines Co. v. BoardFirst, L.L.C., 3:06-CV-0891-B, 2007 WL 4823761 (N.D. Tex. Sept. 12, 2007).

[16] *Id.* at 5.

[17] *Id.* at 2.

[18] *Id.*

BoardFirst has had knowledge of the Terms as early as" when it received Southwest's cease-and-desist letter in which it was informed of the violation.[19]

In *Schnabel v. Trilegiant Corp.*,[20] however, the court found that the terms of a clickwrap agreement did not include the terms that were provided via hyperlink in a later e-mail. In that case, the plaintiffs were purchasers at various sites who were prompted, after completing their transaction, to sign up for "an online discount program called 'Great Fun.'"[21] The program appeared to be a cashback award from the site where the purchase was made when it was in fact operated by defendant Trilegiant.[22] In order to receive the award, the plaintiffs had to enter a password and other information and simultaneously enroll in the discount program. At the bottom of the pop-up advertisement or prompt, there was information that by signing up for the program, the plaintiffs would be charged a monthly fee.[23] After clicking on the "Yes" icon, the plaintiffs were shown a screen welcoming them to the program and alerting them to an e-mail with instructions on how to receive their gift and information about the subscription fee. The plaintiffs believed that they were signing up to receive money back from their purchase site and claimed that they did not realize they had enrolled in a discount program. Shortly thereafter, the plaintiffs received a welcome e-mail from the defendants, which contained information about their account number. At the bottom of the message, in smaller font, were the "Great Fun Membership Terms & Conditions."[24] Monthly subscription charges from the defendants were made to the plaintiffs' credit cards.

The defendants argued that the plaintiffs were bound by the arbitration clause contained in their terms and conditions. The court noted that the registration process did not mention arbitration or that additional terms would follow.[25] It found that even if a contract had been formed, it would only have included the terms in the online registration process and not those contained in the e-mail:

> By the time Edward and Brian received an email from Trilegiant, any contract had already been formed. Both Edward and Brian claim to have never seen the email in question, but, assuming they had and assuming that they had

---

[19] *Id.* at 7.

[20] Schnabel v. Trilegiant Corp., 3:10-CV-957 JCH, 2011 WL 797505 (D. Conn. Feb. 24, 2011) aff'd and remanded, 697 F.3d 110 (2d Cir. 2012).

[21] *Id.*

[22] *Id.* at 1.

[23] *Id.* at 1 and 2.

[24] *Id.* at 2.

[25] *Id.* at 4.

understood it as an attempt by Trilegiant to bind them to the terms and conditions contained in the email, neither Edward nor Brian manifested assent to these terms at the time the contract was formed.[26]

The court distinguished *ProCD v. Zeidenberg* because the plaintiffs in the case before it had "received no notice of the eventual receipt of additional terms and were never given the opportunity to 'reject' the email they eventually received."[27] The court also noted that unlike in *Register.com v. Verio*, the plaintiffs were not aware of the proposed terms and conditions prior to the acts constituting contract formation.[28] Finally, the court noted that the plaintiffs did not receive a benefit *after* being informed of the proposed terms, as neither plaintiff received coupons or even cashed in the original rebate.[29]

The language in cases such as *Register.com v. Verio*,[30] *Southwest Airlines v. BoardFirst*,[31] and *Schnabel v. Trilegiant Corp.*[32] indicates that the effectiveness of the notice applies to actions of the user undertaken after receipt of the notice—in other words, notice received after the initial interaction may be effective with respect to ongoing interactions where the user continues to receive benefits from the website.

Another case, *Van Tassell v. United Marketing Group*[33], involved a membership program similar to that in *Trilegiant*. The plaintiffs alleged that after making a purchase on certain websites, those websites transferred their credit or debit card information to United Marketing without their permission.[34] United Marketing then enrolled them in a negative-option marketing program which, after a thirty-day trial period, resulted in charges to the plaintiffs' credit or debit card accounts of between $10 and $20 a month.[35] In some cases, consumers were enrolled in multiple membership programs.[36] The program purported to provide discounts to its members, but because its members were not aware that they were enrolled, practically speaking they received nothing in return for what they paid.[37] The defendants claimed that the plaintiffs were subject to the arbitration clause located in the conditions

---

[26] *Id.*

[27] *Id.* at 5.

[28] *Id.*

[29] *Id.*

[30] Register.com v. Verio, 356 F.3d 393 (2d Cir. 2004).

[31] Sw. Airlines Co. v. BoardFirst, L.L.C., *supra* note 15.

[32] Schnabel v. Trilegiant Corp., *supra* note 20.

[33] Van Tassell v. United Mktg. Group, LLC, 795 F. Supp.2d 770 (N.D. Ill. 2011).

[34] *Id.* at 774.

[35] *Id.*

[36] *Id.*

[37] *Id.*

of use. The hyperlink to the conditions of use did not appear on the home page or the checkout page. The link was accessible only after scrolling to the bottom of the web page and clicking on the "Customer Service" link, and then scrolling to the bottom of the Customer Service page or by clicking on the "Conditions of Use, Notices & Disclaimers" link located near the end of a list of links on that page.[38] The court stated:

> instead of merely scrolling down to find the terms on a submerged screen when there was no reason to do so, the users of ChefsCatalog.com, also without any reason to do so, must scroll down the home page, make the illogical leap that "Customer Service" means binding "Conditions of Use" and click on that link. They must next scroll down a lengthy page containing unrelated information to find the Conditions of Use, or click on the "Conditions of Use, Notice & Disclaimers" link sandwiched between "Price Adjustments" and "CHEFS Gift Card & Product Giveaway" links.... This multi-step process to find the Conditions of Use is especially problematic because ChefsCatalog.com lacks any reference to the existence of the Conditions of Use or that they are binding on all users of the website outside of the Conditions of Use themselves.[39]

In *Hoffman v. Supplements Togo Management, LLC*,[40] the plaintiff Hoffman had purchased Erection MD, which were pills that defendant advertised as enhancing sexual performance.[41] The plaintiff sued, claiming among other things, fraud.[42] The forum selection clause was contained in its website disclaimer, which required scrolling down to a "submerged portion of the webpage."[43] A purchaser could click on an item and add it to his shopping cart and complete the transaction without being forced to click "I agree" or otherwise acknowledge the terms.[44] The New Jersey Superior Court found that the forum selection clause was "unreasonably masked from the view of the prospective purchasers because of its circuitous mode of presentation."[45] Therefore, the court found that "the absence of reasonable notice to consumers, and the manifestly unfair manner in which defendants' website was

[38] *Id.* at 792.
[39] *Id.* at 792–93.
[40] Hoffman v. Supplements Togo Mgmt., LLC, 18 A.3d 210 (N.J. Super.App.Div. 2011).
[41] *Id.* at 213.
[42] *Id.* at 214.
[43] *Id.* at 219.
[44] *Id.*
[45] *Id.*

structured" rendered the forum selection clause presumptively unenforceable.[46] The court left open the issue whether the presumption that the forum selection clause was unenforceable for lack of reasonable notice could be overcome if Hoffman had actually read the clause prior to purchasing the product.[47]

Agreements viewable only by scrolling (such as in a scroll box) have been upheld where notice that terms applied to the transaction were visible, even if the terms themselves were not. The court in *Feldman v. Google, Inc.*[48] explained that as long as there was notice that terms were contained in a particular location, requiring users to scroll in order to view them was permissible:

> The facts in *Specht*… are easily distinguishable from this case. There, the internet users were urged to click on a button to download free software. There was no visible indication that clicking on the button meant that the user agreed to the terms and conditions of a proposed contract that contained an arbitration clause. The only reference to terms was located in text visible if the users scrolled down to the next screen, which was "submerged." Even if a user did scroll down, the terms were not immediately displayed. Users would have had to click onto a hyperlink, which would take the user to a separate webpage… Only on that webpage was a user informed that the user must agree to the license terms before downloading a product.… Through a similar process, the AdWords Agreement gave reasonable notice of its terms… Unlike the impermissible agreement in *Specht*, the user did not have to scroll down to a submerged screen or click on a series of hyperlinks to view the Agreement. Instead, text of the AdWords Agreement was immediately visible to the user, as was a prominent admonition in boldface to read the terms and conditions carefully, and with instruction to indicate assent if the user agreed to the terms. That the user would have to scroll through the text box of the Agreement to read it in its entirety does not defeat notice because there was sufficient notice of the Agreement itself and clicking "Yes" constituted assent to all of the terms. The preamble, which was immediately visible, also made clear that assent to the terms was binding. The Agreement was presented in readable 12-point font. It was only seven paragraphs long—not so long so as to render scrolling down to view all of the terms inconvenient or impossible.

---

[46] *Id.* at 220.

[47] *Id.*

[48] Feldman v. Google, Inc., 513 F. Supp. 2d 229 (E.D. Pa. 2007).

A printer-friendly, full-screen version was made readily available. The user had ample time to review the document.[49]

In *Scherillo v. Dun & Bradstreet*,[50] the court upheld the terms in a scrollable box that was on "the bottom quarter to third" of the registration page.[51] The terms were not presented until after the user had already expended time inputting personal information.[52] The court found that the agreement was enforceable because the user could not proceed without clicking.[53]

If the user is not asked to click to indicate assent, the terms need to be visible without scrolling. In *Hines v. Overstock*,[54] for example, the plaintiff Hines sued the defendant Overstock.com for charging her a restocking fee after she was told that she could return without cost a vacuum purchased on the company's website. Overstock sought to enforce a mandatory arbitration provision contained in the company's browsewrap. Hines, however, argued that she was never made aware of the terms because they could be viewed only by scrolling to the bottom of the web page. Hines stated that she "did not scroll down to the end of the page(s) because it was not necessary to do so, as I was directed each step of the way to click on to a bar to take me to the next step to complete the purchase."[55] The court found that Hines had neither actual nor constructive notice because she was never advised of the terms and conditions, could not view the link without scrolling to the bottom of the screen, which was not required to complete her purchase, and "unlike in other cases where courts have upheld browsewrap agreements, the notice that 'Entering this Site will constitute your acceptance of these Terms and Conditions,' was only available within the Terms and Conditions." The court stated that "[v]ery little is required to form a contract nowadays—but this alone does not suffice."[56]

Another court held a similar browsewrap unenforceable in *In re* Zappos.com, Inc., Customer Data Security Breach Litigation.[57] The plaintiffs were Zappos.com customers who were suing for damages resulting from a security breach that occurred when hackers attacked the company's server and tried to download files containing

---

[49] *Id.* at 237.

[50] Scherillo v. Dun & Bradstreet, Inc., 684 F.Supp. 2d 313 (E.D.N.Y. 2010).

[51] *Id.* at 320 (E.D.N.Y. 2010).

[52] *Id.*

[53] *Id.* at 321.

[54] Hines v. Overstock.com, Inc., 668 F. Supp. 2d 362 (E.D.N.Y. 2009) aff'd 380 Fed. Appx. 22 (2nd Cir. June 03, 2010).

[55] *Id.* at 367.

[56] *Id.*

[57] In re Zappos.com, Inc., Customer Data Sec. Breach Litig., 3:12-CV-00325-RCJ, 2012 WL 4466660 (D. Nev. Sept 27, 2012).

customer information. Zappos.com tried to compel arbitration pursuant to its terms of use. The court framed the issue as one of notice: "Where, as here, there is no evidence that plaintiffs had actual notice of the agreement, the validity of a browsewrap contract hinges on whether the website provides reasonable notice of the terms of the contract (citations omitted)."[58]

The Zappos.com' terms of use were found on every Zappos.com web page "between the middle and bottom of each page, visible if the user scrolls down." The court noted that when the home page is printed, "the link appears on page 3 of 4. The link is the same size, font, and color as most other non-significant links." Furthermore, the user was not directed to the terms of use when creating or logging in to an account or when making a purchase. The court concluded that

> [t]he Terms of Use is inconspicuous, buried in the middle to bottom of every Zappos.com webpage among many other links, and the website never directs a user to the Terms of Use.[59]

Interestingly, the court added that, "[n]o reasonable user would have reason to click on the Terms of Use, even those users who have alleged that they clicked and relied on statements found in adjacent links, such as the site's 'Privacy Policy.'"[60]

Multiwrapping raises even more complicated issues because it provides more opportunities for the drafter to give legal notice, which, in turn, increases the burden on the nondrafting party, who must now undertake increased efforts in order to access the actual terms. Where the multiwrapping involves paper and digital forms, the application of traditional contract law may render different results than the application of wrap doctrine as illustrated by comparing two cases with remarkably similar facts, *Manasher v. NECC Telecom*[61] and *Briceño v. Sprint Spectrum*.[62]

In *Briceño v. Sprint Spectrum*, the plaintiff brought her Sprint camera-telephone into a Sprint store for repair. She alleged that Sprint employees asked for her password, accessed her e-mail account, and obtained and distributed "personal photographs of her body to third persons via the Internet."[63] Briceño sued Sprint for, among other

---

[58] *Id.* at 3.

[59] *Id.* at 4.

[60] *Id.*

[61] Manasher v. NECC Telecom, 06-10749, 2007 WL 2713845 (E.D. Mich., Sept. 18, 2007) aff'd in part, 310 F. App'x 804 (6th Cir. 2009).

[62] Briceño v. Sprint Spectrum, L.P., 911 So.2d 176 (Fla. Dist. Ct. App. 2005).

[63] *Id.* at 178.

things, invasion of privacy.[64] Sprint filed a motion to compel arbitration pursuant to its terms and conditions which contained a mandatory arbitration clause.

The court noted that Briceño did not read the terms and conditions that were posted on the website. The court's skeptical, scolding tone is worth citing:

> Sprint's customary business practice is to include the Terms and Conditions in the packaging of its telephone. Briceño and Sprint dispute whether she was given the Terms and Conditions with her original telephone. However, it is undisputed that Briceño had access to the Terms and Conditions and its subsequent amendments via Sprint's website. Sprint printed a "*Notice of Changes*" on the front of the June 16, 2003 invoice that it mailed to Briceño. This notice informed her that amendments to the original Terms and Conditions were posted on Sprint's website. Briceño stated that she never read any of the original or amended Terms and Conditions, either on the internet or in hard-copy, because it was "not important" to her. She also stated that she saw the "*Terms and Conditions of Service*" internet link, but did not care to click it.

The court's use of quotations seems to fault Briceño for failing to locate and read the terms on the website. The court chides Briceño for her lack of interest in reading the terms even though it appears that there was, in addition to the original Terms and Conditions, subsequent amendments. The court also notes that from 2000 to 2003, Briceño changed her phone equipment four times and that "it was customary for Sprint to include the applicable Terms and Conditions in each telephone box."[65] It is unclear how many times Sprint issued amendments, but the court notes that it did so "periodically."[66] Sprint could not prove that Briceño received the terms and conditions in the box because it did not ask her to sign anything and there was no way to prove otherwise. Yet, the court concluded that Briceño received notice when she received her invoice, which stated:

> **Important Notice Regarding Your PCS Service from Sprint**
>
> The Terms and Conditions of PCS Service from Sprint have changed. To view the current version, please visit www.sprintpcs.com or press *2 on your PCS Phone and request a copy from a PCS Customer Solutions Specialist.[67]

---

[64] *Id.*

[65] *Id.* at 178–179.

[66] *Id.* at 180.

[67] *Id.*

The court upheld the mandatory arbitration clause in the terms and conditions. In doing so, the court noted that the clause had been "completely capitalized" in the relevant amendment.[68] Yet, in so stating, the court confuses the notice of the amendment with the amendment itself. The so-called notice on the invoice was not capitalized. The court imposes upon Briceño the obligation to visit the website in order to obtain the amendment even though the notice is given in a different medium, rather than imposing upon Sprint the obligation to enclose the amendment with the invoice.

Briceño entered into the contract with Sprint in December 2000; the court states that the mandatory arbitration clause had been in the terms and conditions "since 2001" although apparently not "completely capitalized" until 2003. Thus, the so-called notice on the invoice was to unilateral amendments to an existing contract. Traditionally, contract law requires that modifications to an agreement require consideration;[69] even in those jurisdictions that don't require consideration, the modification must be "fair and equitable," due to unanticipated circumstances, and voluntary.[70] (The agreement at issue in *Briceño* was a service contract—and most likely did not fall under the Uniform Commercial Code.)[71] The unilateral amendment is made all the more egregious when considered in light of Sprint's early termination policy. Under that policy, customers were obliged to pay $200 for terminating their policies prior to the expiration of their contract. The claim, therefore, that customers could "reject" the changes is particularly troubling. The court states:

> Further, Sprint gave Briceño the opportunity to opt out of her contract if she so decided. Balancing these factors, we find nothing inherently unfair which would lead to a finding of unconscionability. The only troubling fact is the uncertainty regarding whether or not Sprint would have enforced its early termination penalty clause in the event that Briceño had sought termination upon disagreeing with a proposed amendment to the Terms and Conditions. However, there is no evidence that Sprint charged any other customers a termination penalty for cancellation of a contract due to their refusal to accept amendments to its Terms and Conditions. We note that enforcement of an early termination fee, coupled with more onerous terms or amendments, could render an amendment unconscionable and, thus, unenforceable.[72]

---

[68] *Id.* at 178.

[69] 17A C.J.S. Contracts § 562

[70] 17A C.J.S. Contracts § 563; RESTATEMENT (SECOND) CONTRACTS, § 89 (1981).

[71] U.C.C. § 2-102; U.C.C. § 2-209.

[72] *Id.* at 180–81.

The court's rationale is convoluted, to say the least, and unreasonably favorable to Sprint. Pursuant to the terms and conditions, customers can reject the modification by terminating the service, even though Sprint has an obligation under the existing contract to continue providing service and no right to terminate the service at will. The active rejection requirement unilaterally imposed by Sprint is further complicated by the possibility that a customer would have to pay the not insubstantial amount of $200 in order to do so. The court acknowledges that imposing this termination fee on users who decline the changes may be problematic but concludes that an active rejection requirement in this context is not unconscionable because there is "no evidence" that Sprint has charged other customers who have actively rejected the terms.[73] The point is specious given that it fails to consider those customers who would otherwise have actively rejected the terms but did not because they did not wish to incur the termination fee (and did not want to test the enforceability of the clause in court). It also ignores that very few Sprint customers registered awareness of the notice, much less bothered to read the posted terms. Sprint may not have had the opportunity to enforce the termination clause against actively rejecting customers simply because there weren't any.

The court's opinion indicates that it is aware of this contracting reality. Sprint's provision of notice is a mere formality, designed to meet formalistic requirements of assent—and not designed to elicit knowing assent. The court assumes—probably correctly—that Briceño would not have read the terms regardless of how they were presented. The court goes through the song and dance regarding notice because it is required to do so under contract law. The court's opinion reflects a belief that the attenuated provision of notice was justified because Briceño would not have read the terms even if they were more clearly, and conveniently, presented.

To this court, what matters is the nature of the unilaterally imposed terms—or at least the ones that are subject to the dispute. If the disputed terms are benign or socially beneficial, then the court wants to enforce them. The court contorts the analysis of notice and assent to support enforceability, essentially replacing analysis of formation with analysis of the terms. It thus conflates the doctrine of assent with that of unconscionability. Furthermore, the court turns its unconscionability analysis into one focusing wholly on the substantive fairness of the terms, without considering the effect of procedural unconscionability. In ruling that the arbitration clause is not unconscionable, the court makes a supposition about the relevance of the clause to Briceño. As the court notes, "Briceño claimed that she would not have terminated her Sprint subscription because she published her Sprint telephone

[73] *Id.* at 180.

number in a book of babysitters given to area concierges, and that she derived much of her business from calls received through that service. She also claimed that she could not change the telephone number in the book."[74] The implication is that it doesn't matter that notice was ineffective because even if Briceño had read the provision she wouldn't have terminated her contract over it. The court fails to consider that Briceño's dependence upon her phone service exacerbates the unfairness of a unilaterally imposed modification.

Notice is relevant in order to show contract formation, but it is also relevant in establishing whether a document is incorporated by reference. In *Manasher v. NECC Telecom*,[75] the relevant website terms of use were also referenced in a paper invoice but the court concluded that they did not apply to the transaction between the parties. The defendant, NECC, was a telecommunications company that provided phone service. The plaintiffs were customers who sought to bring a class action lawsuit claiming, among other things, fraud based on the defendant's billing practices. The plaintiffs signed up with the defendant's phone service after receiving a telemarketing call during which they discussed the financial terms of the service. After service began, the plaintiffs received an invoice. The invoice contained charges which the plaintiffs claimed they did not agree to and which were different from what they were told during the initial sales call.[76] The second page of the invoice contained the following statement:

> NECC's Agreement "Disclosure and Liabilities" can be found online at www.necc.us or you could request a copy by calling us at (800) 766-2642.[77]

The Disclosure and Liabilities Agreement contained a mandatory arbitration provision and precluded class arbitration. The plaintiffs argued that the single reference in the invoice was insufficient to make the Disclosure and Liabilities Agreement part of the contract between the parties. The court agreed, and distinguished *Briceño*. The court stated:

> Here, the issue is not whether the arbitration agreement is unconscionable or whether Defendant attempted to conceal it. Rather, the issue is whether the statement on the invoice regarding Disclosure and Liabilities was sufficient

---

[74] *Id.* at 178.

[75] Manasher v. NECC Telecom, 06-10749, 2007 WL 2713845 (E.D. Mich. Sept. 18, 2007) aff'd in part, 310 F. App'x 804 (6th Cir. 2009).

[76] *Id.* at 1.

[77] *Id.* at 2.

to incorporate that document by reference into the contract between the parties. Unlike Briceño, who was initially, and several times thereafter, provided with the actual Terms and Conditions Agreement from Sprint, there is no indication that Plaintiffs were ever given the actual Disclosure and Liabilities Agreement. The only reference to the Disclosure and Liabilities Agreement is the fifth statement on the second page of the Plaintiff's invoice. Notably, in Briceño, the notice was on the first page of the invoice, just below the amount due, and the first sentence was in bold print. Additionally, the notice stated that it regarded "*Your* PCS Service from Sprint." In contrast, Defendants reference to the Disclosure and Liabilities Agreement was the last of five statements in plain type on the second page of the invoice, and did not explicitly state that it applied to the consumer's agreement with Defendant. Thus, Briceño, does not have similar facts, and does not decide a similar legal issue.[78]

The court concluded that the arbitration clause contained in the Disclosure and Liabilities Agreement was unenforceable because "[n]othing in the statement clearly indicates that the Disclosure and Liabilities Agreement applies to the service contract between the parties, that it forms any part of the agreement between the parties, or that it is intended to be incorporated in the agreement between the parties."[79]

In *Durick v. eBay, Inc.*,[80] by contrast, the court found that hyperlinked documents contained in a browsewrap were incorporated by reference. In that case, the court ruled that eBay's user agreement "incorporates a Restricted and Prohibited Items Policy," which in turn incorporated "a Prescription Drugs and Devices Policy as well as a Hazardous, Restricted, and Perishable Items Policy."[81] A glance at eBay's agreement indicates that the user had to click at least three times and scroll several pages in order to access the relevant policy that was incorporated by reference.

In offline/online multiwrapping cases, it may be that courts will apply traditional contract law standards of notice with respect to the paper contract while continuing to apply the standards of notice specific to wrap contracts to the online contract(s). Traditional contract law requires that the document clearly evidence intent by the parties to incorporate another agreement by reference. Incorporation by reference language should be conspicuous. On the other hand, hyperlinked terms contained in an online agreement will likely be deemed incorporated by reference if there is constructive or actual notice of the online agreement containing the hyperlinked

---

78 *Id.* at 5–6.

79 *Id.* at 6.

80 Durick v. Ebay, Inc., 2006 Ohio 4861 (Ohio App. 7 Dist. Sept. 11, 2006)..

81 *Id.* at 3.

terms. For example, courts will likely find hyperlinked terms in a clickwrap incorporated by reference even if the hyperlink requires scrolling in order to be viewable. In other words, when seeking to incorporate an online agreement in a mailed document, expect the notice standards generally to be tougher than when incorporating hyperlinked agreements in an online agreement.

As the foregoing cases illustrate, what constitutes sufficient notice varies from case to case. While it may seem that courts have tended to invalidate contracts in cases involving consumer fraud, it would be a mistake to conclude that the courts are making a decision based solely on the substance of the claim. Terms that are sneaky or difficult to find may create the basis for a consumer fraud claim; this doesn't mean, however, that courts will find that terms are sneaky simply *because* a consumer fraud claim is raised.

Despite the range of these cases, some generalities regarding what constitutes sufficient notice can be gleaned from them. The validity of notice can be categorized based upon the two primary ways that consumers are deemed to "manifest consent," through action (i.e., clicking) or inaction (i.e., browsing a website or failing to return software).

There is generally sufficient notice when the consumer must click in order to proceed and

1. terms are immediately viewable and there is a meaningful opportunity to read them;
2. terms are contained in a scrollable box;
3. terms are contained in a hyperlink placed above or below the icon that requires clicking.

There is generally sufficient notice when the consumer uses the website but does not click in order to proceed and

1. consumer receives actual notice of terms, such as in a cease-and-desist letter (but notice is deemed effective only with respect to actions undertaken thereafter);
2. a hyperlink indicating the existing of applicable terms are visible on website without scrolling and labeled as "Terms of Use" or the like to indicate they are contractual.

Furthermore, there is generally insufficient notice when

1. there is no indication that terms are applicable or forthcoming at the time of transaction (purchase or use of website);

2. There is no indication that terms are applicable or forthcoming at time of transaction but they arrive afterward (via e-mail or post) and user does not receive benefits or engage with website after receiving communication that terms apply to transaction;
3. terms are not labeled as "Terms of Use" or the like to indicate they are contractual or they are obscured or disappear and there is no meaningful opportunity to read them;
4. "clicking" is associated with an activity other than contractual assent and terms are not clearly labeled.

Finally, as a general rule, there is generally insufficient notice when the user does not receive benefits after receiving constructive or actual notice.

The following flow chart may be helpful:

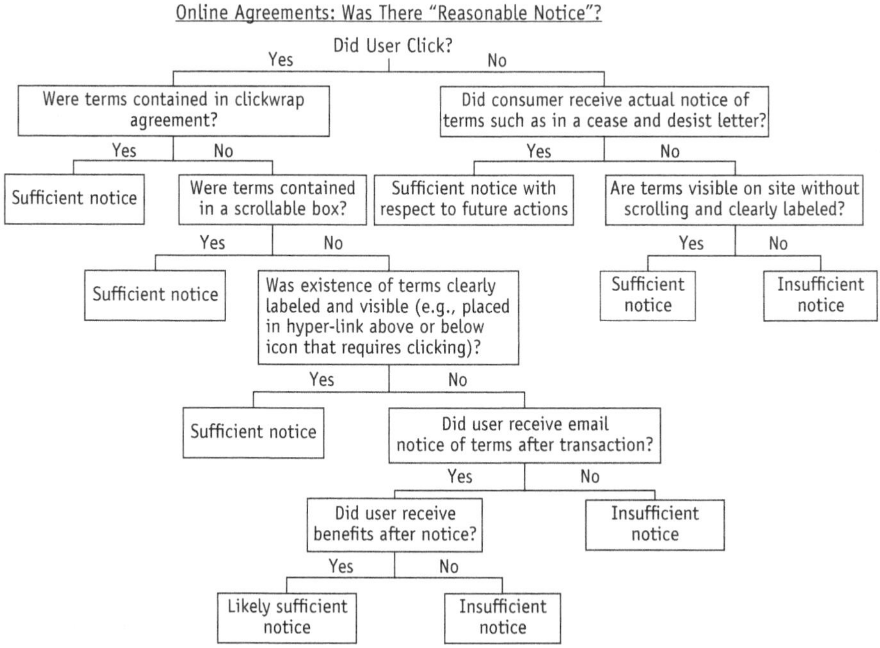

Yet another way to organize and understand the cases is to consider whether the user has a continuing relationship with the company. If the user continues to receive the benefits of the services provided by the drafting company after receiving actual notice of the terms, the courts are likely to find sufficient notice regardless of when the non-drafting party entered into the transaction or when the notice was given. As elaborated in subsection C, rather than adhering to formalistic rules of contract formation, the courts seem to be deferring to the business need to assess and minimize risk, especially where new business models are involved.

As the guidelines above reveal, courts have adopted an expansive view of notice in wrap contract cases. If the drafter follows certain technical requirements, such as employing a click box or presenting a clearly labeled hyperlink that doesn't require scrolling, the courts will find sufficient notice even if the user was not actually aware of the terms and the terms were not immediately viewable. On the other hand, if the drafter fails to follow this formalistic version of notice, actual notice will suffice even if it is provided *after* the acts occurred which constituted the transaction provided that the user continues to receive benefits from the drafter. Terms that arrive via email after a completed transaction (without notice at the time of the transaction that terms were forthcoming) are not enforceable, however, and should be distinguished from actual notice via a cease-and-desist letter. The distinction seems to be that the terms that arrive in an e-mail purport to be applicable to a transaction that has already been completed, whereas in the latter scenario, the notice applies to a continuing or ongoing relationship between the website and the user (i.e. one where the user continues to receive benefits from the website).

B. An Outline of Wrap Contract Doctrine

Despite the protestation by courts that contract law is the same regardless of the contracting medium, many courts have applied that law differently when the case involved a wrap contract. The rules of wrap contract law differ from traditional contract law. The following list summarizes the doctrinal rules that are unique to wrap contracts, by comparing each rule to its traditional doctrine counterpart.

1. **Wrap doctrine**: The assent of the nondrafting party is demonstrated by "notice" of legal terms and "manifestation of consent." The offeree may receive notice after undertaking the acts that constitute acceptance. Manifestation of consent may mean that the adhering party has accepted by acting in a way that does not clearly indicate intent to accept the terms.

   Traditional contract doctrine: Reasonable notice must be given prior to the acts constituting acceptance. The conduct of a party is not effective as a manifestation of consent unless he intends to engage in the conduct and knows or has reason to know that the other party may infer from his conduct that he assents.
2. **Wrap doctrine**: Manifestation of consent can mean the adhering party has not actively rejected the terms.

Traditional contract doctrine: Silence generally does not constitute acceptance. The offeror cannot require the offeree to actively reject unless otherwise agreed by the parties.

3. **Wrap doctrine**: Manifestation of consent may mean that the adherent was in the process of undertaking an action, such as viewing content on a website or purchasing a product on a website, when the terms presented an impediment which the adhering party then removed. The terms may also be imposed without impediment while the adhering party is engaged in an activity, so that the activity continues in a seamless manner.

   Traditional contract doctrine: Luring users to an activity (such as advertising a big sale at a store) and then imposing a contract after the user has commenced an activity in an unobtrusive (i.e., "sneaky") manner could be viewed as a "bait-and-switch" tactic. Traditional contract law recognizes fraud, unilateral mistake, and unconscionability as contract defenses to bait-and-switch tactics. Section 5 of the Federal Trade Commission Act prohibits unfair and deceptive trade practices,[82] and state legislation also prohibits bait-and-switch tactics.[83]

4. **Wrap doctrine**: Notice means that some terms were visible that indicated legal terms applied to the activity that was being undertaken by the adhering party. Notice does not mean that the legal terms themselves were visible.

   Traditional contract doctrine: Contract wording must be conspicuous.

5. **Wrap doctrine**: Where a party has the power of acceptance, contract is not formed by acceptance but can be later modified and integrated by reference to other agreements.

   Traditional contract doctrine: Where a party has the power of acceptance, act of acceptance triggers contract formation. Modifications and addendums to contract require new consideration.

6. **Wrap doctrine**: Constructive notice is effective to incorporate other documents by reference.

   Traditional contract doctrine: In order to incorporate another document by reference into an agreement, the agreement must clearly evidence intent that the document be made a part of the agreement.

7. **Wrap doctrine**: The terms of an offer can be indefinite and modified at will.

[82] 15 U.S.C. § 45.

[83] For an overview of the various laws governing "bait-and-switch" tactics, see David Adam Friedman, *Explaining "Bait-and-Switch" Regulation*, 4 Wm. & Mary Bus. L. Rev. 575 (2013).

Traditional contract doctrine: Offer and acceptance must express a present intent to enter into a contract and terms of an offer must be definite.

8. **Wrap doctrine**: The nondrafting party bears the burden of contracting ambiguities and opaqueness.

   Traditional contract doctrine: Contract ambiguities and opaqueness are construed against the drafting party.

9. **Wrap doctrine**: Every contract should be analyzed as though it were a negotiated paper agreement that is signed by both parties.

   Traditional contract doctrine: Special rules apply to certain standard form contracts, such as airline tickets or insurance contracts. The "reasonable communicativeness" test considers both the physical characteristics of the contract and extrinsic factors, such as the contracting environment.

10. **Wrap doctrine**: A reasonable prudent offeree is one that is uniquely diligent, overly cautious, highly knowledgeable about wrap contract doctrine, exceptional at multitasking, infinitely patient, and likely does not exist in the real world.

    Traditional contract doctrine: A reasonable offeree is judged based upon the standard of an ordinary person standing in the shoes of the offeree.

One might object that the foregoing are not characteristics of wrap contracts at all—they are doctrinal aberrations. Unfortunately, these are not aberrations when it comes to wrap contracts; on the contrary, they have come to define what wrap contracts *are*. Wrap contracts are terms created by businesses, but, as the next section explains, they are deemed contracts only through judicial construction.

C. A New Kind of Judicial Activism

When the term "judicial activism" crops up in the context of contract cases, it is typically associated with a contract drafted by a large corporation that a court refuses to enforce against a vulnerable member of society. The court is seen as siding with David over Goliath, even though the contract appears to be validly formed. Judicial activism also may be associated with a court interpreting a term in accordance with the intent of the parties contrary to the strict language of the document. But the wrap contract cases flip the conventional understanding of judicial activism by enforcing terms drafted by the stronger party against the weaker party *despite* defects in formation.

The problem that software and web-based businesses sought to remedy through the mechanism of contract was activity that they considered to be unfair competition.[84] The activity at issue was not necessarily illegal, not because it was fair or just but because law and policy makers had not yet foreseen the problems created by new technologies. There were no rules or opinions governing practices such as web scraping, deep linking, or reselling digital databases (which, although costly to compile, were unprotected by copyright laws if they were lacking in originality). The technology had advanced ahead of legislation addressing these potential conflicts and conduct. Given the absence of public legislation, companies engaging in these new technologies used private legislation to craft rules to protect their business models and resolve anticipated problems.

Unfortunately, as courts issued rulings that felt instinctively right, they had to reason around existing rules that, strictly applied, would have led to different results. Thus, while courts continue to recite well-established doctrinal rules, some have engaged in analysis and rendered results that are inconsistent with a strict application of those rules in order to achieve a result that they believe is "fair." The liberties that some courts took with doctrinal rules then became binding precedent.

An example of this type of judicial activism is *ProCD v. Zeidenberg*, where the court took liberties with the rules of offer and acceptance in order to enforce the shrinkwrap terms. The shrinkwrap agreement in that case stated as follows: "Please read this license carefully before using the software or accessing the listings contained on the discs. By using the discs and the listings licensed to you, you agree to be bound by the terms of this License. If you do not agree to the terms of this License, promptly return all copies of the software, listings that may have been exported, the discs and the User Guide to the place where you obtained it."[85] In a typical sales scenario, however, the transaction would have been completed at the time payment was rendered and the product physically handed to the purchaser; the terms in the box would have been proposals for modification. The drafter thus unilaterally changed the default rules of contract law with respect to offer and acceptance in a way that burdened the nondrafting party.

One might be tempted to ask whether there is any real harm where courts are reaching a substantively justifiable result (e.g., establishing the boundaries of what constitutes fair business practices with respect to a new type of business) even if via

[84] *See* Register.com, Inc. v. Verio, Inc., 356 F.3d 393 (2d Cir. 2004);Ticketmaster Corp. v. Tickets.com, Inc., CV 99-7654 HLH(BQRX), 2000 WL 525390 (C.D.Cal. Mar. 27, 2000); Cairo, Inc. v. Crossmedia Services., Inc., C 04-04825 JW, 2005 WL 756610 (N.D.Cal. Apr. 1, 2005).

[85] ProCD v. Zeidenberg, 908 F. Supp. 640, 644 (W.D. Wisc. 1996) rev'd, 86 F.3d 1447 (7th Cir. 1996).

an unjustifiable or inexplicable application of doctrinal rules. In other words, do the ends justify the means?

A common objection to judicial activism is that judges should not legislate. They should simply apply the rules and accept wherever the rules lead. The objection ignores the spaces in contract law doctrine that expressly permit judicial discretion, such as interpretation of terms or standards. The determination of what constitutes "reasonableness," for example, depends upon the judge's experiential viewpoint.[86] It also ignores the reality of what actually happens in the courtroom—as the wrap cases illustrate, judges do have their politics and their priorities.

But there are dangers in *misapplying* doctrinal rules that should be distinguished from judicial discretion. Not all courts will reach the right result, and some may simply reach the wrong result because they followed the reasoning established in a prior case without understanding the nuances that distinguished that case.[87] The role of the court in a common law system is not simply to reach a decision but to provide a coherent analysis to provide guidance in future cases.

Another related concern is that seemingly arbitrary decisions may undermine the predictive value of contracts. Wrap contract cases seem to run the gamut; for every case, there seems to be one with similar facts where the court reaches the opposite conclusion. As Juliet Moringiello observes, "[a]lthough courts have considered numerous click-wrap and browse-wrap agreements, it is difficult to find in their reported decisions a coherent framework for analyzing electronic agreements."[88] For example, in *Briceño v. Sprint Spectrum, LP*,[89] the court upheld the terms of service available on a website which were referenced in a mailed invoice, whereas the court in *Manasher v. NECC Telecom*[90] refused to enforce terms that were referenced in the same way.

Drafting parties might engage in inefficient contracting behavior or spend too much on legal fees—a serious concern for smaller, online-only businesses.[91]

---

86 *See* Nancy S. Kim, *Reasonable Expectations in Socio-Cultural Context*, 45 WAKE FOREST L. REV. 641 (2010).

87 Mark Lemley cautions that "courts must resist the temptation to slide further down the slippery slope, enforcing browsewraps in other contexts because they have enforced them in this one." Mark A. Lemley, *Term of Use*, 91 MINN. L. REV. 459, 481 (2006).

88 Juliet M. Moringiello, Signals, Assent and Internet Contracting, 57 Rutgers L. Rev. 1307, 1319 (2005).

89 Briceño v. Sprint Spectrum, L.P., 911 So.2d 176 (Fla. Dist. Ct. App. 2005).

90 Manasher v. NECC Telecom, 06-10749, 2007 WL 2713845 (E.D. Mich. Sept. 18, 2007) aff'd in part, 310 F. App'x 804 (6th Cir. 2009).

91 Schwartz and Scott write of gap-filling standards, "The state wastes resources in drafting them; the parties waste resources in contracting out; and when courts are expected to use standards actively to police bargain, parties may create sets of rules they would otherwise have preferred to omit." Alan Schwartz & Robert E. Scott, Contract Theory and the Limits of Contract Law, 113 Yale L.J. 541, 604 (2003).

Uncertainty may also increase the possibility of litigation as inconsistent rulings may encourage plaintiffs to test their particular set of facts.

Finally, in some cases, what a court considers to be the substantively "correct" results may not be without controversy. For example, in *A.V. et al. v. iParadigms, LLC*,[92] the federal district court upheld a clickwrap against the plaintiffs who were minors and high school students.[93] The defendant company, iParadigms, owned a proprietary technology system, Turnitin, which evaluated the originality of written work with the goal of detecting plagiarism by comparing it to the material in its database consisting of other student work and certain periodicals and journal articles.[94] Educational institutions signed up with the company and authorized it to archive student submissions to add to their growing database of material.[95] The plaintiff-students were required by their high school to submit their papers to Turnitin, which then produced reports for their teachers and archived their submissions.[96] If students refused to submit their work via Turnitin, they received a "zero" on the assignment.[97] The plaintiffs wrote a disclaimer on their submissions indicating that they did not consent to the archiving of their work.[98] They then sued defendants, claiming copyright infringement based upon the defendants' digital archiving of their papers.[99] As part of the submission process, a plaintiff had to click to the terms of the website's user agreement, which included the following limitation of liability provision:

> In no event shall iParadigms, LLC and/or its suppliers be liable for any direct, indirect, punitive, incidental, special, or consequential damages arising out of or in any way connected with the use of this web site or with the delay or inability to use this web site, or for any information, software, products, and services obtained through this web site, or otherwise arising out of the use of this web site, whether based in contract, tort, strict liability or otherwise, even if iParadigms, inc. or any of its suppliers has been advised of the possibility of damages.[100]

---

[92] A.V. v. iParadigms, Ltd. Liab. Co., 544 F. Supp. 2d 473 (E.D. Va. 2008), *aff'd in part, rev'd in part sub nom* A.V. *ex. rel.* Vanderhye v. iParadigms, LLC, 562 F.3d 630 (4th Cir. 2009).

[93] *Id.* at 478–81.

[94] *Id.* at 477–78.

[95] *Id.* at 478.

[96] *Id.*

[97] *Id.*

[98] *Id.*

[99] *Id.*

[100] *Id.*

The defendants claimed that the limitation of liability provision precluded the copyright claim.[101] The district court agreed and found that "a contract was formed based on the terms of the Clickwrap Agreement." It also upheld the very broad limitation of liability provision, stating that it means that "iParadigms cannot be held liable for any damages arising out of Plaintiffs' use of the Turnitin web site, which includes the submission and archiving of their written works."[102]

The plaintiffs raised the infancy doctrine and duress as defenses to the contract.[103] The court rejected both defenses. Regarding the infancy defense, the court stated the rule that if "an infant enters into any contract subject to conditions or stipulations, he cannot take the benefit of the contract without the burden of the conditions or stipulations." It then found that the plaintiffs received "benefits" from entering into the agreement with iParadigms because they "received a grade from their teachers, allowing them the opportunity to maintain good standing in the classes in which they were enrolled."[104] They also cited as a "benefit" of the contract, legal "standing to bring the present suit." [105]

The court also rejected the plaintiffs' duress defense, finding that "there is no evidence that anyone was coerced in any fashion by Turnitin or iParadigms." It further notes that "[i]nsofar as Plaintiffs' duress defense is asserted against Plaintiffs' respective schools, rather than Defendant iParadigms, there is no support for the proposition that a contract can be invalidated on the basis of third party duress."[106] On appeal, the Fourth Circuit skirted the sticky contract law issues and ruled for the defendants under copyright law, finding that the use of their papers constituted fair use.[107]

The Fourth Circuit's refusal to resolve the case on contract law grounds leaves unsettled the many contract law issues raised by the district court's opinion. Cheryl Preston notes that the district court's opinion and the facts of *iParadigms* suggest "that the court's reasoning would not necessarily translate to other cases" and that even if the court's comments on the infancy doctrine are taken seriously, "the district court's conclusion misapprehends the retained benefit exception to the infancy doctrine. Reliance on this case as a basis to deny minors a right to avoid a TOS is unfounded."[108] On the other hand, Julie Cromer Young worries that the district

---

101 *Id.* at 479-80.
102 *Id.* at 480.
103 *Id.* at 480-81.
104 *Id.* at 481.
105 *Id.*
106 *Id.*
107 *Id.* at 481-82.
108 Cheryl B. Preston, *CyberInfants*, 39 PEPPERDINE L. REV. 225, 239 (2012).

court's decision makes it clear that "in the wrong context the infancy doctrine could be little more than a speed bump for the party contracting with the minor to overcome" in which a "minor author could be left without recourse upon discovering the number and nature of the rights that the author has unknowingly licensed away."[109]

The district court may have felt compelled to rule against the plaintiff minors in *iParadigms* in order to save the defendants' "highly beneficial"[110] business model. In its fair use analysis, the court described iParadigms' use of student papers to

> prevent plagiarism and protect the students' written works from plagiarism... Though iParadigms makes a profit in providing this service to educational institutions, its use of the student work adds "a further purpose or different character" to the works... and provides a substantial public benefit through the network of educational institutions using Turnitin.[111]

To permit the use of the infancy doctrine to invalidate the contract between the plaintiff minors would have put at risk the company's entire business since many, if not most, of its users were minors.

While the implications for the plaintiffs in the case before it were benign precisely because iParadigms' business provided a social benefit (reducing plagiarism) and minimal harm (as there was no commercial use of the students' work), the broader implications are more disturbing. Cromer Young observes that social networking sites aimed at young users often grant the websites broad, royalty-free, perpetual, irrevocable licenses to use and distribute content posted by users.[112] She notes that one site, Club Penguin, created by the Disney Company, even appoints Disney representatives to act as agent on behalf of authors to execute contracts and includes a waiver of enforcement of moral rights.[113] That particular site also appears to assume copyright to content created by its users:

> All information, materials, functions and other content (including Submissions, as defined in Section 3, entitled "SUBMISSIONS") ("Content") contained on DIMG Sites are our copyrighted property or the copyrighted property of our licensors or licensees. All trademarks, slogans, service marks, trade names, and trade dress are proprietary to us and/or our licensors or licensees. We may

---

109 Julie Cromer Young, *From the Mouths of Babes: Protecting Child Authors from Themselves*, 112 W.VA. L. REV. 431, 458 (2010).

110 A.V. v. iParadigms, Ltd. Liab. Co., *supra* note 92, at 483.

111 *Id. at* 482.

112 Cromer Young, *supra* note 109, at 443–47.

113 *Id.* at 445. *See* http://www.clubpenguin.com/terms.htm (last visited Jan. 7, 2013).

> change the DIMG Sites or delete Content or features at any time, in any way, for any reason....[114]

In section 3, it defines submissions

> to mean text, messages, ideas, concepts, pitches, suggestions, stories, screenplays, treatments, formats, artwork, photographs, drawings, videos, audiovisual works, musical compositions (including lyrics), sound recordings, characterizations, your and/or other persons' names, likenesses, voices, usernames, profiles, actions, appearances, performances and/or other biographical information or material, and/or other similar materials that you submit, post, upload, embed, display, communicate or otherwise distribute (collectively, "Distribute") on or through a DIMG Site.[115]

But just to cover its bases, Club Penguin's terms of use provides the following broad license grant:

> You hereby grant us and our licensees, distributors, agents, representatives and other authorized users, a non-exclusive, irrevocable, fully-paid, royalty-free, sublicensable and transferable (in whole or part) worldwide license for an indeterminate period (or for such maximum period permitted by applicable law) under all copyrights, trademarks, patents, trade secrets, privacy and publicity rights and other intellectual and industrial property rights you own or control to use, reproduce, transmit, display, exhibit, distribute, index, comment on, modify (including removing lyrics and music from any Submission or substituting the lyrics and music in any Submission with music and lyrics selected by us), create derivative works based upon, perform and otherwise exploit such Submissions, in whole or in part, in all media formats and channels now known or hereafter devised (including on DIMG Sites, on third party web sites, on our broadcast and cable networks and stations, on our broadband and wireless platforms, products and services, on physical media, and in theatrical release) for any and all purposes including, without limitation, entertainment, news, advertising, promotional, marketing, publicity, trade or commercial purposes, all without further notice to you, with or without attribution, and without the requirement

114 *See id.*

115 *Id.*

of any permission from or payment to you or to any other person or entity (the "Submissions License").[116]

The terms of use also state that they "do not limit any past or future grant of rights, consents, agreements, assignments and waivers you may have made or make with respect to Submissions."[117]

The precedent established in one case reverberates and often amplifies in subsequent cases. Courts striving to reach the right result, might apply contract law in a way that compels future courts considering the same *type* of contract to reach the wrong result. For example, the court's enforcement of the browsewrap in the *iParadigms* case, and its refusal to permit the infancy doctrine as a defense, may sway a court to enforce a contract like Club Penguin's that contains very broad and overreaching terms of use, even though the social benefit/individual harm calculus differs.

The erosion of doctrinal integrity can lead to some pretty dramatic changes over time. One notable example is the U.S. Supreme Court's decision in *M/S The Bremen v. Zapata Off-Shore, Co.*[118] In *The Bremen*, the Supreme Court upheld a forum selection clause in a negotiated towage contract entered into by two sophisticated commercial entities who were based in different countries. The Court acknowledged that such agreements were generally not enforceable but distinguished the case before it because it was between two commercial entities with equal bargaining power.[119]

Several years later, the U.S. Supreme Court used the *Bremen* holding in another case, *Carnival Cruise Lines v. Shute*, to enforce a forum selection clause in a non-negotiated cruise ship passenger ticket.[120] In *Carnival Cruise Lines*, the Shutes were cruise ship passengers who made payments for cruise tickets from an agent in the state of Washington.[121] Their payment was forwarded to Carnival Cruise Lines headquarters in Miami, Florida, where their tickets were prepared and sent to them in Washington.[122] The left-hand, lower corner of the face of each ticket stated: "SUBJECT TO CONDITIONS OF CONTRACT ON LAST PAGES **IMPORTANT!** PLEASE READ CONTRACT—ON LAST PAGES 1,2,3."[123] The first page of the contract contained the forum selection clause.

---

116 *Id.*

117 *Id.*

118 M/S Bremen v. Zapata Off-Shore Co., 407 U.S. 1 (1972).

119 *Id.* at 6.

120 Carnival Cruise Lines, Inc. v. Shute, 499 U.S. 585 (1991).

121 *Id.* at 587.

122 *Id.*

123 *Id.*

The Shutes boarded the ship in Los Angeles, and Edith Shute was injured while in international waters off the coast of Mexico when she slipped on a deck mat.[124] The Shutes sued in the state of Washington.[125] At issue was the enforceability of the forum selection clause that required that all disputes be litigated in Florida.

The Supreme Court noted that *The Bremen* decision "did not define precisely the circumstances that would make it unreasonable for a court to enforce a forum clause."[126] It then proceeded to "refine the analysis of *The Bremen* to account for the realities of form passage contracts."[127] The Court cited three such realities:

> First, a cruise line has a special interest in limiting the fora in which it potentially could be subject to suit. Because a cruise ship typically carries passengers from many locales, it is not unlikely that mishap on a cruise could subject the cruise line to litigation in several different for fora (citations omitted). Additionally, a clause establishing *ex ante* the forum for dispute resolution has the salutary effect of dispelling any confusion about where suits arising from the contract must be brought and defended, sparing litigants the time and expense of pretrial motions to determine the correct forum and conserving judicial resources that otherwise would be devoted to deciding those motions. (citations omitted). Finally, it stands to reason that passengers who purchase tickets containing a forum clause like that at issue in this case benefit in the form of reduced fares reflecting the savings that the cruise line enjoys by limiting the fora in which it may be sued.[128]

But as the dissenting opinion pointed out, *The Bremen* decision altered the traditional rule that "contractual provisions, which seek to limit the place or court in which an action… may be brought are invalid as contrary to public policy."[129] The dissent stated that

> [a]lthough adherence to this general rule has declined in recent years, particularly following our decision in *The Bremen v. Zapata Off-Shore Co.* (citations omitted), the prevailing rule is still that forum selection clauses are not

---

124 *Id.*

125 *Id.*

126 *Id.* at 591.

127 *Id.* at 593.

128 *Id.* at 593-94.

129 *Carnival Cruise Lines, Inc. v. Shute*, 499 U.S. 585, 601(1991) (Stevens, K., dissenting).*Id.*

enforceable if they were not freely bargained for, create additional expense for one party, or deny one party a remedy.[130]

The Supreme Court in *The Bremen* underscored that the agreement was "freely negotiated" and recognized that "in the light of present-day commercial realities and expanding international trade" the agreement should be upheld "absent a strong showing that it should be set aside."[131] The *Carnival Cruise Lines* court acknowledged that, given the facts of *The Bremen*, which involved companies from two different nations and the towing of a costly piece of equipment across international waters, it was "entirely reasonable" for *The Bremen* Court to have expected the parties to have "negotiated with care" the forum selection clause. It also acknowledged that the case before it did not involve an unusual transaction, but one that was "purely routine and doubtless nearly identical to every commercial passage contract issued" by most cruise lines, noting that "it would be entirely unreasonable for us to assume that [the Shutes]—or any other cruise passenger—would negotiate with petitioner the terms of a forum-selection clause in an ordinary commercial cruise ticket."[132] Yet, the Court entirely discounts the lack of bargaining in its analysis of whether the forum section clause should be enforceable.[133] Instead, the *Carnival Cruise Lines* Court emphasizes the business context. Rather than seeing the "crucial differences in the business contexts" as grounds for rejecting the forum selection clause in the case before it, it uses those differences to "refine the analysis of *The Bremen* to account for the realities of form passage contracts."[134]

But, as the dissent in *Carnival Cruise* notes, "*The Bremen*, which the Court effectively treats as controlling the case, had nothing to say about stipulations printed on the back of passenger tickets."[135] While *The Bremen* modified the law governing forum selection clauses, it did not change contract doctrine or the rules governing contract formation. By contrast, *Carnival Cruise* changed the very essence of what could be considered a contract, substituting an analysis of the reasonableness of the substantive terms for an analysis of assent and contract formation. Ironically, the *Carnival Cruise* Court did not intend for this to happen. The Court emphasized that the case involved admiralty law and that it was not considering the issue of

130 Dissenting opinion of *Carnival Cruise* at 601.
131 *Id.* at 591.
132 *Id.* at 593.
133 *Id.* at 585.
134 *Id.* at 593.
135 *Id.* at 601.

reasonable notice because the Shutes had stipulated that they had seen the contract terms.[136]

Yet, just as *The Bremen* decision had set a precedent with unintended consequences, so, too, did *Carnival Cruise* establish an important precedent which would make it easier to enforce unilaterally imposed terms in wrap agreements. Juliet Moringiello notes that "[d]espite its lack of analysis on the notice issue, *Carnival* has made a splash in the emerging jurisprudence of electronic contracting."[137] The court in *ProCD v. Zeidenberg* cited to *Carnival Cruise* to support its argument that

> "[t]transactions in which the exchange of money precedes the communication of detailed terms are common... consider the purchase of an airline ticket. The traveler calls the carrier or an agent, is quoted a price, reserves a seat, pays and gets a ticket, in that order. The ticket contains elaborate terms, which the traveler can reject by canceling the reservation. To use the ticket is to accept the terms, even terms that in retrospect are disadvantageous."[138]

But the *ProCD* court's use of this example is misleading in that often airlines do not permit reservation cancellations without some sort of penalty. A paid ticket is considered a completed transaction by both parties. In that case, receiving terms after payment should be interpreted as a request for modification since there is no way to "reject" the terms without penalty, and the penalty could not be enforced unless there was a contract existing between the parties *before* the terms were sent. In other words, the question of contract formation is ignored and replaced with an evaluation of whether the terms are reasonable. This is highlighted by the example that Easterbrook uses:

> Ours is not a case in which a consumer opens a package to find an insert saying "you owe us an extra $10,000" and the seller files suit to collect. Any buyer finding such a demand can prevent formation of the contract by returning the package, as can any consumer who concludes that the terms of the license make the software worth less than the purchase price.[139]

---

[136] *Id.* at 590 (noting that "this is a case in admiralty" and "we do not address the question whether respondents had sufficient notice of the forum clause before entering the contract for passage. Respondents essentially have conceded that they had notice of the forum selection provision.").

[137] Moringiello, *supra* note 88 . at 1321.

[138] ProCD v. Zeidenberg, 86 F.3d 1447, 1451 (7th Cir. 1996)

[139] *Id.* at 1452.

The example is inapt because the consumer is not likely to have read the terms. Furthermore, it is against the policy of many retailers to accept opened packages of software and other, easily reproducible digital goods. The consumer then is effectively left without a way to signal rejection.

The ability to reject is fictitious because the consumer is not likely to reject the terms. If the consumer returns the software, it will be because it is defective and not because she has read and objected to the terms in the box. Unilaterally imposed terms have become an important, intractable part of modern commercial transactions and an integral part of the economy. But these slips of paper are not true contracts; they are referred to as contracts in order to justify their enforcement by a court. The case law has reached the point that it simply does not matter whether the consumer has read the terms—the assumption, in fact, is that she will not have done so. The labeling of the terms as "contract" gives their unilaterally imposed nature legitimacy, and empowers a court to enforce them.

Although courts analyze them as contracts, traditional contract doctrine often fails to explain wrap contracts. In fact, courts often wriggle free of the constraints of contract law and the formation requirements of offer and acceptance and mutual assent, in order to enforce the terms of a shrinkwrap or browsewrap agreement. In *ProCD*, for example, Judge Easterbrook found mutual assent to enter into the shrinkwrap agreement, even though, logically, how could one enter into a contract for a transaction *after* that transaction has been completed? Similarly, how can users accept the terms of a browsewrap agreement without even being aware of its existence? Most troubling, with both browsewrap and shrinkwrap situations, users are *deemed to have accepted* terms through a failure to actively reject them even though traditional contract law states that an offeror cannot unilaterally impose such a requirement of active rejection. As the Corbin treatise states:

> It should here be plainly set forth that an offeror has no power to cause the silence of the offeree to operate as an acceptance when the offeree does not intend it to do so. The offeree's own conduct may be such as to make his silence operative against him; and the offeror's conduct may be such as to make the offeree's silence a sufficient acceptance binding upon the offeror. But an offer can not, merely by saying that the offeree's silence will be taken as an acceptance, cause it to be operative as such. He can not force the offeree to take his pen in hand, or to spend a two-cent stamp, or to open his mouth, under penalty of being bound by a contract if he does not.[140]

[140] Arthur L. Corbin, Corbin on Contracts (one-volume ed., West Publishing 1952).

Nor would it seem that he could require the offeree to pack up his computer or software disk, get in his car, park, and try to return the product if he rejects the terms—a task made all the more challenging when one considers that few retailers will accept such packages after they have been opened unless they contain a defect. Even then, retailers generally will exchange the defective product rather than provide a monetary refund.

There are certain exceptions to the general rule that silence does not constitute acceptance. All of these exceptions, however, are limited to situations where it is reasonable to assume that the offeree intended to accept the offer. The exceptions are based on a kind of implied contract theory that seeks to prevent unjust enrichment or else on an interpretive theory where it makes sense to view nonverbal acts, such as a nod of the head or a gesture, as acceptance. In a few cases, the offeror has indicated that acceptance need not be communicated, but those cases were upheld only if the communication of acceptance was for the benefit of the offeror—not where the offeree had no intention of accepting the offer. Furthermore, the exceptions apply only to the known terms of the offer, not to any additional terms that are unknown to the offeree.

Assume, for example, that your neighbor suggested that you share the cost of building a fence between your two houses. He tells you the approximate cost and you shrug and make a noncommittal response. The next day, you pull into your driveway and see your neighbor has hired someone who is constructing a fence. You remark to your neighbor that the fence looks good. When your neighbor approaches you afterward to ask you to pay for half the cost of building the fence, a court may very well find that your shrug, noncommittal response, and subsequent inaction to the fence-building activities to be "acceptance" of your neighbor's offer.

But this is not the same situation faced by adherents to wrap contracts who are deemed to have accepted terms that extend beyond what is being exchanged. A more apt analogy would be if your neighbor told you that your "silence" when confronted with the fence-building activities constituted acceptance to him picking the flowers from your garden and using your pool whenever he wanted. Outside of the wrap contract setting, courts have been unwilling to find that offerees have accepted terms that were not expressly part of the bargain.

Clickwrap agreements, although often lumped together with browsewrap and shrinkwrap agreements, are less troubling from a doctrinal perspective in that they require a manifestation of consent by the user. In reality, however, this distinction is one without a difference. While the licensee's click manifests assent to the transaction and to the contractual relationship, often the user does not read—and therefore, cannot actually assent to—the contractual terms themselves.

Courts sometimes compare wrap contracts with other unilaterally imposed terms, such as claim check tickets or airline ticket waivers. This comparison is misleading for several reasons. First, the language on the back of these other unilaterally imposed forms typically attempts to limit the drafter's liability. These limitations are enforceable only to the extent that they conform to requirements of other law, such as applicable legislation, property, tort, or, in the case of warranty disclaimers, commercial law. These areas of law expressly permit disclaimers and limitations of liability, provided that there is adequate notice.

Second, the notice required is not the fantasy that it often is with wrap contracts. A form only has two sides, and there is at least a 50 percent chance that the adherent will see the notice. It also has tangibility, unlike wrap contracts, which raises the likelihood of the recipient actually noticing the legal terms. In addition, the terms are limited by the space on the form itself. There are only so many words that can be squeezed onto the back of a ticket especially given that a court will evaluate font size in determining reasonable notice. Even then, language on the back of tickets may not constitute sufficient notice. For example, in *Wallis v. Princess Cruises, Inc.*,[141] the Ninth Circuit analyzed whether the limitation of liability provision on the back of a passenger's ticket was reasonably communicated to the passenger as required under federal common law and maritime law. The cruise ship passenger was given a ticket containing ticket coupons and a "Passage Contract."[142] At the bottom of the first coupon was the headline "IMPORTANT NOTICE" in 1/8-inch type followed by a statement in 1/16-inch type, which stated:

> THIS TICKET INCLUDES THE PASSAGE CONTRACT TERMS SET FORTH AT THE END OF THIS PACKET WHICH ARE BINDING ON YOU. PLEASE READ ALL SECTIONS CAREFULLY AS THEY AFFECT YOUR LEGAL RIGHTS, PARTICULARLY SECTION 14 GOVERNING THE PROVISION OF MEDICAL AND OTHER PERSONAL SERVICES AND SECTIONS 15 THROUGH 18 LIMITING THE CARRIER'S LIABILITY AND OUR RIGHTS TO SUE.[143]

On pages 6 and 7 of the Passage Contract, paragraph 16 limited the carrier's liability in accordance with the "Convention Relating to the Carriage of Passengers and Their Luggage by Sea."[144] The court found that

> [u]nder the reasonable communicativeness test, a disincentive "to study the provisions of the ticket" is considered an extrinsic factor impeding "the passenger's

[141] Wallis v. Princess Cruises, Inc., 306 F.3d 827 (9th Cir. 2002).
[142] *Id.* at 830.
[143] *Id.*
[144] *Id.* at 831.

> ability to become meaningfully informed" and that it "would require some legal and financial sophistication" to understand the provision.[145]

Consequently, the court found that the limitation of liability provision was not reasonably communicated and was therefore unenforceable. Contrast that decision with the wrap contract cases which have upheld browsewraps accessible only via hyperlinks generically labeled "Legal Terms."

To be sure, new contracting forms create new problems and, thus, new doctrinal challenges. Yet, with wrap contracts, courts have vehemently denied that different rules should apply and have not made adjustments to recognize the ways that wrap contracts differ from traditional paper contracts. Rather than acknowledging the importance of form, courts insisted that electronic contracts were the same as paper contracts and that the same rules applied.[146]

This may be a case of courts doth protesting too much, methinks. Despite their claims to the contrary, courts *have* created new law. They have instinctively focused their analysis on attaining the result that felt right, and have done so by maneuvering around existing rules, leaving doctrinal chaos in their wake. They recite law that originates from the paper-based contracting world to this brave new digitally based world when they might be better off acknowledging the difference that contract form and function make to the reasonable expectations of the parties. The problem with adhesion contracts is not that they are nonnegotiable or that they are unlikely to be read; the real problem is that their terms may be unexpected and unfair. Wrap contracts, by their form, permit companies to impose more objectionable terms than paper contracts of adhesion. Judicial adoption of a one-size-fits-all approach to agreements has resulted in companies sneaking into standard contracts terms that are ill-suited to them and unexpected by the nondrafting party.

---

145 *Id.*

146 Moringiello, *supra* note 88, at 1320 (stating that "[i]f there is any coherent theme in the judicial rulings on the enforceability of electronic contracts it is that such contracts are really no different from paper contracts.").

9 Form, Function, and Notice

A DISCUSSION OF the relevance of notice in online contracting requires a preliminary discussion of the so-called duty to read. In order to implicate the duty to read, a reasonable person must have believed that the conduct of the other party indicated assent. A party can manifest assent in several ways. For example, a party can sign a contract, or accept a document such as an airline ticket, where the act of doing so implies assent.[1] Parties are bound by their outward manifestations. Thus, if a party signs a contract, it is reasonable to assume that she or he has read the terms. In some situations, such as those involving bills of lading, passenger tickets, and receipts, no signature is required and mere acceptance of the document may be deemed acceptance of the terms.[2] Online, a

[1] *See* JOSEPH M. PERILLO, CALAMARI & PERILLO ON CONTRACTS § 9.41 (6th ed., West 2009)) (stating that the "duty to read" applies "even without a signature if the acceptance of a document, which purports to be a contract implies assent to its terms. Thus, for example, the mere acceptance of documents such as bills of lading, passenger tickets, insurance policies, bank books and warehouse receipts may give rise to contracts based upon the provisions contained therein. The recipient has a duty to read.").
[2] *Id.*

party manifests assent by clicking "I agree" to the terms of a clickwrap or by continuing to use a website after notice of the terms.

Notice takes center stage with wrap contract formation because there is no handwritten signature affixed to a legal document to clearly indicate awareness and acceptance of terms. The act of consent has significance only if it can be clearly tied to intent. Intent is tied to knowledge, and knowledge is tied to awareness. This is where notice steps in.

Notice must be sufficiently called to the attention of the nondrafting party. Notice can be either actual or constructive. Actual notice may mean that the user actually saw and read the terms at the time they were initially presented or that the user received notice of the terms sometime thereafter, including via communication from the drafting party, such as a cease-and-desist letter informing the other party of the terms.[3]

Constructive notice arises in those cases where the offeree claims that she did not see the terms. Constructive notice means that a reasonably prudent offeree would have known about the terms. In order to assess the reasonableness of the offeree's conduct or awareness, the court must first determine whether the notice itself was reasonable. As explained in chapter eight, the courts have not provided uniform guidelines for what constitutes constructive notice in wrap cases, but the cases tend to focus on the visibility of the terms and wording that indicates that the terms are meant to be legally binding. By contrast, effective notice in the offline world must be presented alongside the terms themselves. Liability limitations are presented with the coat claim ticket. Warranty disclaimers are presented in the box with the product. Online, however, notice of terms is often notice that terms are available on another page, not on the same page with the notice itself. The burden on adherents then is much greater—not only do they have to read the fine print, they have to track it down. Because the terms don't necessarily accompany the notice, there are often more of them.

In addition to notice, the offeree must manifest consent to the terms. There are two ways that an offeree can manifest consent under wrap contract doctrine. The offeree can act affirmatively by clicking on an icon that indicates acceptance. The offeree can also manifest consent by a failure to act in certain circumstances. These circumstances include opening merchandise with notice of the terms and then failing to return the merchandise, acting in a way that is designated by the notice as manifesting consent, and continuing to browse a website or use a website's services after having notice of legal terms. In these situations, the offeree is required to actively reject the terms.

---

[3] *See* Southwest Airlines Co. v. BoardFirst, LLC, 2007 WL 4823761 (N.D. Tex.) (finding that BoardFirst had "actual knowledge of Southwest's Terms" at least since receiving a cease-and-desist letter informing it of Southwest's Terms). *Id.* at 7.

Courts justify an active rejection requirement under the theory that the offeree presumably knew that the service or product was rendered pursuant to the terms. One court stated

> "While new commerce on the Internet has exposed courts to many new situations, it has not fundamentally changed the principles of contract. It is standard contract doctrine that when a benefit is offered subject to stated conditions, and the offeree makes a decision to take the benefit with knowledge of the terms of the offer, the taking constitutes acceptance of the terms, which accordingly become binding on the offeree."[4]

Yet, the court could just as easily have applied a different rule to reach a contrary result, which is that "the conduct of a party is not effective as a manifestation of assent unless he intends to engage in the conduct and knows or has reason to know that the other party may infer from his conduct that he assents."[5]

Courts routinely enforce wrap contracts where consumers have no intent of entering into a contract. The requirement of manifestation of consent seems to be subsumed in wrap contract cases with the issue of notice. In other words, what courts mean when they talk about manifestation of consent in online contracting scenarios is really presumptive notice—the manifested act which supposedly indicates consent really only indicates that the offeree received actual or constructive notice. The affirmative act of clicking, rather than being an act of assent, is a mechanistic act that signals that notice was given—and only because courts have designated it as such. Where there is no affirmative act required to manifest consent (i.e., with shrinkwraps or browsewraps), courts may *construct* the manifestation of consent if there is notice. In other words, the manifestation of consent requirement has been swallowed up by notice so that if the drafter can show notice, the nondrafting party will be deemed to have assented to the wrap contract.

To state that notice and manifestation of consent may be judicially constructed in wrap cases means that the nondrafting party does not actually need to either receive notice or understand or intend the meaning attributed by the courts to a particular action. In shrinkwrap cases, a failure to return the product after an opportunity to read the terms constitutes a manifestation of consent. Realistically, many consumers are not even aware of the terms so it is not reasonable to infer from their inaction that they are manifesting consent. Even with clickwraps, the act of "clicking" is not

---

[4] Register.com v. Verio, 356 F.3d 393, at 403 (2d Cir. 2004) (citations omitted).

[5] Restatement (Second) of Contracts § 19 (1981).

perceived the same way as signing a legal document.[6] Users, habituated to the common act of clicking, are often not even aware of what they have done. The plaintiff in one case, *Scherillo v. Dun & Bradstreet, Inc.*,[7], argued that he had "no recollection of checking the box or reading the terms and conditions, and he must have inadvertently hit the space bar as he was tabbing through the application."[8] The court rejected the plaintiff's argument as "simply not credible."[9]

The plaintiff in that case does not seem to be the only one with click amnesia. During one of my recent law school classes, I asked my students—nearly all of whom were users of Facebook—whether they remembered what that website's contract terms were. Nobody did. Then I asked whether anyone bothered clicking on the link to view the terms of service. Nobody did. In fact, nobody said anything. They just looked at me. I asked them, "Why are you all looking at me like that? Is it because you're ashamed that you didn't read the contract before agreeing to it?" (This was a contract law class, after all.) Finally, one brave soul raised his hand and said, "I think it's because we don't remember seeing a contract at all." The nodding of heads indicated that he was indeed speaking for the others.

There's a famous study having to do with perception that indicates that my students were not unusually inattentive—and that the plaintiffs in wrap cases are not so much unreasonably click-happy as they are typical. In the study, subjects were asked to watch a videotaped basketball game. One team wore white shirts, the other black shirts. People were asked to silently count the number of passes made by players on the white shirted team while ignoring passes made by those wearing black shirts. The video was less than a minute. Halfway through the video, a person wearing a gorilla suit stopped in the middle of the players and thumped her chest. Approximately half of the participants in the study did not notice the gorilla.[10] If observers fail to notice someone wearing a gorilla suit in the middle of a basketball game, how can we expect consumers to register a click in the middle of an interactive and visually distracting website?

Yet, once the bulwark of assent was overcome by constructive notice and judicially constructed manifestations of consent, there was little to restrain companies from

---

[6] Rainer Böhme & Stefan Köpsell, 2010 ACM Conference on Human Factors in Computing Sys., Trained to Accept? A Field Experiment on Consent Dialogs 2403 (2010), *available at* http://www1.inf.tu-dresden.de/~rb21/publications/BK2010_Trained_To_Accept_CHI.pdf.

[7] Scherillo v. Dun & Bradstreet, Inc., 684 F.Supp.2d 313 (E.D.N.Y. 2010).

[8] *Id.* at 321.

[9] *Id.* at 322.

[10] Christopher Chabris & Daniel Simons, The Invisible Gorilla: How Our Intuitions Deceive Us 5–6 (2009) (discussing their famous "Invisible Gorilla" study which was reported in the article D. J. Simons & C. F. Chabris, *Gorillas in Our Midst: Sustained Inattentional Blindness for Dynamic Events*, 28 Perception 1059–74 (1999)).

employing even more unobtrusive contracting forms, such as browsewraps. Mark Lemley speculates that

> the clickwrap and shrinkwrap cases may have conditioned courts to abandon the idea of assent when it comes to browsewraps. Legally there is a big difference between a unilateral statement of desires and a statement of terms to which the other party has agreed. But once we have expanded agreement to include clicking on a Web site or engaging in conduct that we would expect the buyer to engage in anyway, it seems only a small step to enforce a unilateral statement of terms. As the argument goes, if we refuse to enforce browsewraps, a site owner will simply impose the same restrictions via clickwrap or shrinkwrap. Since no one reads the latter forms of contract anyway, and owners can include whatever terms they want, it seems a sort of formalism to require them to go through the effort of requiring some weak manifestation of assent.[11]

Contract form became less important than the existence of notice for purposes of determining wrap contract formation. But, as this chapter explains, a notice is not a contract and what suffices as reasonable notice for certain purposes should not be mistaken for contractual assent in all contexts.

A. What is a Notice?

While most courts in paper contract cases have construed reasonable notice to mean that terms must be both conspicuous and accessible, many courts assessing the enforceability of wrap contracts have interpreted notice to mean that only the notice itself, and not the legal terms, must be conspicuous and accessible. For example, courts have enforced contracts that were only accessible via hyperlinks.

This construction of notice threatens to place an undue burden on the nondrafting party because of the duty to read. Notice of terms triggers a duty to read on the part of the nondrafting party. In other words, if you sign a twenty-page agreement, you are presumed to have read the terms. When you unwrap a software package and a piece of paper falls out with the words, "IMPORTANT—PLEASE READ," courts believe that you have notice of legal terms which triggers your duty to read. If, however, the piece of paper says, "IMPORTANT—LEGAL AGREEMENT,"

---

[11] Mark A. Lemley, *Terms of Use*, 91 MINN. L. REV. 459, 469–70 (2006).

and you open it up and it says, "Please log on to our website to read your legally binding agreement," you might feel it unreasonable for the company to expect you to do so. You may feel this even more strongly if, upon visiting the company's website, you discover that the relevant page contains several hyperlinks to other pages which the company may modify at will.

Notices are intended to draw attention. Consequently, they are posted where they are likely to be read, meaning they are usually posted where they are most relevant. Imagine passing a sign that stated: "Warning—please read sign on Alexander Street." Alexander Street is the next block over and would require a detour, so you don't bother to read the sign. You cross the street and narrowly miss getting hit by an oncoming car. Later, you find out that the sign on Alexander Street stated: "Traffic Light Broken—Watch for Traffic Both Directions!" The first warning sign would hardly be considered effective notice of the broken light. Effective warning signs are posted near the dangerous condition, not miles away from it.

Another purpose of a notice is to make certain information salient. Accordingly, notices should provide some substantive information, not just direct the reader to where information can be found. A package of cigarettes warns the user of the harmful effects of smoking; the label does not simply state, "Warning," and tuck information of the harmful effects inside the package.

The American Bar Association Joint Working Group on Electronic Contracting Practices (ABA Working Group)[12] posited that a user assents to a browsewrap if four elements are satisfied:

(i) The user is provided with adequate notice of the existence of the proposed terms.
(ii) The user has a meaningful opportunity to review the terms.
(iii) The user is provided with adequate notice that taking a specified action manifests assent to the terms.
(iv) The user takes the action specified in the latter notice.[13]

---

[12] The ABA Working Group is formed with members from within the Electronic Commerce Subcommittee of the Cyberspace Law Committee and within the Uniform Commercial Code Committee of the Business Law Section of the American Bar Association

[13] Christina L. Kunz, John E. Ottaviani, Elaine D. Ziff, Juliet M. Moringiello, Kathleen M. Porter, & Jennifer C. Debrow, *Browse-Wrap Agreements: Validity of Implied Assent in Electronic Form Agreement*, 59 Bus. Law. 279 (Nov. 2003). The working group had completed an earlier project focusing on clickwrap agreements, which is discussed in chapter 11. *See* Christina L. Kunz, Maureen E. Del Duca, Heather Thayer, & Jennifer Debrow, *ClickThrough Agreements: Strategies for Avoiding Disputes on Validity of Assent*, 57 Bus. Law. 401 (Nov. 2001).

The ABA Working Group stated that what constitutes adequate notice should be based upon both the "physical presentation of the notice" and the "content of the notice."[14] The ABA Working Group wrote:

> In an electronic setting, the user can be given adequate notice of the existence of terms by a scroll box revealing a portion of the terms or by a well placed phrase or sentence in a format calculated to be apparent to the typical user of that Web site or CD-ROM.... we suggest that care be taken to make sure that any linking capability of the phrase or sentence is clear to the reasonable user.[15]

With respect to the content of the notice, the ABA Working Group wrote that

> "clear language in a hyperlink that the terms constitute a proposed agreement is more likely to result in a binding contract. For example, a hyperlink that makes the statement, 'Use of this Web site is subject to our terms of use, click here to read,' is more informative than a hyperlink that states simply 'Terms of Use.' Even more informative would be a hyperlink that states the following: 'By going beyond this page, you are deemed to have agreed to our terms of use.'"[16]

The ABA Working Group recommendations reflect traditional contract law principles applied to electronic contracts. Unfortunately, many courts have not followed these recommendations and have instead, swapped the signpost for the information, disregarding that notice requires both attracting user attention *and* providing at least some of the relevant information.

The substitution of "notice of notice" for "notice" threatens to unduly burden the offeree, given the variety of electronic tools at the drafting party's disposal. A drafter can send an offeree written notice of terms on a card sent in the mail, which references the terms which can be found on a website. That website may contain a clickwrap that contains several hyperlinks. Under wrap contract doctrine, the card provides notice, and the clickwrap provides both notice and manifestation of consent. As a practical matter, however, the hyperlink acts as a barrier, concealing the actual terms. But in the judicially constructed alternative universe, the use of a hyperlink is viewed—not as the obstruction that it is—but as notice. Under wrap contract doctrine, since "notice" and "manifestation of consent" equals "assent," the consumer has assented, and so is bound by the so-called contract.

---

[14] *Id* at 291.

[15] *Id.* at 293.

[16] *Id.* at 294.

In *Major v. McCallister*, the website user sued a referral website after she became dissatisfied with its "prescreened" construction contractors.[17] As part of the referral process, Major entered information about her project on several website pages. Each page was hyperlinked to ServiceMagic's browsewrap.[18] After inputting the information about her project, a new page appeared where Major had to submit her contact information and press a "Submit for Matching Pros" button.[19] Next to this button was a blue hyperlink to the browsewrap and the words, "By submitting you agree to the Terms of Use."[20] Not surprisingly, Major pressed the "Submit for Matching Pros" button without clicking on the hyperlink to the browsewrap. [21]

The court emphasized the consumer's failure to read the terms as an indication that she did not care for them—not as an indication that the notice was ineffective. Yet, the court should have considered the provision of notice from the user's perspective. The hyperlink to the terms and conditions was on the page where the user was inputting information. To read the terms and conditions would have required a disruptive process of toggling from one page to another and back again, interrupting the "flow" of the transaction. Similarly, when Major was presented with the hyperlink to the terms at the same time as she was presented with the "Submit for Matching Pros" button, she could not perform both functions at once. In this author's experience, clicking on a hyperlink when filling out an online form sometimes results in loss of data in the form fields. Major may have been aware of that. Given the time and care she had already expended in inputting information on the website pages, she may have been reluctant to disrupt the process by clicking on a link that might require her to start the process over again. On the other hand, she may simply not have seen it. The two wrap contracts, presented concurrently, compete for the user's attention and require diverging actions. A user is much more likely to read the agreement if it is presented consecutively rather than concurrently. Because the primary task is filling out and completing the form, the online multiwrapping practically guarantees that the hyperlink will be ignored and the browsewrap terms unread.

The court noted that it "should honor the forum selection clause unless it is unfair or unreasonable to do so,"[22] suggesting that the substance of the disputed provision is of more concern than the validity of assent. The court's analysis rationalized attenuated notice in order to enforce what it viewed as a substantively reasonable contract clause. The court reached its conclusion regarding the substance of the contract

---

[17] Major v. McCallister, 302 S.W. 3d 227 (Mo. App. S.D. 2009).

[18] *Id.* at 228.

[19] *Id.* at 229.

[20] *Id.*

[21] *Id.*

[22] *Id.*

first, then backed into the assent analysis in a way that supported its conclusion. But the court's substitution of its own will for that of the nondrafting party contravenes contract law.

The substitution of notice for consent is a legal construct to establish contract formation. Notice provided by the offeror is not the same thing as the offeree intentionally engaging in conduct that a reasonable person would interpret as assent to the terms of a contract. Although intent to be legally bound is not a requirement for contract formation,[23] the offeree must intend to engage in the conduct that would signal to a reasonable person the making of a promise or commitment.[24] The offeree may not realize the legally binding nature of her actions, but she must intend to engage in those actions that, to a reasonable person, would indicate the making of the promise or commitment. In the case of wrap contracts, the act that constitutes assent is often undertaken for reasons other than to signal promise making. Furthermore, most reasonable drafters of wrap contracts are fully aware that the vast majority of offerees are oblivious to the existence of contracts—they specifically design contracts to make them unobtrusive (something which is further discussed in chapter 11). This is especially true where the contract terms are not readily available, such as with shrinkwraps or where terms are viewable only by clicking on a hyperlink.

Some companies use a variety of wrap agreements to ensure that users receive formalistic notice while making it difficult for users to actually view the terms. They might mail a notice to users rather than sending the entire agreement, and then indicate on the notice where to find the agreement online. The online agreement may be hidden behind a clickwrap and one or more hyperlinks, placing the burden upon the user to uncover the terms.

Finally, multiple versions of the same notice and/or agreement increase the burden on users, who are then required to sort through the different forms to determine whether there are conflicting terms. For example, a user may receive a contract in the box with a product, and then later an invoice referencing an online agreement. When she visits the website, she may encounter one or more hyperlinks to terms and one or more clickwraps. She may be confounded as to which terms actually govern the relationship with the drafter. Courts, however, courts may find that the delivery of notice in any one of these forms constitutes reasonable notice even when the abundance of terms may actually compel the user to disregard all of them.

---

[23] Restatement (Second) of Contracts § 21 (1981) ("Neither real nor apparent intention that a promise be legally binding is essential to the formation of a contract, but a manifestation of intention that a promise shall not affect legal relations may prevent the formation of a contract.").

[24] *Id.*at § 19 ("The conduct of a party is not effective as a manifestation of his assent unless he intends to engage in the conduct and knows or has reason to know that the other party may infer from his conduct that he assents.").

In short, to equate constructive notice and constructive manifestation of consent with assent is a fiction which imposes unreasonable burdens upon the user. So why have courts turned notice into contract? The next section suggests that it had something to do with the role of notice and contracts in tort and property law.

B. Intent and Consent in Contracts, Torts, and Property

What constitutes reasonable notice should depend upon the contracting environment. The essential problem with wrap contract doctrine is that courts mistake the role of notice with that of contract and thus, substitute visibility of terms for consent. The role of notice, however, is very different from contract. A notice can be used for several different purposes. It can be used in the context of property to inform others of the status of that property and the owner's rights. It can grant permission to others. It can also seek to modify existing duties of care or rights. Finally, it can be used as a contract. The courts have not distinguished these different types and functions of notices and have collapsed them all into the last one—contract.

A property owner can use a sign as a notice, to inform others that property belongs to her. Her status as a property owner allows her to impose certain rules relating to the use of its property but only to the extent that she has the right to do so under property law. She may inform others of those rules by using a notice.

For example, a property owner (P) may place a notice in the form of a sign on her property: **Private Property. Visitors Only From 9 am To 5 pm. Keep off the grass.** The sign indicates that P will not exercise her property right to kick visitors off her property and/or sue them for trespass if they comply with the stated conditions—they can only be on the property during the hours of 9 a.m.–5 p.m., and they must keep off the grass. If a visitor (V) violates either restriction, P can exercise her property rights (i.e., her right to exclude) by ejecting V from the premises.

Notice may also be relevant in determining damages. Good faith on the part of the trespasser may exclude punitive damages.[25] If, for example, V claims that she did not know that she was on P's property, a large conspicuous sign indicating **KEEP OUT—PRIVATE PROPERTY** would make her claim less believable.

A notice can also determine whether P owed a duty of care or whether a duty of care was breached.[26] Assume that P places a sign on her property —**PRIVATE**

---

[25] DAN B. DOBBS, THE LAW OF TORTS, at § 56, p. 115 (2nd ed 2000) (noting that "deliberate and known trespass, coupled with factors such as repetition, destruction or taking of property, or other aggravating elements, warrant substantial punitive awards.")

[26] *Id.* at §211, p. 534(noting that cases "formerly resolved under assumed risk rationales can now be resolved by (1) applying comparative fault rules, (2) holding that the defendant had no duty of care, or (3) holding that the defendant did not breach a duty.") *Id.* at § 211, page 534.

PROPERTY—WARNING: FALLING ROCK! OWNER ASSUMES NO LIABILITY FOR INJURIES! PROCEED AT YOUR OWN RISK! If V enters the property and is injured by falling rock, the notice may play a pivotal role in determining whether V consented to accept the risk of falling rock, thereby limiting P's duty of care.[27]

Tort law, however, recognizes limits to consent. The Dobbs treatise on torts states, "[a]lthough the plaintiff may consent to accept a risk of the defendant's conduct either by express agreement or by implication—the so-called primary sense of assumed risk—the conclusion that she relieves the defendant of a duty does not necessarily mean that she has consented to relieve the defendant of all possible duties of care."[28] Tort law provides a backstop to what contract law might permit when the relevant term has to do with a duty imposed by tort law.

Without contract, the ability of the property owner to set rules is governed by property law and limited by tort law. The rights of the property owner over her property does not give her rights over the property (or entitlements) of others. Imagine that in the above example, the sign said : **Private Property. $5 entrance fee.** If V entered the property, would V have to pay the entrance fee? P can impose whatever rules P wants on her property but whether she can *enforce* those rules depends upon whether she is legally permitted to do so. In other words, P has rights to control use of her property but those rights don't extend to control over V's property (i.e. V's $5).

There are two situations where P could collect the $5 in the above circumstances. The first is if there is some law, such as an ordinance, that permits her to exercise her rights as a property owner in this manner. A city ordinance may, for example, allow a property owner to impose a fine or fee for unauthorized entry. The second situation is if P enters into a contract with V whereby V agrees to pay $5 for entry onto P's property. This is where notice is also a contract.

If V saw the sign, there is an implied contract to pay for entry onto P's land. If, however, V did not see the sign, the situation becomes more complicated because it involves *V*'s property (the $5) as well as P's property. Whether V will be obligated to pay the $5 will depend upon whether the notice was so conspicuous that the terms of entry were clear; it will also depend upon whether V's act of entering onto the property could reasonably be construed as assent to the terms of the notice. If V should have seen the sign because it was unavoidable, it is reasonable to assume that she

[27] *See id.* at § 212, p. 540 (noting that the "effect of the plaintiff's consent to accept the risk is that the defendant has no duty to the plaintiff with respect to that risk. By agreement, responsibility has been shifted to the plaintiff.")

[28] *Id.*, at section 214, p. 546.

intended to accept the terms of the notice by entering onto the premises. If, however, the sign was obscured or not conspicuous, then V's act of entering onto the premises does not clearly indicate her intent to pay the $5.

Consequently, whether there is an implied contract depends upon how conspicuous the notice was and whether it was reasonable to infer from V's subsequent action that she intended to accept the posted terms. If the notice was unavoidable, then it would be reasonable to infer that the subsequent act of entering on the property by V would indicate consent to the terms. (There is one caveat, further discussed below, which is that this inference is only reasonable if P owns the property and thus has the power to unilaterally set the terms for entry onto P's property.) If the notice was not reasonably conspicuous, V should not be obligated to pay the $5; *however*, V may then be liable for trespass *as permission to enter was conditioned* upon payment of the $5 fee.

By contrast, consider a scenario involving a conspicuous sign scrawled by P and placed upon public property (i.e., that P does not own): **Please pay P $5 entrance fee.** Assuming V knows that P does not own the property, V's entry onto the property even after receiving actual notice, could not reasonably be construed to mean consent to the terms of the notice. Even if V believed that P owned the property, because that belief was incorrect, P would not be able to enforce the terms of the notice. P does not have any power under property law to impose the contractual terms upon V, and P could not force V to pay under a contract theory (or any other theory, for that matter). In other words, P can impose whatever rules she is entitled to impose under property law (including any local ordinances or regulations)—provided they do not violate any other law. P's rights as a property owner do not give her rights over the world—only over her own property. To the extent that she seeks an entitlement belonging to another (in this case, V), she can only do so, not because P owns the property visited by V, but because V has consented. If V has not consented, P's remedies are those permitted by property law, not contract.

Although there are restrictions regarding what one can impose under property and tort law, there are few limits to what parties can agree to in contract law. Consent to a contract does more than simply limit the consenting party's right to sue the other party in tort—a binding contract can impose affirmative obligations or commit a party to do something in the future. In the example above where the sign, **Please pay P $5 entrance fee**, placed upon P's property is construed as a contract, V has to give up something that is not within P's rights to take. P needs V's permission to access V's money, whereas P does not need V's permission to tell V to keep off the grass or leave the premises after 5 p.m.—or, for that matter, to be careful of falling rocks. A notice does not need consent to be effective—it needs only to meet certain visibility and disclosure requirements where such requirements are applicable. By contrast, consent is an essential requirement of a contract.

The requirement of consent guides courts in determining whether a party intended to enter into an agreement. As it is difficult (if not impossible) for courts to discern whether a party is telling the truth, external manifestations of consent substitute for admissions of consent. These external manifestations, such as a signature on the dotted line, mean that, according to our society's norms of conduct, it is reasonable to assume the party consented to the agreement.

But these external markers of consent can take on a life of their own in contract law, so that "manifestation of consent" becomes a construct, divorced from the reality of whether there was in fact consent. Jean Braucher describes consent as a "conclusion based on a complex set of normative judgments" and not "a simple description of fact."[29] She writes:

> In the event of a dispute between contracting parties, some external power must first decide whether the parties have consented in a valid manner and, if so, determine the scope of the consent. Legal decisionmakers, serving collective societal norms, construct consent. This process is unavoidably a means of regulation, one which fosters one view or another of beneficial contractual relations.[30]

Whereas the manifestation of consent was intended to provide evidence of actual subjective consent, now it has replaced it, rendering unnecessary an actual inquiry regarding consent. The construct of consent—its manifestation—suffices in wrap contract cases even in situations where it is unreasonable to assume that it indicates actual consent.

This substitution of manifestation for meaning and of construct for reality is evident with wrap agreements and glaringly so in the case of browsewraps. Clicking "I agree" has come to mean acceptance to the terms of an agreement, even though most people don't consider this act the equivalent of entering into a legally binding commitment. Instead, most users view this act as simply another step in the processing of a transaction. Even more surprising, in the context of browsewraps, notice (such as a hyperlink at the bottom of a website home page) and the continued use of a website has been interpreted by some courts as consent, even though most website visitors are not aware of the terms.

---

[29] Jean Braucher, *Contract versus Contractarianism: The Regulatory Role of Contract Law,* 47 WASH. & LEE L. REV. 697, 699 (1990).

[30] *Id.* at 699-700.

One of the essential functions of contract law is to fulfill the reasonable expectations of the parties. Where a party is ignorant of the terms, it is a fiction to claim that she reasonably expected to be held to them. A notice is not the same thing as a contract. The objective of contract law is the fulfillment of the intent of the parties. Without intent, there is no contract.

A contract requires a promise, and a promise requires intent. The Restatement (Second) of Contracts defines a contract as "a promise or a set of promises for the breach of which the law gives a remedy, or the performance of which the law in some way recognizes as a duty."[31] It defines a promise as a "manifestation of intention to act or refrain from acting in a specified way, so made as to justify a promisee in understanding that a commitment has been made."[32] This modified objective standard means that the silent intent of the parties doesn't matter; what matters is what a reasonable person in the shoes of one party would think of the words or actions of the other party. Unfortunately, that is not what manifestation of consent means under wrap contract doctrine. Most reasonable people would not believe that surfing a website, opening a software package, or even clicking on an icon constitute intent to enter into a contract—unless, of course, they were familiar with the wrap contract cases.

Consent is used in contract law in place of subjective intent because the latter is too hard to discern; judges aren't mind readers. The objective standard simply recognizes that parties may lie and that judges are not omniscient. But that does not mean consent should be a complete fiction or that intent is irrelevant. Consent is supposed to reveal intent; instead, courts have imputed meaning to acts to create consent, divorcing the act from the state of mind that should be attributable to it. The role of courts in contract disputes is, and always should be, to enforce the reasonable expectations of the parties. But courts have constructed consent in an entirely unreasonable fashion by twisting doctrinal rules, conjuring up notice, inferring action from inaction, and blithely ignoring the central role of intent in contracts. They engage in this hocus pocus in order to enforce transactions that they believe provide a net benefit to society.[33] Yet certain parameters should be set around these makeshift rules to

---

[31] RESTATEMENT (SECOND) OF CONTRACTS § 1 (1981).

[32] *Id.*at § 2.

[33] As Richard Craswell states, in some cases, the costs of obtaining a party's "proper" consent depends heavily on "just what is deemed necessary for [such party's] consent to be proper." Richard Craswell, *Property Rules and Liability Rules in Unconscionability and Related Doctrines*, 60 U. CHI. L. REV. 1, 9–10 (1993). Craswell further states that as a result, in some cases, such as fine-print contracts, it may be appropriate to adopt a liability rule to avoid the unnecessary expense of ensuring consent is proper. *Id.* at 10–11; *see also* Richard A. Epstein, *Contract, Not Regulation: UCITA and High-Tech Consumers Meet Their Consumer Protection Critics*, *in* CONSUMER PROTECTION IN THE AGE OF THE "INFORMATION ECONOMY" 205, 208–14 (Jane K. Winn ed., 2006) (observing that different software products require different kinds of solutions which cannot be anticipated by the government and that current licensing practices have "unleashed an unprecedented wave of new firms and products" that have benefited consumers).

avoid undermining the purpose of contract law and to ensure that entitlements are not extracted from unwitting parties through the vehicle of wrap contracts.

C. Contract Functionalism

Wrap contract doctrinal confusion originated with software and shrinkwraps. Software companies generally license software instead of selling it in order to maintain proprietorship rights. The practice of licensing rather than selling software stemmed from an understanding on the part of software producers that, given the ease with which their product could be duplicated, certain unauthorized uses could potentially destroy or substantially diminish the economic value of the underlying property right for the licensor. Many courts, understanding the practical aspects and limitations of selling software and digital information, contorted existing contract doctrine to enforce agreements that in other contexts would be unenforceable. The cases governing nonnegotiated software licenses frame the issue as one of contract formation. But in order to understand the wide range of judicial opinions, it is necessary to move beyond a discussion of contract doctrine and consider the business environment in which these software licenses were created.

As many commentators have argued, these types of agreements (and form agreements in general) provide a societal benefit by facilitating transactions. In other words, they should be enforced not because they manifest the classic signs of bargaining, but because they are good for society and are generally not harmful to the licensee.

In nearly all the cases upholding the terms of a nonnegotiated software license, the licensor was suing because the licensee was using the software or product in a manner expressly prohibited by the licensor, not because the licensor wished to enforce an onerous obligation (such as payment of additional money). The courts, while using the language of contract law, were reacting to what they considered unfair business practices.

The courts used the language of contracts because the contract was the vehicle through which the license was made; however, it was the transfer of (some) rights that affected the analysis of the contract. In ProCD v. Zeidenberg, for example, if the shrinkwrap license were not enforceable as a contract due to lack of assent, then the licensor would have lost control over how the software was used. If Zeidenberg used the data stored in the software to undermine the licensor's business, ProCD would be unable to prevent it. Database information might not be protected under copyright law if it lacked sufficient creativity. Without a legal right to stop the licensee from using the software to the licensor's detriment, there would be no economic incentive for the licensor to develop and distribute the data in the first place.[34]

A contract was often the most practical way to constrain the licensee's undesirable but lawful behavior. For example, if you used my website and accompanying services to solicit my unwitting customers to your competing website, I probably could not stop you unless I had a contractual right to do so. Generally, the early court decisions recognized the technology provider's dilemma and supported businesses by enforcing wrap contracts where there was notice.

Judge Easterbrook's opinion in *ProCD* dismissed the importance of formal rules of offer and acceptance, noting that in certain industries, transactions in which the exchange of money precedes detailed terms is common and requiring consumers to actually sign contractual terms would result in higher prices and greater inconvenience:

> Consider the purchase of insurance. The buyer goes to an agent, who explains the essentials (amount of coverage, number of years) and remits the premium to the home office, which sends back a policy.... Or consider the purchase of an airline ticket. The traveler calls the carrier or an agent, is quoted a price, reserves a seat, pays, and gets a ticket, in that order. The ticket contains elaborate terms, which the traveler can reject by canceling the reservation. To use the ticket is to accept the terms, even terms that in retrospect are disadvantageous.... Just so with a ticket to a concert. The back of the ticket states that the patron promises not to record the concert; to attend is to agree. A theater that detects a violation will confiscate the tape and escort the violator to the exit. One could arrange things so that every concertgoer signs this promise before forking over the money, but that cumbersome way of doing things not only would lengthen queues and raise prices but also would scotch the sale of tickets by phone or electronic data service. Consumer goods work the same way. Someone who wants to buy a radio set visits a store, pays, and walks out with a box. Inside the box is a leaflet containing some terms, the most important of which usually is the warranty, read for the first time in the comfort of home. By Zeidenberg's lights, the warranty in the box is irrelevant; every consumer gets the standard warranty implied by the *U.C.C.* in the event the contract is silent;

---

[34] *See generally* Frank H. Easterbrook, *Contract and Copyright*, 42 HOUS. L. REV. 941 (2005). *See also* Maureen A. O'Rourke, Drawing the Boundary Between Copyright and Contract: Copyright Preemption of Software License Terms, 45 Duke L. J. 479, 496–99 (1995) (discussing why licensors may feel the need to include particular provisions that track the Copyright Act).

> yet so far as we are aware no state disregards warranties furnished with consumer products. Drugs come with a list of ingredients on the outside and an elaborate package insert on the inside. The package insert describes drug interactions, contraindications, and other vital information—but, if Zeidenberg is right, the purchaser need not read the package insert, because it is not part of the contract.[35]

Yet, Easterbrook's analogies ignore certain important differences between the shrinkwrap at issue and the examples he cites. In the insurance policy example, the provisions that require an obligation from the insured, such as premium amounts, are explained over the phone. The obligations of the insured are limited by the duration of the phone call—even a curious and prudent would-be insured would lose patience after a few minutes. The policy that comes afterward should contain only those provisions that do not require the insured's consent because they do not seek to impose an affirmative obligation upon the insured, such as additional payments that were undisclosed over the phone. (Those that do are susceptible to claims of consumer fraud.) The policy likely covers the scope of the protection offered by the insurance company—exclusions, coverage explanations—but nothing that would deprive the insured of a noncontingent entitlement. In other words, the policy limits what the insurance company must pay; it does not (or should not) contain provisions regarding what the insured must pay that deviate from what was communicated in the phone call.

Furthermore, courts have adopted special interpretation rules for insurance contracts. They interpret insurance policies against the insurance company and subject their enforceability to a "reasonable expectations" [36] standard so that if there are any terms that the insurance company believes the insured would not have agreed to, those terms do not belong in the agreement. State statutes also impose certain minimum requirements regarding both the substance of insurance policy provisions as well as the form (i.e., conspicuousness requirements) in which they are presented.

The other examples ignore the role of other law in permitting terms to provide notice. Airlines can set parameters around their services (they don't have to offer biscuits or free meals), but some terms are expressly regulated by the Federal Aviation Administration and the Warsaw Convention. The concert hall can enforce its property right to set the rules for entry on to its premise, but its enforcement measures are limited by property law and tort law. Easterbrook's example of the consumer purchasing a radio is misleading because the Uniform Commercial Code and the

---

[35] *ProCD, Inc.*, 86 F.3d. at 1451.

[36] Restatement (Second) of Contracts § 211.

Magnuson Moss Act specifically permit warranties, warranty disclaimers, and limitations of liability, and each regime specifies what constitutes sufficient notice. Drugs are regulated by the Food and Drug Administration, which mandates certain disclosures—which also means, that it permits the conveyance of the disclosures through terms contained with the drug.

But most significantly, and troubling, the *ProCD* court ignores the importance of form itself. The terms on the back of a ticket typically can't be missed because they are placed on the same form as the terms necessary to utilize the ticket. Furthermore, the volume of the terms is contained by the space available on the back of a ticket. While the shrinkwrap terms also have space constraints and an unavoidable physicality (i.e., a consumer cannot bypass the terms if he wants to access the product), subsequent cases have used the decision in *ProCD* to enforce digital terms that are not similarly restricted by space and tangibility.

For example, in *Pollstar v. Gigmania Ltd.*,[37] the court cited to the *ProCD* court's rationale, concluding that

> [w]hile the court agrees with Gigmania that the user is not immediately confronted with the notice of the license agreement, this does not dispose of Pollstar's breach of contract claim. Taking into consideration the examples provided by the Seventh Circuit—showing that people sometimes enter into a contract by using a service without first seeing the terms—the browser wrap agreement may be arguably valid and enforceable.[38]

The significance of form was lost amidst the focus on the formalities of offer and acceptance.

What Easterbrook should have argued was that as the owner of the software code, ProCD has the right to establish the way in which its property may be offered to the public, subject to limitations of other law (i.e., copyright law). It doesn't matter whether Zeidenberg assented to the terms—he exceeded the permission that the company granted to him. Easterbrook missed the opportunity to explain why the shrinkwrap in *ProCD v. Zeidenberg* should be enforceable given the business environment and the conduct of the parties. Instead of mangling contract doctrine, he could have reached for a quasi-contract approach.[39] As Corbin explains, "[c]ontracts are formed by expressions of assent; quasi contracts quite otherwise. The

---

[37] Pollstar v. Gigmania, Ltd., 170 F. Supp. 2d 974 (E.D. Cal. 2000).

[38] *Id.* at 982.

[39] Corbin describes a quasi-contractual obligation as one "that is created by the law for reasons of justice, without any expression of assent and sometimes even against a clear expression of dissent." ARTHUR L. CORBIN, CORBIN ON CONTRACTS, § 19, p. 27 (one-volume ed., West Publishing Group 1952).

legal relations between contractors are dependent upon the interpretation of their expressions of assent; in quasi contract, the relations of the parties are not dependent on such interpretation."[40]

Instead, Easterbrook stated that the shrinkwrap was enforceable because it was no different from other contracts. The contracts he cited, however, *were* different from other contracts. They were contractual in a very limited sense, but in another way, they were not contracts at all because they did not require the consent of the other party in order to be imposed; they only needed to effectively notify the other party. An insurance company can limit its coverage, a concert hall its liability, and a radio manufacturer its warranty provided each meets the disclosure and visibility requirements required under whatever other law is applicable, such as state consumer laws, tort law or applicable legislation. These terms are presented in a contractual manner in order to avoid future conflict and to set expectations. This may be what Easterbrook was getting at since the ProCD shrinkwrap, too, was intended to establish parameters around ProCD's business and the use of its software.

Courts instinctively understand the different functions of contracts but shy away from acknowledging the difference that function makes, and I suspect this may be because it has been drilled into judges' heads that they should not consider the adequacy of consideration. It is easier to justify a decision by claiming that it is the result of following formalistic rules of contract formation than it is to justify it on substantive grounds. The terms of adhesive contracts are not the product of bargaining and consent to them is dictated by the drafter. The fact of their nonnegotiability, however, should not make them any less enforceable if consent is not necessary to enforce them in the first place. In those instances, consent, rather than being necessary to the imposition of a term, is useful in the attempt to enforce it.

In wrap cases, notice has been interpreted as including an "opportunity to read," even where such opportunity was in practicality fictitious. The decisions reveal that the lack of notice and a lack of an opportunity to read prior to the transaction did not necessarily render an agreement invalid, although it may have suspended performance. For example, in *Register.com v. Verio, Inc.*,[41] the defendant Verio sold a variety of website design, development, and operation services which competed with the plaintiff Register.com's website development business. Verio obtained daily updates of information from Register.com's computers relating to newly registered domain names via an automated software program. Verio's practice of e-mail solicitations to those registered names was inconsistent with the terms of the restrictive legend Register.com attached to its responses to Verio's queries. Some of the recipients of

---

[40] *Id.*

[41] Register.com., Inc. v. Verio, Inc., 356 F.3d 393 (2d Cir. 2004).

Verio's solicitations believed they were coming from Register.com (or an affiliate) and were sent in violation of the registrant's election not to receive solicitations from Register.com.[42] Register.com sent Verio a cease-and-desist letter, but to no avail. Verio claimed that it never became contractually bound to the conditions imposed by Register.com's restrictive legend because, in the case of each query Verio made, the legend did not appear until after Verio had submitted the query and received the WHOIS data.[43] Verio contended that it did not receive legally enforceable notice of the conditions Register.com intended to impose and therefore, should not be deemed to have taken WHOIS data from Register.com's systems subject to Register.com's conditions. The court rejected Verio's argument, stating that

> Verio's argument might well be persuasive if its queries addressed to Register's computers had been sporadic and infrequent. If Verio had submitted only one query, or even if it had submitted only a few sporadic queries, that would give considerable force to its contention that it obtained the WHOIS data without being conscious that Register intended to impose conditions, and without being deemed to have accepted Register's conditions. But Verio was daily submitting numerous queries, each of which resulted in its receiving notice of the terms Register exacted. Furthermore, Verio admits that it knew perfectly well what terms Register demanded. Verio's argument fails.[44]

In other words, even if Verio *was* unaware of Register.com's terms of use at the time it entered into the transaction, it subsequently became aware of the terms. While Verio did not have an opportunity to read the terms prior to each transaction, because it engaged in multiple transactions, it had actual notice of such terms at the time Register.com contacted it. If, however, Register.com had sued Verio for breach of contract after the first transaction (and assuming that it had not sent Verio a cease-and-desist letter), the results would likely have been otherwise. As the court notes:

> The situation might be compared to one in which plaintiff P maintains a roadside fruit stand displaying bins of apples. A visitor, defendant D, takes an apple and bites into it. As D turns to leave, D sees a sign, visible only as one turns to exit, which says "Apples—50 cents apiece." D does not pay for the apple. D believes he has no obligation to pay because he had no notice when he bit into the apple that 50 cents was expected in return. D's view is that he never agreed to pay for the

---

42 *Id.* at 396–97.
43 *Id.* at 401.
44 *Id.*

> apple. Thereafter, each day, several times a day, D revisits the stand, takes an apple, and eats it. D never leaves money. P sues D in contract for the price of the apples taken. D defends on the ground that on no occasion did he see P's price notice until after he had bitten into the apples. D may well prevail as to the first apple taken. D had no reason to understand upon taking it that P was demanding the payment. In our view, however, D cannot continue on a daily basis to take apples for free, knowing full well that P is offering them only in exchange for 50 cents in compensation, merely because the sign demanding payment is so placed that on each occasion D does not see it until he has bitten into the apple.[45]

Verio's claim of "lack of notice" is disingenuous, not because it had such notice at the time the transaction was entered into but because it subsequently had notice and chose not to comply with such terms. Similarly, in *Pro CD*, the defendant was being sued for using the ProCD data in a manner that the defendant knew was contrary to the licensor's business model given the pricing differential of the commercial and noncommercial versions of the product.

The courts in *ProCD* and *Register.com* enforced wrap contracting forms where the nondrafting party deliberately and consciously acted in a way that undermined the drafting party's new business model. In doing so, however, these cases approved contracting forms that could be used in all types of transactions, including those having nothing to do with software or digital content. The Internet is a vital part of many businesses. Not surprisingly then, clickwraps and browsewraps are common features on all kinds of websites. Businesses that sell clothing, housewares, and books use clickwraps and browsewraps to impose terms upon transactions that were made without contracts a decade ago.

Adhesive contracts can provide an essential function by establishing the parameters of a developing business or industry (such as the software industry), thus enabling it to grow. In this capacity, contracts are not plans, promises, or tools for coordination so much as they are manuals and instructions, a set of permissions and prohibitions. License agreements are the quintessential instructive contract because they establish parameters of use. But courts have failed to make distinctions based upon the function of different contracts and the purpose of different provisions. Instead, they have twisted doctrinal rules to accommodate legitimate business needs. In the process, they established undesirable precedent which, as the next chapter explains, may have unintended consequences.

---

[45] *Id.*

10 Contracts in Wonderland

SIGNS OF WRAP contracts are everywhere yet the terms themselves are harder to find than their traditional counterparts. The obscurity of the terms tempts drafters to engage in overzealous drafting. Multiwrapping and hyperlinking turn the "duty to read" into a hunt for terms. All of this makes it even more likely that the consumer will ignore the terms governing her interaction on a website. Even for those users savvy enough to understand that wrap terms can be legally binding, the nuisance of locating the myriad terms, the difficulty of understanding legalese, and the inability to negotiate terms means that these terms often go unread, more so than even paper contracts of adhesion. In addition to the above, the lack of signaling and the ubiquity of terms practically guarantee that the user will "manifest assent" automatically, without realizing that she has entered into a legal relationship. Yet, despite all this, some may remain skeptical that wrap contracts are a problem. What real harm can they cause anyway?

I'm glad you asked.

Scenario 1

It is September, and you are planning a vacation in February to a South Pacific Island. You check several airlines, and the best deal you discover is a round-trip ticket on Pacific Island Express for $550. It's about a thousand dollars cheaper than the other airlines you've checked. You figure the low price has to do with the fact that the airline is not as well known as the others you considered. You congratulate yourself on your web-searching skills and quickly book two tickets for yourself and your significant other. It's an anniversary present, and you are both thrilled about the trip. You spend many hours researching fun activities for the two of you to do. You book a hotel for the time you plan to be on the island. You can feel the sunshine on your bare shoulders.

Unfortunately, four months after you booked the ticket, you get an e-mail from Pacific Island Express. They tell you that the price they posted was a mistake. A round-trip ticket to your island will cost $1800. You check the prices on other airlines, but they have all gone up. You will either have to pay $1800 or forfeit your plans to go to the South Pacific. Your significant other is not pleased.

You contact the airline and threaten to sue. The company representative gently points you to your agreement with Pacific Island Express. Under the terms of service, accessible via a hyperlink at the bottom of the page, and the clickwrap agreement that you can't even remember clicking, it turns out that you "agreed" that Pacific Island Express has the right to cancel without penalty any tickets due to pricing errors.

Scenario 2

You have just broken up with your significant other. (You were having problems that you hoped to resolve during your romantic getaway to the South Pacific. We know what happened to that trip.) You are feeling depressed and lonely. A coworker tells you about this great new dating website, Lonely Hearts. You tell your coworker that you're not sure about online dating. You're kind of shy and not quite ready to put yourself out there so soon after you've broken up with someone who you thought was the love of your life. Your coworker tells you, "Give it a try. If you don't like it, you don't have to continue." You figure, your coworker is right. What can it hurt?

You sign up with Lonely Hearts. You fill out personal information, your dating preferences, your favorites things ("piña coladas and walks in the rain"). You fudge a little on your weight, shaving off twenty pounds, rationalizing it by telling yourself that by the time you actually meet someone through the site, you will have lost the extra weight. You also "round down" your age to the nearest number ending in zero. You upload a picture that your significant other took of you when you went to the beach—it shows off your abs when they were at their best. You click "I agree" and voila! You are officially a member of Lonely Hearts.

As luck would have it, the next day you run into your significant other. You have coffee. You laugh. You have drinks (piña coladas, of course). You tell your former significant other that you have been heartbroken and unable to eat or sleep since your breakup. Your significant other is touched by your sincerity and your loyalty. Drinks turn into dinner, then a walk during which it lightly rains. Suffice it to say, you are back together. One is no longer the loneliest number.

You practically float to work the next morning. It's a great day. Things are finally going your way—until you log on to your computer.

There you are, at the top of the Gloogle home page, decked out in your skimpiest swim suit, muscles flexed, abs in all their glory. The most popular home page in the universe. Above your head is a banner that reads, "DESPERATE? SO WAS I—UNTIL I JOINED THE LONELY HEARTS CLUB! COME MEET ME—I LOVE PINA COLADS AND LONG WALKS IN THE RAIN! CLICK HERE TO SEND ME AN E-MAIL."

You peer over your cubicle and look around. Is everyone in the office snickering at you or is it your imagination?

You check your e-mail. You have 745 new messages.

A coworker walks by, humming a familiar song. Another coworker slips you a note, "It's 'colad-A.' Next time, don't forget the 'A.'" You frantically call up Lonely Hearts, but nobody answers. You send Gloogle and Lonely Hearts e-mails and beg them to take down your picture. No response. You threaten to sue. You receive this e-mail back from Lonely Hearts:

> "Thank you for your e-mail. As you know, you were required to agree to the terms of service and the terms of our membership agreement when you registered with Lonely Hearts. You specifically agreed in paragraph 8.1 of the Membership Agreement and paragraph 3.4 of our Terms of Service to let us use your personal information for our marketing purposes. You also agreed to paragraph 2.5, which requires any disputes to go through our dispute-resolution process and, if necessary, mandatory arbitration with one of our authorized arbitrators."

You look at both agreements and sure enough, the language clearly states that you give Lonely Hearts a "perpetual, irrevocable license" to use any content you provide them, including personal information and pictures, for any purpose whatsoever "including to third parties for our marketing purposes." There is also a mandatory arbitration clause which you are pretty sure the U.S. Supreme Court would enforce.

You don't think the day can get any worse. Of course, you're wrong. Your significant other texts you, "U Lly Hrt Lsr. I tht u misd me. Dont call evr."

Scenario 3

You are blinded with hurt by your ex's rejection. Seeking revenge, you log on to Don'tDateThatPsycho.com. In your emotionally wrecked state, you decide to "Tell Your Story" via a link on the website. You post a picture of your ex, identifying your ex by name, and add the following words, "This is a psycho. If you ever get a chance to date this person, don't do it! This person is absolutely nuts!" You provide some examples from your time together to prove why you think this person is "psycho."

The website allows you to post this information anonymously. Without thinking twice, you hit "Send." Almost immediately, you regret what you've done. But it's too late, your post is on the home page of Don'tDateThatPsycho.com for all the world to see.

You send an e-mail to Don'tDateThatPsycho.com and beg them to take down your post, claiming that it was a mistake.

Somebody from Don'tDateThatPsycho emails you back and tells you that the website won't take down your post. You beg, plead, and finally threaten. You tell the representative that your post is "your property" and that you "own the copyright" to it and that if the company continues to "distribute my copyrighted material, I will sue you for copyright infringement." The Don'tDateThatPsycho representative responds that the company has the right to keep your post on the website since you gave them a *perpetual, irrevocable* license to do so. "Section 3.7 of our Terms of Service, which you were required to agree to prior to posting, states as follows: 'By posting information or content to any public area of the Service, you automatically grant, and you represent and warrant that you have the right to grant, to the Company and other Registered Users an irrevocable, perpetual, nonexclusive, fully-paid, worldwide license to use, copy, publicly perform, publicly display, and distribute such information and content and to prepare derivative works of, or incorporate into other works, such information and content for any purpose whatsoever pursuant to our sole discretion, and to grant and authorize sublicenses of the foregoing.'"

Scenario 4

A few days later, you receive a letter from your former significant other's attorney. You are being sued for defamation and invasion of privacy, although your significant other will drop the claims if you remove the post immediately.

You send another frantic e-mail to the good people at Don'tDateThatPsycho.com and inform them of the lawsuit. You inform them that the likelihood of damages increases the longer the material stays on the website. You tell them that they should save themselves the attorney fees and take down the material.

Someone from the company emails you back to inform you that under federal law, the Communications Decency Act, the company is immune from tort liability for content posted by others (i.e., you). The representative adds that they wish you the best of luck with your lawsuit.

Scenario 5

You are so angry with Don'tDateThatPsycho.com that you post an update on your Mugbook page: "Don't Use Don'tDateThatPsycho.com." Mugbook is a very popular social networking website, and you have been using it for years. You have lots of fond digital memories on the site, including digital images and conversations with your grandparents, who are now deceased.

The next time you log on to your Mugbook page, nothing appears. All of your content has been deleted. This time, before e-mailing Mugbook, you check their terms of service. Sure enough, in paragraph 6.3, it states as follows: "If you violate the letter or spirit of this Statement, or otherwise create risk or possible legal exposure for us, we can stop providing all or part of Mugbook to you. We will notify you by e-mail or at the next time you attempt to access your account."

Scenario 6

Just when you thought things couldn't get worse, you get an e-mail from Don'tDateThatPsycho.com stating that your significant other's father is suing the website for copyright infringement. The image of your ex that you uploaded to the site was taken by him and so he owns the copyright. The company writes that it is seeking indemnification from you since you are the one who posted the picture, reminding you that "pursuant to section 15.2, if anyone brings a claim against us related to your actions, content or information on our site, you will indemnify and hold us harmless from and against all damages, losses, and expenses of any kind (including reasonable legal fees and costs) related to such claim."

When you write back that it is the company's own inaction that created this problem, you receive this terse e-mail: "As stated in section 3.2 of our terms of service, you are solely responsible for the content you post. Furthermore, you represent and warrant that you own the rights to any content you post." To make matters worse, the company informs you that, in addition to indemnification, it is suing you for breach of contract.

Scenario 7

You decide that you need to listen to some old familiar music to lift your spirits. You log on to your eTunes account and try to buy one of your favorite songs from a happier time in your life. You find the pricey "Greatest Hits of the Whiney Indies" and click to see whether the title you are looking for is included as an individual download. Unfortunately, your frayed nerves make your fingers twitchy, and you accidentally press the button twice instead of once, thus converting the "View" to a "Buy." You frantically disconnect the Wi-Fi, but that only stops the download since your card has been charged and the item purchased. You try to obtain a refund but, after reading the Terms of Service, discover that "all sales are final." You can't figure out who to contact to fight the charge; anyway, you are too demoralized to try to contact eTunes and certain you'd lose anyway based upon the contract language.

At this point, you vow never to use the Internet or any wireless device ever again. You cancel your e-mail account, your online banking account, your I-netflix and eTunes, and every other online account that you have. You log off, forever.

Scenario 8

You spend the next few weeks indoors, reading novels, handwriting letters, and using your landline telephone to order in pizzas and Chinese food. One afternoon, the doorbell rings. You peek outside. There are uniformed federal enforcement officers standing on your porch. You open the door and politely inquire as to their purpose. They tell you that you are under arrest for violating the Computer Fraud and Abuse Act.

"The what?"

"It's a federal law that makes it a crime—a *federal* crime—to access a computer without authorization. You accessed Lonely Hearts computers without authorization when you violated their membership agreement and used their website. You are only authorized to use their website as long as you comply with their terms of service."

"But I had authorization," you protest. "I signed up. I ended up all over the Gloogle home page. It ruined my life!"

"You violated their terms of service. Under section 12.4, you are obligated to keep your contact information updated. You failed to keep your contact information updated. They tried to send you e-mail and it bounced back. It turns out your account has been closed for at least a week." The agent eyes you skeptically. "It seems you also lied about your weight. You look at least twenty pounds heavier than what you posted on your profile. That's a violation of section 1.3 of their agreement."

"But it's only because I've been eating so much take-out!"

"You can tell that to the judge."

They lead you away in handcuffs.

You might think that these scenarios sound so far-fetched, they could never happen. On the contrary, all of the scenarios are based, to varying degrees, on actual cases or news stories (admittedly, with certain details filled in for dramatic effect). Scenario 1, for example, is based upon two different mistaken pricing incidents involving two major airlines. The first one involved British Airways, which posted fares from the United States to India for $40. The erroneous price was listed for only a few minutes before it was discovered. The second incident involved Korea Air, which posted the wrong prices for flights from various cities to Palau, an island nation in the South Pacific.[1] The erroneous price was posted for several days, but Korea Air failed to notify customers for over two months. It offered ticket holders a full refund on the ticket and travel-related expenses or an opportunity to buy a more expensive ticket at a price equal to the lowest fare on the route or a similar route, and a $200 voucher for a future Korean Air flight. (Note: A Department of Transportation rule passed since then prohibits postpurchase increases.)[2]

Ticket purchasers may have viewed the lengthy (forty-four pages) contract as a potential hurdle to contesting the airline's right to retroactively increase the fare.

---

[1] David Segal, *Your Ticket Is Void (Unless You Pay More)*, N.Y. TIMES, Dec. 11, 2011, *available at* http://travel.nytimes.com/2011/12/11/your-money/korean-air-and-the-canceled-ticket-the-haggler.html (last visited January 14, 2013).

[2] 14 CFR § 399.88 (effective Jan. 26, 2012).

Interestingly, under the terms of its Contract of Carriage, neither airline was expressly permitted to cancel tickets due to mistaken pricing.[3] The proliferation of wrap contracts contributes to a type of learned helplessness on the part of consumers where they not only fail to read the term prior to engaging in the transaction, they also assume the contract strips them of all rights. The existence of the contract itself—in all its lengthy, intimidating, fine print glory—seems to deter consumers from pursuing legal action.

The other scenarios are a blend of actual court cases and news stories with contract language borrowed from real websites. The indemnification clause from Scenario 6, for example, was copied from Facebook's terms of use.[4] These scenarios illustrate the unintended consequences of other laws with contract law. One of those laws is constitutional law, specifically the Fourth Amendment. The primary bulwark against unreasonable searches and seizures is a "reasonable expectation of privacy." But what if a suspect consents to such a search by clicking "I agree" on a mobile device or by signing a car rental agreement which incorporates the terms of an online agreement which expressly permits it? The possibility is chilling—and not fantastical. Global positioning systems (GPS) are used in a variety of devices, including phones and cars. Cookies and other online tracking software can follow one's online movements. One court stated that "the terms of service agreement or subscriber agreement between plaintiffs and the internet service provider are relevant to characterizing objective privacy interests."[5] While the court in that case was considering whether such an agreement created a reasonable expectation of privacy, it could also show that such an expectation is *unreasonable*. A judge recently relied upon Twitter's privacy policy in a case involving Wikileaks.[6] In that case, Judge Liam O'Grady upheld an order allowing federal prosecutors to gain access to information on Twitter accounts held by Wikileaks and by three Wikileaks associates. The judge held that the individuals had no reasonable expectation of privacy in the Twitter account information, in part, because they were notified via Twitter's privacy policy that the company may retain IP address information.[7] The standard in determining

---

3 *See, e.g.*, The Points Guy, *Korean Air Bungles Palau Fare Mixup, available at* http://thepointsguy.com/2011/11/korean-air-bungles-palau-fare-mixup/ (last visitedJanuary 14, 2013) (stating that Korean Air may have the right to unilaterally cancel valid tickets under their Contract of Carriage).

4 Facebook, Statement of Rights and Responsibilities, Http://www.facebook.com/legal/terms (last visited January 14, 2013).

5 Lukowski v. The County of Seneca, 08-CV-6098, 2009 WL 467075 (W.D.N.Y.Feb. 24, 2009) modified on reconsideration, 08-CV-6098, 2010 WL 1038607 (W.D.N.Y. Mar. 19, 2010).

6 *In re* Application of the United States of America for an Order Pursuant to 18 U.S.C. § 2703(d). 830 F. Supp. 2d 114 (E.D. Va. 2011).

7 *Id.* at 136. *See also* Wired.com, "Judge Rules Feds Can Have WikiLeaks Associates' Twitter Data," Nov. 10, 2011, http://www.wired.com/threatlevel/2011/11/wikileaks-twitter-ruling/.

"reasonable expectation of privacy" under the Fourth Amendment typically requires consideration of whether any subjective expectation of privacy was objectively reasonable in light of all the circumstances which, in this case, included the privacy policy. While the judge specifically did not rule on whether the privacy policy was binding as a contract, it was relevant as "notice."[8] With online contracting practices affecting offline ones in a feedback loop, a normative standard such as "reasonable expectations of privacy" may shift to reflect changing business practices, such as intrusive tracking by companies, online *and* offline.

The reasonable expectation of privacy standard also arises in state claims based upon privacy invasions. A court recently dismissed a plaintiff's intrusion upon seclusion claim because it found that "there is no reasonable expectation of privacy when a plaintiff has been notified that his Internet activity may be forwarded to a third party to target him with advertisements."[9] In that case, the plaintiff had been informed of the defendants' data-sharing practices in an online privacy policy. The court found that the defendants, who were Internet service providers, had provided notice of the policy when it sent an e-mail to its subscribers which contained a hyperlink to the privacy policy.[10]

The rest of this chapter explains how wrap contract doctrine may affect the application of laws in other areas in unexpected—and disturbing—ways.

A. Contract Law and the Right of Publicity

The right of publicity is a common law or state statutory right that enables an individual to control the commercial use of his or her identity. The right is treated as an intangible property right which can be assigned or licensed. A license is typically granted via a contract. Furthermore, consent is a defense to claims that a right of publicity has been violated. If a wrap contract is a *real* contract, it can be used to license rights of publicity and to establish consent. Given the reality of consumer behavior (i.e., nobody reads wrap contracts) and the fiction of constructive assent, a person can license or consent to the commercial use of his or her image without even knowing it.

Not long ago, I received an electronic greeting card that contained images of dancing elves with the giant faces of my sister and her family attached. I laughed myself silly and thought I might want to make a card of myself. I clicked on the link

---

8 *Id.*

9 Deering v. CenturyTel, Inc., CV-10-63-BLG-RFC, 2011 WL 1842859 (D. Mont. May 16, 2011).

10 *Id.* at 3.

that said, "Elf yourself," which brought me to the Office Max "Elf Yourself" website. After reading the promotional materials, and just prior to uploading the images, a clickwrap agreement appeared that contained the following:

> 2.5 *Grant of License to Registrant Content.* By posting Registrant Content to the Website or by otherwise submitting Registrant Content to us, Registrants automatically grant, and represent and warrant that they have the right to grant to Office Max, a non-exclusive, perpetual, irrevocable, sublicensable (through multiple tiers), assignable, fully paid, royalty-free, worldwide license to use, copy, modify, publish, make, sell, create derivative works of or incorporate into other works such Registrant Content, derive revenue or other remuneration from, communicate to the public, distribute (through multiple tiers), perform or display such Registrant Content (in whole or in part) and/or to incorporate such Registrant Content in other works in any form, media, or technology now known or later developed… for any purpose, including for purposes of advertising and publicity on the Website and elsewhere. Office Max shall not be limited in any way in its use, commercial or otherwise, of any such Registrant Content…. Further, we have the explicit right to incorporate any Registrant Content posted to the Website… into any further work, in any medium, without prior consent or review, and without payment of any royalty or fee whatsoever.

In other words, by simply taking advantage of their dancing elf offer, the consumer offers the digital images of himself and his family for Office Max to use in advertising and in any other way it wants—forever.

Okay, you might argue, a company *might* have the right to do that, but they won't. And you may believe they won't because so far, they haven't. But then I have to gently remind you about two companies that you probably use every day—and who use you, too.

Facebook uses you in "sponsored stories," which means that they use you in ads to promote a product or service. They get paid although you don't. For example, if you write on your wall, "Am having a liquid lunch at The Sloppy Donkey," Facebook can pluck that message right off your wall and post it again on the top right hand column of your friends' home pages with other sponsored ads. Although you may not know it, you gave Facebook the right to spam your friend with your words and your image when you (unknowingly) agreed to their online contract.

If it were up to Facebook, you wouldn't have a choice in the matter. As the company made very clear in a hard-to-find statement: "You can't opt out of being featured in Sponsored Stories."[11] The only choice Facebook would give you is to stop using Facebook, which might not be so easy to do after you have invested so much time and energy in the site.

Fortunately for you, Facebook implemented the program without clearly drafting the license that would give it a right to use you in it. In California, class action plaintiffs sued, claiming (among other things) that Sponsored Stories violated their right to publicity.[12] Facebook defended itself by claiming that the plaintiffs had consented when they signed up under its terms.[13] The plaintiffs argued that they did not consent because Sponsored Stories was not a feature at the time they registered. The court found that the issue of consent was a factual matter and allowed the suit to continue. The parties settled instead. Under the $20 million dollar proposed settlement, plaintiffs can claim a $10 payment and Facebook will provide a way for users to opt out.[14] But given the realities of user behavior and the complexities of Facebook's privacy settings, few users will actually benefit from an opt-out mechanism. Furthermore, by more clearly drafting its terms of use to specifically allow programs like Sponsored Stories, Facebook may be able to avoid similar lawsuits in the future.

Given the market capitalization of Facebook, the Sponsored Stories proposed settlement is mild and Facebook persists in its efforts to exploit user information. Instagram, a company acquired by Facebook in September 2012, alarmed its users several months after the acquisition when it announced the following change to its terms of service:

> Some or all of the Service may be supported by advertising revenue. To help us deliver interesting paid or sponsored content or promotions, you agree that a business or other entity may pay us to display your username, likeness, photos (along with any associated metadata), and/or actions you take, in connection with paid or sponsored content or promotions, without any compensation to you.[15]

---

11 Facebook, Interacting with Ads, Sponsored Stories, *available at* http://www.facebook.com/help/?page=154500071282557(last visited Dec. 1, 2012).

12 Fraley v. Facebook, 830 F. Supp. 2d 785 (N.D. Cal. 2011).

13 *Id.* at 23.

14 Jessica Guynn, *Facebook's "Sponsored Stories" Settlement Gets Judges Tentative OK*, L.A. TIMES, Dec. 4, 2012, *available at* http://www.latimes.com/business/technology/la-fi-tn-facebook-sponsored-stories-settlement-gets-judges-tentative-ok-20121204,0,4550961.story.

15 Roberto Baldwin, *Instagram Backtracks to 2010 Terms of Service for Advertisers*, WIRED.COM, Dec. 21, 2012, *available at* http://www.wired.com/gadgetlab/2012/12/instagram-backtracks-to-2010-tos/.

Instagram users, afraid that their personal photos could be used in advertisements, defected in droves. The company reverted to its original terms, prompting some users to return. Others, however, have moved on, concerned that the company could again change course.[16]

At least defection was still an option for these users. Instagram is a young company, and competition continues to thrive in its market segment. It's a different story for Facebook, which is really the only game in town when it comes to socially connecting online.

It's not just Facebook. Another Internet behemoth, Google, recently announced changes to its privacy policy that angered many of its users. These changes would permit information to be accessed across a user's different Google accounts. This would mean, for example, that postings from a user's Google Plus social network might appear in that user's Google search results so that when your friends search for "bathing suit" they might receive in their search results images of you in your new bikini on last year's vacation in Mexico.

One could say that you had only yourself to blame. If you don't like being used as a "sponsored story" or you don't like the idea of helping Google personalize its search results with content that you (or your friends) have posted across its network, you shouldn't have "agreed" to their contracts. Google's terms of service state the following in the third line, "By using our Services, you are agreeing to these terms. Please read them carefully."[17]

A few paragraphs later, Google's terms of service state, "Google's Privacy Policies explain how we treat your personal data and protect your privacy when you use our Services. By using our Services, you agree that Google can use such data in accordance with our privacy policies."[18]

The Privacy Policies state:

> We use the information that we collect from all of our services to provide, maintain, protect and improve them, to develop new ones and to protect Google and our users. We also use this information to offer you tailored content—such as giving you more relevant search results and ads.... We may combine personal information from one service with information, including personal

---

[16] David Streitfeld & Nicole Perlroth, *Instagram Reversal Doesn't Appease Everyone*, N.Y.Times, B-1, December 22, 2012, *available at* http://www.nytimes.com/2012/12/22/technology/instagram-reversal-doesnt-appease-everyone.html?_r=0.

[17] Google Policies and Principles, Terms of Service, http://www.google.com/intl/en/policies/terms/ (last visited March 9, 2013).

[18] *Id.*

> information, from other Google services—for example, to make it easier to share things with people you know.[19]

Facebook's terms require a little more clicking, so let's start at the beginning. When you signed up with Facebook, you filled in your personal information (your first and last name, your e-mail, your password, your gender, and your birthday). Then you clicked on a big green icon with the words: "SIGN UP." Easy, right? You probably didn't even pay attention to the following words that were in small, but clearly legible, font:

> By clicking Sign Up, you agree to our Terms and that you have read and understand our Data Use Policy.

Unless you worked for a privacy watchdog group, were writing a book on wrap contracts, or were extremely bored, unemployed, or possibly deranged, you likely did not click on either the "Terms" or the "Data Use Policy" hyperlinks. If you had clicked on the "Terms" link, you would have been subjected to a seven- page document in 8.5 font typeface. This document would contain only some of the terms that govern your use of Facebook's website because there are other documents and terms hyperlinked within this document. Nevertheless, as the first paragraph states, "[b]y using or accessing Facebook, you agree to this Statement, as updated from time to time in accordance with Section 14 below."[20]

If you had clicked on the "Data Use Policy" hyperlink, you would have landed on a page with nine more hyperlinks, each one addressing a specific topic. There is a hyperlink to the entire data use policy. If you had clicked on it, you would have been subjected to approximately thirteen pages of 8.5 font which also contain several hyperlinks. Unless you were specifically looking for it, you would probably have missed this provision:

> Your trust is important to us, which is why we don't share information we receive about you with others unless we have:
>
> - received your permission;
> - **given you notice, such as by telling you about it in this policy** (emphasis added); or

---

[19] Google Policies & Principles, Privacy Policy, http://www.google.com/intl/en/policies/privacy/ (last visited March 9, 2013).

[20] Facebook Statement of Rights and Responsibilities Http://www.facebook.com/legal/terms (last visited March 9, 2013).

- removed your name or any other personally identifying information from it.[21]

Researchers have conducted studies to reach a conclusion that Internet users and companies already know: we don't read wrap agreement terms.[22] In fact, most people don't even *see* them. One study, conducted by Yannis Bakos, Florencia Marotta-Wurgler, and David Trosser estimated that only between 0.05 percent and 0.22 percent of users access online end-user license agreements.[23] The authors state that even these few users do not spend enough time on the page with the agreement to have digested more than "a fraction" of its content.[24] In another study, conducted by Nathaniel S. Good, Jens Grossklags, Deirdre K. Mulligan, and Joseph A. Konstan,[25] only 1.4 percent of 222 test subjects reported reading end-user license agreements (EULAs) often, although a greater percentage (24.8 percent) report reading parts of the agreement or browsing its contents. An additional 66.2 percent reported that they rarely read or browse EULAs, and 7.7 percent reported that they had not ever noticed or had never read them.[26] This finding is significant given that the researchers also found that users reported less regret about having engaged in the activity governed by the agreement (the installation of software) if they had spent more time reading it.

While the format of wrap contracts may vary, one common feature in wrap contract cases is the plaintiffs' failure to recall the terms at all. In *Vernon v. Qwest Communications International, Inc.*,[27] for example, none of the class action plaintiffs could recall seeing an agreement:

> During her deposition, (Plaintiff) Vernon could not recall receiving a Welcome Letter and insisted that she never received a written contract for her internet service.... Defendants maintain that Qwest's records show that the Vernons affirmatively accepted the Subscriber Agreement by clicking "accept" while

---

[21] Facebook, Data Use Policy, http://www.facebook.com/full_data_use_policy (last visited March 9, 2013).

[22] For a summary of the empirical studies in this area, see Amy J. Schmitz, *Pizza-Box Contracts: True Tales of Consumer Contracting Culture*, 45 Wake Forest L. Rev. 863 (2010).

[23] Yannis Bakos, Florencia Marotta-Wurgler, & David Trossen, *Does Anyone Read the Fine Print? Testing a Law and Economics Approach to Standard Form Contracts*, at p. 36, *available at* http://papers.ssrn.com/sol3/papers.cfm?abstract_id=1443256.

[24] *Id.*

[25] Nathaniel S. Good, Jens Grossklags, Deirdre K. Mulligan, & Joseph A. Konstan, *Noticing Notice: A Large-Scale Experiment on the Timing of Software License Agreements*, paper presented to the Conference on Human Factors In Computing Systems, Apr. 28 – May 3, 2007, San Jose, CA.

[26] *Id.*

[27] Vernon v. Qwest Communications Int'l, Inc., 857 F. Supp. 2d 1135 (D. Colo. 2012) aff'd sub nom. Vernon v. Qwest Commuications Int'l, Inc., 09-CV-01840-RBJ-CBS, 2013 WL 752155 (D. Colo. Feb. 27, 2013).

> configuring their computer for high-speed Internet service... (Plaintiff) Durkin insists that he did not receive a written contract in 2007 or at any time thereafter.... Asked if he affirmatively accepted the terms and conditions of the Subscriber Agreement, Mr. Durkin testified that he "got the service and if that's the only way that I can get the service, then I must have clicked it."[28]

All the plaintiffs contended that they were never presented with the Subscriber Agreement.[29] Yet, contrary to the facts (and common sense), the court concluded that the plaintiffs had reasonable notice even though neither the Subscriber Agreement nor the arbitration clause was physically presented, because they were "not hidden or difficult to find."[30]

In another case, *Fusha v. Delta Airlines*, plaintiff Fusha booked airline tickets on defendant Airtrade's website.[31] Fusha alleged that due to the actions of the various defendants, including Airtrade, she missed her flight and suffered significant injuries and damages. Airtrade sued to dismiss the complaint for improper venue as the terms and conditions on its website mandated that any suit be brought in Santa Clara County, California. Prior to purchasing her tickets, Fusha had to click to the terms on the website but argued that she had "no recollection of ever reading, much less agreeing to, a forum selection clause."[32] The hyperlink, *Terms of Service*, failed to register in her consciousness.

Yet for many judges, a hyperlink means "notice" and the act of clicking means "manifestation of consent." They have transported rules from cases involving paper contracts into the online environment but failed to consider whether it makes sense to do so. For example, in one recent case involving a browsewrap and plaintiffs under eighteen years of age, the court stated:

> Whether or not Plaintiffs actually read Facebook's TOS (terms of service) is irrelevant, of course, to the matter of the conspicuousness of the TOS and thus Plaintiff's constructive knowledge of the TOS, and Plaintiffs are bound by Facebook's TOS whether Plaintiffs read them or not.[33]

---

[28] *Id.* at 1147

[29] *Id.* at 1148.

[30] *Id.* at 1151.

[31] Fusha v. Delta Airlines, Inc., CIV.A.RDB-10-2571, 2011 WL 3849657, at 1-2 (D. Md., Aug. 30, 2011).

[32] *Id.* at 2.

[33] E.K.D. ex rel. Dawes v. Facebook, Inc., 885 F. Supp. 2d 894 (S.D. Ill. 2012).

The court then blithely quotes another case—one involving two sophisticated parties and a negotiated paper contract—that stated, "a party who agrees to terms… without knowing or investigating those terms does so at his own peril.[34]

Ignoring the factual differences between a case involving a negotiated paper contract in a sophisticated international business transaction and one involving a browsewrap and underaged consumers would earn that judge a failing grade in most law school classes. Facts make the case. To simply borrow phrases from one case and transport them to another without regard for the context for which those words were written is sloppy at best.

In the physical world, visible words trigger a duty to read. But the physical world is different from the digital world in a variety of significant ways. Courts tend to ignore these differences. For example, one court compared online to offline agreements and stated that the hyperlinks "should be treated the same as a multipage written paper contract. The blue hyperlink simply takes a person to another page of the contract, similar to turning the page of a written paper contract."[35] Yet, turning a page is a naturally flowing, progressive act whereas clicking on a hyperlink is a disruptive activity. Clicking on a hyperlink takes a reader from an existing page to another page, which then requires returning to the previous page to continue the interrupted activity.

Another court stated that a person who "checks the box agreeing to the terms and conditions of a purchase on an internet site without scrolling down to read all of the terms and conditions is in the same position as a person who turns to the last page of a paper contract and signs it without reading the terms—namely the clause is still valid."[36] Yet, a person who signs a fifteen-page agreement is more likely to flip through the pages than one who clicks "I agree"; even if she does not read all the terms, the weight of the document alerts her to the nature and gravity of the transaction. One size doesn't fit all in the paper contracts world, yet one click suffices to cover all types of transactions in the digital environment.

B. Wrap Contracts and Federal Laws

Scenario 8, where you are hauled off in handcuffs by federal agents for lying about your weight, illustrates how contract law may affect the interpretation and applicability of other laws with alarming consequences. For example, the federal Computer Fraud and Abuse Act (CFAA) punishes anyone who "knowingly and with intent to

[34] *Id.* (citing Paper Express, Ltd. v. Pfankuch Maschinen GmbH, 972 F.2d 753, 756 (7th Cir. 1992)).

[35] Hubbert v. Dell Corp., 835 N.E. 2d 113, 121 (2005)..

[36] Scherillo v. Dun & Bradstreet, Inc., 684 F. Supp. 2d 313, 322 (E.D.N.Y. 2010).

defraud, accesses a protected computer without authorization, or exceeds authorized access, and by means of such conduct furthers the intended fraud and obtains anything of value."[37] The CFAA was originally directed at computer hacking, but when this broad language is combined with the trend in contract law toward enforcing wrap contracts, the result may be outright alarming. As some commentators have noted, exceeding a website's terms of use by, for example, failing to keep your contact information "accurate and up to date"[38] may mean not only that you have breached a "contract" but that you have committed a federal crime.[39] The contract grants you the authority to access the website, so if you breach the contract, your authority is presumably revoked and your access is "unauthorized."

But would the Department of Justice really bring an indictment based upon a violation of a *wrap agreement*? That seems to depend on the violation. At a congressional hearing on cybersecurity, Richard Downing, deputy chief of the Computer Crime and Intellectual Property Section at the Department of Justice, argued that the CFAA *should* be interpreted to include a violation of the "terms of service or similar contractual agreement with an employer or provider."[40]

In one rather infamous case, Lori Drew, 49, allegedly created a Myspace account pretending to be "Josh," a sixteen-year-old boy. "Josh" engaged in a flirtatious online relationship with a thirteen-year-old girl. Drew reportedly perpetrated the hoax as retaliation against the girl, who had a falling out with Drew's daughter. Shortly after Josh broke off the relationship with the girl—by telling her that the world would be a better place without her—the girl committed suicide. Missouri prosecutors could not find sufficient evidence to bring charges under state criminal statutes so federal prosecutors turned to the CFAA. The indictment claimed that the CFAA was violated when Drew disobeyed Myspace's terms of service to get information from Myspace to further the intentional infliction of emotional distress upon the thirteen-year-old girl. The "terms of service" regulated the conduct of users of Myspace's website. A user could become a Myspace member only by clicking a box that indicated agreement to the terms of service. The terms of service, however, were only visible by

---

[37] 18 U.S.C. § 1030(a)(4) (West 2013).

[38] *See* Facebook, Statement of Rights and Responsibilities http://www.facebook.com.

[39] An August 3, 2011 letter signed by several civil rights organizations expressed concern that the CFAA would criminalize violations of a website's terms of use.*See* Letter from Laura W. Murphy, Director, Washington Legislative Office, American Civil Liberties Union, et al. to Senators Patrick Leahy and Charles Grassley, Aug. 3, 2011, *available at* https://www.cdt.org/files/pdfs/CFAA_Sign-on_ltr.pdf.

[40] Richard W. Downing, "Cybersecurity: Protecting Amercia's New Frontier," presented Nov. 15, 2011, before the U.S. House of Representatives, Committee on Judiciary Subcommittee on Crime, Terrorism, and National Security, *available at* http://judiciary.house.gov/hearings/pdf/Downing%2011152011.pdf. *See also Eyder Peralta, "Is Lying On The Internet Illegal?," The Two-Way: Breaking News from NPR, Nov. 15, 2011, available at* http://www.npr.org/blogs/thetwo-way/2011/11/15/142356399/is-lying-on-the-internet-illegal.

clicking on the link titled "terms of service." In other words, a prospective member must have agreed to the terms of service but Myspace did not require the members to actually read those terms, nor did it facilitate their ability to do so. The jury convicted Drew, although a judge later tossed out the conviction.

While the prosecution of someone like Lori Drew may not be particularly troubling from a moral or emotional standpoint, it does highlight the problem of line drawing. While the basis for most of the scholarly commentary on the case focuses on the broadness of the legislative language itself, the concern comes from the "what if" scenarios raised by standard wrap contract terms, and not any perceived injustice suffered by the universally despised Drew. In other words, what is alarming about the Department of Justice's prosecution of Drew is not the broad language of the CFAA *per se* applied to the Drew situation, but the conjunction of the CFAA language with the even broader language in impossibly wordy and rapacious wrap agreements. For example, one commentator noted that some website terms of service prohibit users from making disparaging remarks about the website owner; "[i]f you write on a blog something disparaging about that company, are you in violation of criminal law?"[41] Another wrote that "[t]he U.S. Department of Justice is defending computer hacking laws that make it a crime to use a fake name on Facebook or lie about your weight in an online dating profile at a site like Match.com."[42] The expansive nature of most wrap agreements makes it easy to fear the worst.

As the Department of Justice noted in a document submitted to the court, the CFAA requires intent to violate the terms of service. Lori Drew claimed that she was not even aware of the terms of service at the time she registered with Myspace. But contract law, through the fiction of constructive assent, imparts upon the defendant knowledge of the terms of service. The website lays out the rules providing authorized access to its services through wrap contracts, but it does so using contracting methods that virtually guarantee that those rules will go unread. Rather than using plain, simple, and minimal language, wrap contracts pile on legalese. Instead of requiring a click to signify every important contractual term, they require only one click—blanket assent—to all the terms, so that the user has no way to distinguish the important obligations from those which are trivial.

Courts have accommodated contracting innovation, which has opened the floodgates to contracting mania on the part of companies. Companies, seeing no cost to piling on terms which appear innocuous when delivered via wrap forms, provide

---

41 Kim Zetter, *Experts Says MySpace Suicide Indictment Sets "Scary" Precedent*, May 15, 2008, *available at* http://www.wired.com/threatlevel/2008/05/myspace-indictm/.

42 Declan McCullagh, *DOJ: Lying on Match.com Needs to Be a Crime*, CNET, Nov. 14, 2011, *available at* http://news.cnet.com/8301-31921_3-57324779-281/doj-lying-on-match.com-needs-to-be-a-crime/.

themselves with maximum protection and leverage, even though they likely have no intention of ever exercising most of these contractual rights against most users. They see no cost to inserting onerous terms in their wrap contracts, so they exercise no restraint. The concern surrounding CFAA and contract law is not that Lori Drew was prosecuted but that the same combination of laws that resulted in her indictment would also result in the indictment of someone who lied about her weight on a dating website.

The Ninth Circuit Court of Appeals expressed precisely these fears in *U.S. v. Nosal*,[43] a case that rejected the argument that the CFAA applies to terms of service violations. The government in that case argued that employees who used their employer's computer system to funnel confidential information to an ex-employee's competing business exceeded their authorized access and, thus, violated the CFAA. The employees entered into agreements that restricted the use of the confidential information and were notified, at the time they logged on to the computer system, that their access was restricted by their employer. The case involved company policies and not website terms of service, yet it raised the same issues. Chief Judge Kozinski, writing the opinion for the Ninth Circuit, acknowledged the troubling implications that might arise through a broad interpretation of the CFAA given the ubiquity of terms of service:

> Our access to those remote computers is governed by a series of private agreements and policies that most people are only dimly aware of and virtually no one reads or understands. For example, it's not widely known that, up until very recently, Google forbade minors from using its services. Adopting the government's interpretation would turn vast numbers of teens and pre-teens into juvenile delinquents—and their parents and teachers into delinquency contributors. Similarly, Facebook makes it a violation of the terms of service to let anyone log into your account. Yet it's very common for people to let close friends and relatives check their email or access their online accounts. Some may be aware that, if discovered, they may suffer a rebuke from the ISP or a loss of access, but few imagine they might be marched off to federal prison for doing so. Or consider the numerous dating websites whose terms of use prohibit inaccurate or misleading information. Or eBay and Craigslist, where it's a violation of the terms of use to post items in an inappropriate category. Under the government's proposed interpretation of the CFAA, posting for sale an item prohibited by Craigslist's policy, or describing yourself as "tall,

---

[43] *United States v. Nosal*, 676 F.3d 854 (9th Cir. 2012).

dark and handsome," when you're actually short and homely, will earn you a handsome orange jumpsuit. Not only are the terms of service vague and generally unknown—unless you look real hard at the small print at the bottom of a webpage—but website owners retain the right to change the terms at any time and without notice. Accordingly, behavior that wasn't criminal yesterday can become criminal today without an act of Congress, and without any notice whatsoever.[44]

The Ninth Circuit decision creates a split among the circuits. While the Ninth Circuit rejected the argument that the CFAA applies broadly, other courts have not,[45] leaving open the possibility that exceeding the authorization granted by terms of service may violate the CFAA and constitute a federal crime.

Other statutes may also be affected by determinations of assent. The Stored Communications Act (SCA), the Electronic Communications Privacy Act (ECPA), the Fair Credit Reporting Act (FCRA), and the Video Privacy Protection Act (VPPA) all require authorization or consent. Wayne Barnes observes that while there is a "well-developed body of statutory provisions in federal law that governs electronic surveillance and unauthorized use of computers... consent is a defense to all" of them.[46]

A trio of recent cases involving a third-party online marketing company illustrate how contractual notions of consent can affect the application of other laws. In *Mortensen v. Bresnan Communication, LLC*,[47] plaintiffs sued an Internet service provider under the ECPA, the CFAA, and for invasion of privacy and trespass to chattels for collecting and diverting their communications to a third-party advertising company called NebuAd., Inc.[48] The EPCA provides an exception from liability where "one of the parties to the communication has given prior consent to such interception."[49] The defendant argued that the plaintiffs had consented to the interception of communication via the defendant's Online Privacy Notice and Online Subscriber Agreement, which informed users of their practices and provided them with the ability to opt out.[50] The court agreed, finding that "through the *Online*

---

[44] *Id.* at 861-62 (9th Cir. 2012).

[45] *See* United States v. Rodriguez, 628 F.3d 1258 (11th Cir. 2010); United States v. John, 597 F.3d 263 (5th Cir. 2010); Int'l Airport Ctrs., LLC v. Citrin, 440 F.3d 418 (7th Cir. 2006).

[46] Wayne R. Barnes, *Rethinking Spyware: Questioning the Propriety of Contractual Consent to Online Surveillance*, 39 UC Davis L. Rev. 1545, 1563 (2006).

[47] Mortensen v. Bresnan Commc'n, L.L.C., CV 10-13-BLG-RFC, 2010 WL 5140454 (D. Mont. Dec. 13, 2010).

[48] *Id.* at 1.

[49] 18 U.S.C. § 2511(2)(d)(West 2013)

[50] Mortensen v. Bresnan Commc'n, L.L.C., *supra* note 47, at 4.

Subscriber Agreement, the *Privacy Notice* and the NebuAd link on Brenan's website, Plaintiffs did know of the interception and through their continued use of Bresnan's Internet Service, they gave or acquiesced their consent to such interception."[51] It also found that because the Subscriber Agreement and the Privacy Notice informed the plaintiffs of their monitoring and diversion, and because the use of the Internet service constituted acceptance of their terms, that the plaintiffs had no reasonable expectation of privacy.[52] (In analyzing the CFAA and the trespass to chattels claims, the court found that the plaintiffs had granted authorization to their computers but allowed those claims to continue because the defendant may have exceeded the scope of that authorization.)[53]

In *Kirch v. Embarq Management Co.*,[54] the court granted a summary judgment motion dismissing a claim based upon the ECPA because the plaintiffs had agreed to the terms of the defendant's online agreement, which referenced the defendant's privacy policy. The defendant Internet service provider collected and diverted customer communications to NebuAd for use in targeted advertising.[55] The court found that "based on the plaintiffs' consent, which is expressly excluded from the category of 'unlawful interceptions,'"[56] the defendant was not liable under the ECPA.

Similarly, in *Deering v. CenturyTel, Inc.*,[57] the plaintiff sued several Internet service providers for, among other claims, invasion of privacy and violation of the ECPA based upon their collection of customer communications and their sharing that information with NebuAd. Defendants disclosed their data sharing and information collection policies in their privacy policy, which was accessible via a hyperlink that was e-mailed to its customers. The court found that "consent is a defense to the EPCA"[58] and granted the defendants' motions to dismiss.

Another area where contract law may mingle with federal laws with unexpected consequences is copyright. Copyright law vests the creator of a work with ownership of the copyright. (The exception to this is where the creator is an employee and the work is created within the scope of employment, in which case the copyright belongs to the employer.)[59] The creator, however, can transfer or license that copyright via a contract. Since courts have deemed wrap contracts to be *real* contracts,

---

[51] *Id.* at 5.

[52] *Id.*

[53] *Id.* at 8.

[54] Kirch v. Embarq Mgmt. Co., 10-2047-JAR, 2011 WL 3651359 (D. Kan. Aug. 19, 2011) aff'd, 702 F.3d 1245 (10th Cir. 2012).

[55] *Id.* at 1.

[56] *Id.* at 7.

[57] Deering v. CenturyTel, Inc., CV-10-63-BLG-RFC, 2011 WL 1842859 (D. Mont. May 16, 2011).

[58] *Id.* at 2.

[59] 17 U.S.C.A. § 101.

constructive assent means that a creator can transfer or license the copyright to a work without actually knowing it.

Don't think this can lead to problems? Alison Chang might disagree. Alison Chang was a sixteen-year-old girl when she received an e-mail from a friend. Her friend informed her that a big picture of Chang was posted on a billboard in Australia promoting Virgin Mobile's text messaging service. At the top of the advertisement, in capital letters, were the words, "DUMP YOUR PEN FRIEND" which indicated that Chang was the friend to dump. In smaller text, across the bottom of her image were the words, "Free Text Virgin-to-Virgin." Alison's youth counselor had taken a photograph of her and posted it to his Flickr account under a Creative Commons (CC) attribution license. Under the terms of that license, anyone (including Virgin Mobile) could use the image provided that they credited the photographer.

As her lawyer stated in the complaint against Virgin Mobile and Creative Commons:

> The photograph immediately incited the interest of news stations, legal commentators, and website bloggers across the world—primarily because Alison is the only minor depicted in the campaign. And in a matter of months, Alison was transformed from a normal high school student to the "dump your pen friend girl" whose name generates over a hundred responsive links on Google. Although Alison, like most teenage girls her age, tried at all costs to avoid humiliating and embarrassing situations, because of Virgin Mobile's opportunistic conduct, she now faces them every day.[60]

The photographer did not realize that the CC attribution license permitted commercial use of the photograph. The complaint, filed by Alison Chang and the photographer, Justin Wong, alleged that Creative Commons was negligent in failing to educate the photographer on the meaning of a "commercial use" license, claiming that if it had, he would "not have released or licensed the picture, eliminating any need for this lawsuit."[61]

As the Virgin Mobile case illustrates, the problems spawned by wrap contracts are much more complicated than the issue of "assent." (The court wisely skirted the complicated contract/copyright/privacy law issues by dismissing the case on the grounds of lack of personal jurisdiction.)[62] Nondrafting parties should not assume

---

[60] *See* Chang v. Virgin Mobile USA, LLC, Virgin Mobile Pty, Ltd., and Creative Commons Corp., Plaintiff's First Amended Petition, 2007 WL 4839797 (N.D. Tex.) (Trial Pleading).

[61] *Id.*

[62] Chang v. Virgin Mobile USA, LLC,, 2009 WL 111570, (N.D. Tex. Jan. 16, 2009).

that wrap terms are innocuous and drafters should not rely upon them to impart important information.

C. Terms of Disservice

To many Facebook users, Scenario 5 seems like an unlikely worst case scenario. They depend upon the service, which is why they stay even when they dislike the treatment they receive from the company. They have too much invested in the site to leave it. They believe that Facebook wants them, too—all one billion of them.

I hate to break this to you, but Facebook doesn't need the entire billion. And when the company's done with a user, it's really done. Facebook has both the power to deactivate user accounts and a history of doing so. It may not exercise that power against many users, but to those who are affected, that power can seem arbitrary and unfair. In one case, *Young v. Facebook*,[63] a user was so incensed by the deactivation of her account that she drove all the way from her home in Maryland to Facebook's headquarters in California—twice.

Mary Beth Young created a Facebook account to engage with others on cancer-related issues and to develop "genuine and heartfelt" relationships with those she met online.[64] She came across another Facebook page implicitly praying for the death of President Obama.[65] She objected to this page and claimed that she was subjected to threats and personal attacks, including the hacking of her profile picture.[66] She joined a petition requesting that Facebook remove the "Prayer for Death" page.[67] She alleged that her account was deactivated in an attempt to prevent her from accessing the petition. According to an e-mail from Facebook, however, her account was disabled for harassing or threatening other Facebook users, including sending friend requests to people she didn't know and soliciting others for dating or business purposes.[68] Young claimed that she made "numerous email and telephone inquiries" regarding her deactivation but was denied "human interaction."[69] Finally, Young drove from her home in Maryland to Facebook's headquarters in order to talk to a human being from the company.[70]

---

[63] Young v. Facebook, Inc., 5:10-CV-03579-JF/PVT, 2010 WL 4269304 (N.D. Cal. Oct. 25, 2010).

[64] *Id.* at 1.

[65] *Id.*

[66] *Id.*

[67] *Id.*

[68] *Id.*

[69] *Id.*

[70] *Id.*

If Young thought driving to California would impress anyone, she was mistaken. When she got to Facebook headquarters, the only human being who would see her was the receptionist, who told her that she could fill out a form, but nobody would meet with her in person or speak to her by telephone.[71] According to Young, the receptionist told her that driving to Facebook's headquarters from Maryland was not "a big deal" as others had done the same thing, some from as far away as Canada.[72] Talk about lousy customer service.

Shortly thereafter, Young's account was reactivated with a warning that actions that violated Facebook's Statement of Rights and Responsibilities would result in her account being disabled permanently.[73] Young e-mailed a request for clarification and a personal meeting but received no response.[74] She returned to Maryland only to have her account again deactivated a couple of days later.[75] She received an e-mail informing her that her account had been permanently disabled for violating the Statement of Rights and Responsibilities and that it would not be reactivated for any reason. Facebook refused to provide her with information about the reason for the termination and would not give her an opportunity to appeal. This prompted Young to drive to California a second time where she filed a lawsuit. (Young apparently realized that California has exclusive jurisdiction pursuant to Facebook's terms of use.)[76] Her complaint alleged breach of contract, breach of the implied covenant of good faith and fair dealing, negligence, and fraud.

In its response to Young's complaint, Facebook argued that her breach of contract claim was barred as "the parties agreed to terms expressly disavowing the liability upon which Plaintiff now seeks to sue."[77] The company pointed to its Statement of Rights and Responsibilities, which stated in bold letters:

> WE TRY TO KEEP FACEBOOK UP, BUG-FREE, AND SAFE, BUT YOU USE IT AT YOUR OWN RISK. WE ARE PROVIDING FACEBOOK "AS IS" WITHOUT ANY EXPRESS OR IMPLIED WARRANTIES INCLUDING BUT NOT LIMITED TO, IMPLIED WARRANTIES OF MERCHANTABILITY, FITNESS FOR A PARTICULAR PURPOSE,

---

[71] *Id.*

[72] Plaintiff's Motion in Opposition to Defendant Facebook, Inc's. Notice of Motion and Motion to Dismiss Pursuant to Fed. R. Civ. P. 12 (b)(6) (Sept. 9, 2010), Case No. C10-03579-JF, 2010 WL 4786091, at 12.

[73] *Young v. Facebook, Inc., supra* note 63, at 2.

[74] *Id.*

[75] *Id.*

[76] *See Facebook, Statement of Rights and Responsibilities* http://www.facebook.com/legal/terms. (last visited March 9, 2013)

[77] Defendant Facebook, Inc.'s Notice of Motion and Motion to Dismiss Plaintiff's First Amended Complaint Pursuant to Fed. R. Civ. P. 12(b)(6) (Jan. 13, 2011), Case No. C10-03579-JF, 2011 WL 1041187.

> AND NON-INFRINGEMENT. WE DO NOT GUARANTEE THAT FACEBOOK WILL BE SAFE OR SECURE. FACEBOOK IS NOT RESPONSIBLE FOR THE ACTIONS, CONTENT, INFORMATION OR DATA OF THIRD PARTIES, AND YOU RELEASE US.... FROM ANY CLAIMS AND DAMGES, KNOWN AND UNKNOWN, ARISING OUT OF OR IN ANY WAY CONNECTED WITH ANY CLAIM YOU HAVE AGAINST ANY SUCH THIRD PARTIES.[78]

In response to Young's claims that Facebook "failed to provide adequate site management," failed to provide a "secure environment," and showed a "lack of concern for public safety and health," the company merely replied that they "never agreed that Facebook would do any of these things."[79] Essentially, Facebook argued that the covenant of good faith and fair dealing did not require it to actually act in good faith and fairly deal with Young because the browsewrap did not require it and, in fact, expressly disclaimed it.[80]

For the most part, the judge agreed with Facebook, citing the disclaimers to support its finding that Facebook had no affirmative obligation to enforce its own Statement of Rights and Responsibilities.[81] The court noted, however, that "Facebook has an implied duty not to frustrate the other party's right to receive the benefits of the agreement actually made." The court noted that the Statement of Rights and Responsibilities is an "operative contract" and that it is "at least conceivable that arbitrary or bad faith termination of user accounts, or even termination of user accounts with no explanation at all, could implicate the implied covenant of good faith and fair dealing."[82] The court leaves open the possibility that an amendment to the contract could close even this possible opening for future plaintiffs by noting that while Facebook expressly reserves the right to terminate the accounts of users who violate the Statement or create risks for Facebook, "it does not expressly reserve the right to terminate an account for any reason."[83] It may be that amending the online contract to expressly reserve the right to terminate for any reason would permit Facebook to terminate accounts arbitrarily without violating the implied covenant of good faith and fair dealing.

The court concluded that "Young's current complaint does not allege that the termination of her account was undertaken in bad faith or violated Facebook's

---

[78] *Id.*

[79] *Id.*

[80] *Id.*

[81] Young v. Facebook, Inc., *supra* note 63, at 4–5.

[82] *Id.*

[83] *Id.*

contractual obligations."[84] It is not surprising that Young failed to adequately and convincingly present her case—she represented herself, *in pro se*. Facebook, on the other hand, was represented by Orrick, Herrington & Sutcliffe, a large, elite international law firm.[85] The sad fact, as illustrated by *Young v. Facebook, Inc.* is that as a practical matter, most plaintiffs seeking to overcome the enforceability of wrap contracts will simply be outgunned by attorneys for the company unless they are members of a class action lawsuit. Unfortunately, as previously noted, class action is often barred, due to the existence of a class action waiver and/or a mandatory arbitration clause and the preclusion of class arbitration. The company has the resources to spend on costly lawyers and the plaintiffs may not even know the law.

Young was a determined exception to the typical victim of an unsavory wrap term in that she actually went through the trouble of filing a complaint. Often, the matter never even reaches the court as disgruntled consumers often just throw up their hands rather than fight. A contract is often used by a company as a deterrent to litigation. A consumer, unhappy with the functioning of a product, might scan the online contract only to believe that she is subject to the warranty disclaimers. (Mary Beth Young herself might not have sued if someone had bothered to explain to her what provision of the Statement of Rights and Responsibilities she had violated.) The costs of litigation are too high for most individual consumers and the expected benefits too low. Consequently, the company's overreaching terms then may prevail, not because they are reasonable or fair but because it is more rational, using a cost-benefit analysis, for the consumer to suffer the transactional loss than incur the cost of fighting the contract term.

The result is that a Facebook user may lose all the content that she has painstakingly curated and posted to her account, including posts by her family and friends, with only a vague canned statement from the company as to why her account has been permanently deactivated. No further explanation may be required or warranted if the wrap contract doesn't require it.

Not a Facebook user? The same thing could happen to you if you use e-mail or text messaging since wrap contract terms tend to be similar across industries. For example, Yahoo's e-mail terms state:

> You agree that Yahoo! may, *without prior notice*, immediately terminate, limit your access to or suspend your Yahoo! account, any associated email address, and access to the Yahoo! Services. Cause for such termination, limitation of access or suspension shall include, but not be limited to, (a) breaches or

---

[84] *Id.* at 5.

[85] *Id.*

> violations of the TOS or other incorporated agreements or guidelines, (b) requests by law enforcement or other government agencies, (c) discontinuance or material modification to the Yahoo! Services (or any part thereof), (d) unexpected technical or security issues or problems, (e) extended periods of inactivity, (f) engagement by you in fraudulent or illegal activities, and/or (g) nonpayment of any fees owed by you in connection with the Yahoo! Services. Further, you agree that all terminations, limitations of access and suspensions for cause shall be made in Yahoo!'s sole discretion and that Yahoo! shall not be liable to you or any third party for any termination of your account, any associated email address, or access to the Yahoo! Services.[86]

Google's Gmail states more simply:

> Google may also stop providing Services to you, or add or create new limits to our Services at any time.[87]

These companies provide essential communication services and wield nearly absolute power through the mechanism of wrap contracts containing unilateral modification clauses, disclaimers, limitations of liability, and broad power to terminate services. The users of these sites, accustomed to using the site frequently, could lose years of accumulated messages containing valuable information. Many important transactions, such as financing of homes, are now done via e-mail. Correspondence with loved ones may be erased. Users of these services may be left with nothing but memories of the old-fashioned kind as the digital ones have all been erased—with their constructive assent.

---

[86] Yahoo! Terms of Service, *available at* http://info.yahoo.com/legal/us/yahoo/utos/en-us/ (last visited Jan. 15, 2013).

[87] Google Terms of Service, *available at* http://www.google.com/intl/en/policies/terms/ (last visited Jan. 15, 2013).

11 Reshaping Wrap Contract Doctrine

THE OPPRESSIVENESS OF wrap contracts has become a joke—literally. One South Park episode took the implications of the iTunes contract terms to a hilariously gruesome extreme, ending with one character being tortured in obscene ways because he had clicked assent to the agreement without reading it. Despite the lack of seriousness associated with the contracting of everything, wrap contracts are not harmless. They have the power to change business norms and practices and to deprive users of important rights and entitlements. These changes are often surreptitious and incremental, but, like termites, they have the potential to wreak substantial havoc.

Businesses should have the ability to establish certain limits on their obligations to their customers and to enter into agreements with them. The exploitation of wrap contracts shouldn't mean that *no* wrap contract should be enforceable. There are many good reasons for companies to employ standard form contracts, chief among them is that they reduce transaction costs.

In the case of wrap contracts, however, the balance has tipped too far in favor of convenience to the drafting party without regard to the burden on the nondrafting party. It is unduly burdensome to expect a website visitor to ferret out the various terms associated with a multi-hyperlinked terms of service, for example, even if he or she has notice that the terms exist. The contracting landscape has changed dramatically in the last twenty years, and a failure to recognize these changes risks undermining the legitimacy of contracts.

Although wrap contracts are similar to other contracts of adhesion, they differ in ways that warrant special consideration. Courts should move away from a one-size-fits-all approach that requires them to twist and shove doctrinal rules into ill-suited contractual forms. The result in too many wrap contract cases has been a verdict that may be appropriate for the occasion, but which leaves stretched and misshapen precedent.

Scholars have recognized that changing times and evolving forms necessitate legal adaptations. As Friedrich Kessler wrote, "freedom of contract must mean different things for different types of contracts. Its meaning must change with the social importance of the type of contract and with the degree of monopoly enjoyed by the author of the standardized contract."[1] Juliet Moringiello observes, "[t]raditional contract rules, based on the model of two individuals meeting face-to-face to negotiate written terms, have been modified over the years to accommodate diverse methods of communicating those terms. In developing these modifications, courts recognized the traditional cautionary function served by the signed paper contract and fashioned new rules to account for the different signals sent to offerees by novel methods of contracting."[2] But, as discussed in chapter 8, courts have stubbornly refused to recognize the different signals sent by wrap contracts.

Currently, blanket assent forces the burdens of innovative contracting to fall solely upon the consumer while the business garners all the advantages. Companies aim to minimize the obtrusiveness of online agreements. Unobtrusive contracts, however, primarily advantage companies by allowing more onerous terms without also enhancing consumer awareness. Contract doctrine places the onus of manifesting assent on the wrong party in a digital contracting environment because the non-drafting party lacks control over how the contract is presented. In the context of intellectual property, Jacqueline Lipton writes that "traditional Property theories remind us that along with Property rights come important responsibilities. The responsibilities will vary with the nature of the rights in question and with the nature of the competing interest in those rights. Nevertheless, any kind of Property rights,

---

[1] Friedrich Kessler, Contracts of Adhesion—Some thoughts About Freedom of Contract, 43 Colum. L. Rev. 629, 642 (1943).

[2] Juliet M. Moringiello, Signals, Assent and Internet Contracting, 57 Rutgers L. Rev. 1307, 1309 (2005).

including information property rights, should be tempered by necessary legal duties imposed on the right holder as an incident of property ownership."[3] Contract law, too, should recognize the responsibility that drafting parties have by virtue of their ability to control the contract form and contracting environment.

Contract law is flexible enough to accommodate changes, yet wrap contract case law has failed to recognize the unique issues raised by contracting form. This chapter proposes several doctrinal adjustments to existing contract law that recognize the difference contractual form makes. These adjustments are the following: recognizing a duty to draft reasonably; replacing blanket assent with specific assent; considering contract function when applying existing doctrinal rules, and reinvigorating unconscionability.

A. Imposing a Duty to Draft Reasonably

The problem of wrap contracts is essentially one of framing. In evaluating whether a contract is enforceable, courts impose upon the nondrafting party a duty to read without also imposing upon the other party a duty to draft reasonably. The determination of reasonable notice, too, involves considering the behavior of only the nondrafting party, without also considering the conduct of the drafting party.

The so-called duty to read is not really a duty in the sense of an affirmative obligation; rather, it is an assumption by the court that a signatory to a contract has read its terms. An exception to the duty to read is that if a writing does not appear to be a contract and the terms are not called to the party's attention, there is no contract formed with respect to the undisclosed term.[4] Companies draft their online agreements to meet the requirements of legal notice by putting certain wording in large lettering at the beginning of their contracts. On Target.com, for example, the terms of use state as follows:

> Welcome to target.com. These Terms & Conditions apply to the Target website located at www.target.com and all other sites, services, and tools where these Terms & Conditions appear or are linked (collectively, the "Site"). As used in these Terms & Conditions, "Target", "us", or "we" refers to Target Corporation and its subsidiaries and affiliates.

---

[3] Jacqueline Lipton, *Information Property: Rights and Responsibilities*, 56 FL. L. REV. 135, 148–49 (2004).

[4] *See* Specht v. Netscape Communications Corp., 306 F.3d 17, 30 (2d Cir. 2002).

> **YOUR USE OF THIS WEBSITE IS GOVERNED BY THESE TERMS & CONDITIONS**
>
> BY ACCESSING OR OTHERWISE USING THE SITE YOU AGREE TO THESE TERMS & CONDITIONS. Any person or entity who interacts with the Site through the use of crawlers, robots, browsers, data mining or extraction tools, or other functionality, whether such functionality is installed or placed by such person or entity or a third party, is considered to be using the Site. If at any time you do not accept all of these Terms & Conditions, you must immediately stop using the Site. Certain areas within the Site may be governed by additional terms ("Additional Terms"). By using those areas of the Site, you agree to the Additional Terms. The Additional Terms are incorporated into these Terms & Conditions, and any reference to these Terms & Conditions includes the Additional Terms.[5]

The first two paragraphs clearly provide notice that the terms are contained in the browsewrap. Unfortunately for the visitor to Target.com, the notice that these terms exist is accessible only by clicking on the unobtrusive "terms & conditions" link at the bottom of the home page. It is only after clicking on this link—which few consumers are likely to do prior to using the site—that the terms are actually viewable.

Some might argue that courts will refuse to enforce the browsewrap for lack of notice (and therefore, lack of assent) since it is located at the bottom of the home page and requires scrolling in order to be visible. But it is not the browsewrap which would be the trigger for formation—it would be the subsequent clickwrap that appears toward the end of the transaction.

To illustrate, let us imagine a potential customer on the Target website. She selects an item and adds it to her virtual shopping cart. She then clicks the "checkout" icon, which takes her to the checkout page. This page permits her to continue the checkout process without creating an account. She clicks on the "continue" icon, which takes her to a checkout page, which requires her to fill out personal information, such as her shipping address. She then presses the "continue checkout" icon at the bottom of the page. She is taken to the "review & place order" page where she is asked to verify the items in her cart and her billing address, and place her order. It is only at this juncture that she is asked to manifest consent to the Terms and Conditions. In order to complete the transaction, she must click on the red icon that states, "place order." (See Figure 11-1)

---

[5] Target.com, Terms & Condition, last updated July 25, 2012, http://www.target.com/spot/terms-conditions (last visited March 10, 2013).

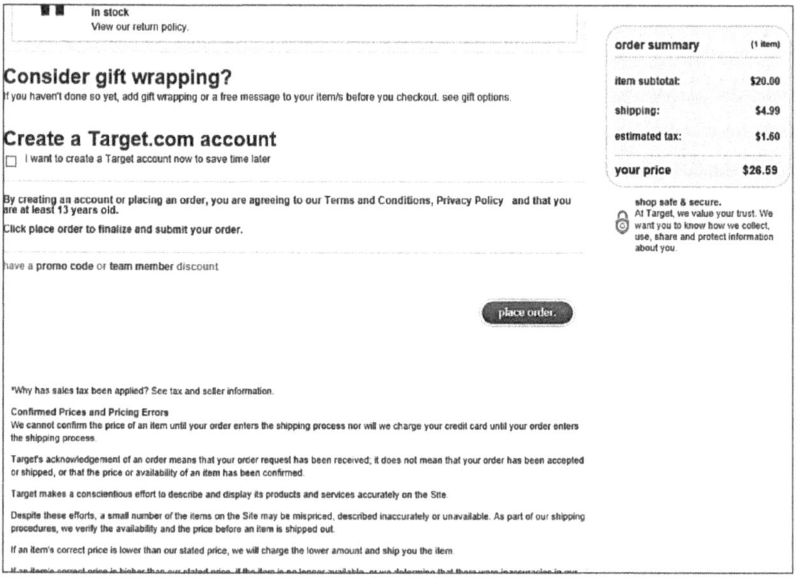

FIGURE 11-1

Directly above this icon, is the following language:

> "By creating an account or placing your order, you are agreeing to our *Terms and Conditions*, *Privacy Policy* and that you are at least 13 years old." (Italics denote hyperlink.)

Most courts will find reasonable notice because the hyperlink to the browsewrap terms were reasonably visible at the time the shopper manifested assent by clicking on the "place order" icon. The multiwrap thus accomplishes two tasks that benefit the company and burden the user—it provides notice and manifestation of consent (via the click) and virtually ensures that the user will not read the Terms or Privacy Policy (because they are accessible only via a hyperlink that competes for user attention with the click).

In addition to notice, the presentation of the contract matters because it signals the contract's importance. Contracts that are accessible only by clicking or scrolling can be easily dismissed by the user as unimportant if they are noticed at all.

The appearance of the contract at the end of the transaction does something more than simply downplay the importance of the contract—it ambushes the consumer and forces an active manifestation of consent after the consumer has already invested in the transaction. The consumer, who has already expended time and energy browsing the various offerings, has at this point selected an item and added it to her cart.

She has spent time inputting personal and payment information. She may have developed an emotional attachment to the selected item. Given her sunk costs, she is less likely to abort the transaction when the clickwrap appears.

Furthermore, in order to read the terms now, she must interrupt the transactional flow by clicking on the two hyperlinks and resisting the urge to click "place order." Even if she has read the Terms during past visits, she must review them each time she visits as Target has the following modification-at-will provision:

> Target may at any time: (i) modify or discontinue any part of the Site; (ii) charge, modify or waive fees required to use the Site; or (iii) offer opportunities to some or all Site users. Target reserves the right to make changes to these Terms & Conditions at any time, and such changes will be effective immediately upon being posted on the Site. Each time you use the Site, you should review the current Terms & Conditions. You can determine when these Terms & Conditions were last revised by referring to the "LAST UPDATED" legend at the top of these Terms & Conditions. Your continued use of the Site will indicate your acceptance of the current Terms & Conditions; however, any material change to these Terms & Conditions after your last usage of the Site will not be applied retroactively. Except for such material changes, the Terms & Conditions that were in effect at the time any claim or dispute arose between you and us will be applied.[6]

Why doesn't Target make it easier for customers to read the legal terms? It *could* design the website so the customer must read the terms before perusing the store offerings. But they don't because they want to attract and retain customers, not scare them away. Rather than presenting the terms up front, when the visitor has less invested in the site, Target presents the terms in such a way, and at such a time, that the likelihood the customer will read them is diminished. The presentation of the terms at the end of the transaction makes them seem like an afterthought, further reducing their salience. There may be valid aesthetic reasons for presenting terms in this way, but contract law should not have to bow to the dictates of Target's marketing department.

Reasonable notice is a misnomer. Given the time and effort it takes to locate and read terms and the low probability that consumers will be affected by them, it is quite reasonable to ignore wrap terms. Reasonableness is—or should be—based on rationality and how most people behave. But reasonable notice as applied by courts in wrap contract cases doesn't refer to something that most people would

---

[6] Target Terms and Condition, http://www.target.com/spot/terms-conditions#?lnk=fnav_t_spc_2_4 (last visited March 10, 2013).

have noticed; it has, unfortunately and erroneously come to mean wording that is reasonably *visible* to a party looking for it.

In *Feldman v. Google, Inc.*,[7] the plaintiff was an attorney who had participated in Google's AdWords program. Pursuant to that program, Feldman purchased certain keywords so that when a user searched using those terms, his advertisement would appear.[8] If the user clicked on Feldman's advertisement, Google would charge Feldman. Feldman claimed that he was the victim of "click fraud" whereby a user clicked on his ads with no interest in his services in order to drive up his costs.[9] He claimed that Google had the capacity to determine which clicks were fraudulent and did not warn him or investigate his complaints.[10] Feldman alleged that Google had charged him more than $100,000 over a two-year period and sued for damages, disgorgement of profits, and restitution. The court noted that click fraud in the AdWords program was the subject of a class action lawsuit that was settled. The plaintiff opted out of the class in order to pursue an individual lawsuit. The issue before the district court of the Eastern District of Pennsylvania was whether the following forum selection clause in Google's clickwrap agreement was enforceable: "The Agreement must be construed as if both parties jointly wrote it, governed by California law except for its conflicts of laws principles and adjudicated in Santa Clara County, California."[11]

As part of the AdWords process, advertisers were required to go through an online sign-up process which required agreeing to the terms of a clickwrap before advancing to the next step.[12] At the top of the page displaying the contract, a notice appeared in bold, which stated, "**Carefully read the following terms and conditions.** If you agree with these terms, indicate your assent below." The terms themselves, however, were contained in a scroll box that required the advertiser to scroll down to read the entire contract.[13] The court observed,

> "The contract itself included the preamble and seven paragraphs, in twelve-point font. The contract's preamble, the first paragraph, and part of the second paragraph were clearly visible before scrolling down to read the rest of the contract. The preamble, visible at first impression, stated that consent to the terms listed in the Agreement constituted a binding agreement with Google. A link

[7] Feldman v. Google, Inc., 513 F. Supp. 2d 229 (E.D. Pa. 2007).
[8] *Id.* at 231-232.
[9] *Id.* at 232.
[10] *Id.*
[11] *Id.* at 232-233.
[12] *Id.* at 233.
[13] *Id.*

to a printer-friendly version of the contract was offered at the top of the contract window for the advertiser who would rather read the contract printed on paper or view it on a fullscreen instead of scrolling down the window. At the bottom of the web page, viewable without scrolling down, was a box and the words, "Yes, I agree to the above terms and conditions." The advertiser had to have clicked on this box in order to proceed to the next step."[14]

The plaintiff claimed that he did not have notice of and did not assent to the agreement. The court disagreed. It stated that in order to determine the enforceability of a clickwrap agreement, "courts presented with the issue apply traditional principles of contract law and focus on whether the plaintiffs had reasonable notice of and manifested assent to the clickwrap agreement."[15]

That passage was cited in a subsequent case, *Major v. McCallister*, to uphold a browsewrap agreement that was accessible only by clicking on a hyperlink. The court concluded that because the *hyperlinks* were visible, there was "immediately visible notice of the existence of license terms."[16]

Courts expect too much from consumers, and far too little from companies that draft these agreements. For example, the court in *Vernon v. Qwest Communications, Int'l, Inc.* stated, "While the Qwest Defendants undoubtedly could provide more 'user friendly' access to the Subscriber Agreement, the undisputed facts in this case demonstrate that Plaintiffs had reasonable notice and access to the terms and conditions of the arbitration clause."[17] The court placed the burden of finding contract terms on the nondrafting party, who did not necessarily expect them or know where to find them, rather than require that the drafting party make those terms likely to be found. (Recall that in *Vernon*, the notice was a mailed letter that incorporated by reference an online agreement containing additional hyperlinked terms.)[18]

What passes for notice in wrap contract cases is often devoid of content or information. In *Lebowitz v. Dow Jones & Co.*,[19] subscribers to the *Wall Street Journal Online* signed an agreement that provided them with access to the *Wall Street Journal Online* and *Barron's Online*. Dow Jones (parent of both companies) decided to spin off the *Barron's* service and wanted to change its policy so that subscribers could continue to access one service but could only access the other for an additional fee. The notice that Dow Jones gave to inform its subscribers of the change in fees was in the form

---

[14] *Id.*

[15] *Id.* at 236.

[16] Major v. McCAllister 302 S.W. 3d 227, 230 (Mo. Ct. App. 2009).

[17] Vernon v. Qwest Communications Int'l, Inc., 857 F. Supp. 2d 1135, 1152 (D. Colo. 2012).

[18] *Id.* at 1150-51.

[19] Lebowitz v. Dow Jones & Co., 847 F. Supp. 2d 599 (S.D.N.Y. 2012).

of a box on the website's home page with the words, "IMPORTANT NOTICE TO READERS."[20] When a user clicked on the box, a pop-up window appeared that contained the following information: "Beginning Jan. 8, 2006, we will relaunch Barron's Online as a separate subscription site from The Wall Street Journal Online. A subscription to Barron's Online will no longer automatically include access to the Online Journal, and vice versa."[21]

The box on the website did not inform the users of the relevant information; it merely alerted them to where they could find the information. But the court ignored the reality that many website users may be unwilling to click on a box with vague and generic wording that might just as easily contain a malicious virus or an annoying marketing pitch as it might pertinent information. Dow Jones might have simply included the notice itself in the box, such as "Beginning Jan 8, 2006, you will no longer be able to access both the Wall Street Journal Online and Barron's Online." The user could then click on the box to get further information about the spin-off of *Barron's* and the fee pricing.

Unlike other notices, such as those on prescription drug labels or near construction sites, notice of wrap contract terms is notice only that legal terms are available. Often, they do not provide information about the nature of the terms. Warning labels, by contrast, notify consumers of the most problematic side effects or the most important exhortations: "MAY CAUSE DIZZINESS" or "TAKE WITH FOOD." More detailed information can be found in the insert, but the notice alerts the reader of its importance and relevance.

Physical placement also matters. A sign warning "CAUTION—CONSTRUCTION" is placed near the construction site, not a block away. Hyperlinks, on the other hand, contain terms located "off-site" and not where the consumer is virtually wandering. This is especially true where the notice of the hyperlink is contained offline, in a paper notice. In *Briceño v. Sprint Spectrum*,[22] the court ruled that receipt of a mailed invoice that referenced changes accessible via a hyperlink on a website constituted reasonable notice. The court stated that

> "Kansas law points out that there is a duty to read, especially when the clause language is clear. Briceño stated that she did not read the Terms and Conditions because she did not care about reading them and also stated that she did not like to read. Thus, Briceño failed to avail herself of the information presented to her."[23]

---

[20] *Id.* at 603.

[21] *Id.*

[22] Briceño v. Sprint Spectrum, 911 So.2d 176 (Fla. Dist. Ct. App. 2005).

[23] *Id.* at 180.

The court further noted that "there is no evidence that Sprint concealed the aforementioned original or amended Terms and Conditions," and concluded that since Briceño had "fair and clear warning of changes, conspicuously given on the first page of her invoice" the mandatory arbitration clause was not unconscionable.[24] Yet, to find that a notice received in the mail triggers a duty to read an online agreement that may be unilaterally amended simply makes a mockery of the reasonably prudent offeree standard. It seems a safe bet that very few of Sprint's customers actually felt compelled to read the terms. A reasonably prudent offeree standard cannot mean something that would be inconsistent with what the vast majority of offerees would do.

This is not to say that wrap contracts should be unenforceable; rather, in order to be enforceable the drafting party must make the adhesive terms clear. The drafting party has all the power present terms in the wrap contracting scenario and should make reasonable efforts to make those terms readable. If the drafting party is in fact ready to have the consumer walk away from the transaction if she fails to provide contractual assent, then the presentment of those terms should reflect their significance. In other words, where the terms are offered on a take-it-or-leave it basis, the appropriate inquiry should be—*how would a reasonable person have communicated the mandatory nature of these terms?*

As a result of ineffective notice, some academics and policy makers have called for alternatives, such as mandating certain terms and prohibiting others, which would limit the ability of the drafter to structure transactions. Yet, as others have noted, appropriately designed contracts and truly reasonable notice should be tested before ruling them out as being ineffective. Robert Hillman and Maureen O'Rourke argue that disclosure can "promote values as diverse as economic efficiency, due process, and corrective justice."[25] As reporters for the American Law Institute's Principles of the Law of Software Contracts, they proposed adoption of a disclosure "safe harbor" strategy which included among its requirements that software licensors make their terms available online.[26] Amy Schmitz states that empirical research "indicates that consumers' negative perceptions, feelings of helplessness, and lack of time" may prevent them from reading or negotiating contracts but that data "also indicates that consumers are rational to the extent they read contracts that involve greater choice of terms, more relational context, or larger costs and concerns."[27] M. Ryan

---

[24] *Id.*

[25] Robert A. Hillman and Maureen O'Rourke, *Defending Disclosure in Software Licensing*, 78 U. CHI. L. REV. 95, at 114 (2011).

[26] *See* the American Law Institute's *Principles of the Law: Software Contracts* (2010), section 2.02.

[27] Amy J. Schmitz, *Pizza-Box Contracts: True Tales of Consumer Contracting Culture*, 45 WAKE FOREST L. REV. 863, 888 (2010).

Calo has argued that before denouncing notice as an ineffective regulatory strategy, we should more closely examine ways to provide more effective notice, such as using mechanisms that are associated with user experience.[28] In other words, notice and contract may be effective if we expect more from those who draft them.

Companies can exercise their power over website design to heighten user awareness. One study demonstrated that short notices provided prior to the installation of spyware and in addition to the end-user license agreement significantly reduced the number of installations, thus indicating that these short notices were effective in informing users about the nature of the software.[29] A company could provide a short summary of important legal terms and then ask the user to click for more information. Companies, even small ones, can conduct focus group sessions to gauge the readability and understandability of agreements.

Contract designs should focus on the user's perception and incorporate images and even sounds in appropriate environments. Text bubbles and visual images can capture user interest. A study conducted by researchers Matthew Kay and Michael Terry found that redesigned software agreements which incorporated different font types, graphics, bullets, headings, and other visually oriented strategies (referred to as "textured agreements") improved both reading times and comprehension.[30] Another study found that a standardized privacy "label" similar to a nutritional label allowed users to find information more quickly and accurately—some even found it enjoyable to read.[31] Drafters should consider how an online contracting scenario might differ from a paper-based contracting scenario, taking into account the nature of the user's interaction with the website and the context in which the terms are presented.[32]

---

[28] M. Ryan Calo, *Against Notice Skepticism in Privacy (and Elsewhere)*, 87 NOTRE DAME L. REV. 1027, 1030 (2012).

[29] Nathaniel S. Good, Jens Grossklags, Deirdre K. Mulligan, Joseph A. Konstan, Noticing Notice: A Large-Scale Experiment on the Timing of Software License Agreements,, paper presented to the Conference on Human Factors In Computing Systems, April 28-May 3, 2007, San Jose, CA, USA.

[30] Matthew Kay & Michael Terry, *Textured Agreements: Re-envisioning Electronic Consent*, paper presented to the Symposium on Usable Privacy and Security (SOUPS), July 14–16, 2010, Redmond, WA, USA.

[31] Patrick Gage Kelley, Joanna Bresee, Lorrie Faith Cranor, & Robert W. Reeder, *A "Nutrition Label" for Privacy*, Symposium on Usable Privacy and Security (SOUPS) 2009, July 15–17, 2009, Mountain View, CA, USA.

[32] Stefania Passera and Helena Haapio have proposed that contract terms should be visually represented with flowcharts, drawings, and other graphics. Stefania Passera & Helena Haapio, *User-Centered Contract Design: New Directions in the Quest for Simpler Contracting*, *in* Henschel, René Franz (ed.), paper presented to the International Association for Contract and Commercial Management (IACCM) Academic Forum, Ridgefield, CT, USA, available at http://www.iaccm.com/admin/docs/docs/HH_Paper.pdf.; *see also* Thomas D. Barton, Gerlinde Berger-Walliser, and Helena Haapio, *Visualization: Seeing Contracts For What They Are, And What They Could Become*, Journal of Law, Business and Ethics, 19 JOURNAL OF LAW, BUS. & ETHICS 47 (2013).

A duty to draft reasonably recognizes that in a digital environment, contracts are not only legal terms; contracts are code and code, in the words of Joel Reidenberg, is "Lex Informatica." As Reidenberg explains,

> "In the legal regulatory regime, private contractual arrangements can be used both to deviate from the law's default rules and to customize the relationship between the parties. Such deviations are only available if the law permits freedom of contract and does not preclude the participants' actions: circumstances exist in which the law may not permit customization....Like a legal regime, Lex Informatica offers both customization of rules and inalienable rules. Customization for Lex Informatica occurs through technological configurations."[33]

Similarly, Lawrence Lessig described code as an architecture of control, as "law" in the sense of regulating actions.

There are two levels of regulation with online contracts—one on the level of law and another on the level of code. Contracts as code is an obvious descriptive observation once it is pointed out. Courts have treated online contracts, however, in only the first sense, as (private) law; they have wholly disregarded the function of contracts in the second sense, as code.

Courts have long recognized the power of drafters to select wording. For example, where terms are ambiguous, the courts have interpreted the terms against the drafting party. But a contract can be ambiguous or misleading by its presentation, not just the words used. Unlike paper contracts, digital contracts (contracts as code) can be expressed in multiple ways, and there are multiple ways for them to elude the nondrafting party. Once we truly understand this, we can view the use of such code in relation to the selected means of expression. We can also understand the expression of that code in ways other than words. We are no longer confined to assessing the validity of a digital contract by the size of the font or whether the drafter used all caps. We understand that the use of a hyperlink above a click box could be expressed differently. Drafters are using the contract to direct and control user behavior not just by punctuation and wording but by the coding used to present that wording. Lessig noted that "[t]he code embeds certain values or makes certain values impossible."[34] In selecting the presentation, contract drafters are also expressing certain values or making certain values impossible in the sense that they are permitting, or not permitting, choices.

---

[33] Joel R. Reidenberg, *Lex Informatica: The Formulation of Information Policy Rules Through Technology*, 76 TEXAS L. REV. 553, 571 (1998)

[34] LAWRENCE LESSIG, CODES AND OTHER LAWS OF CYBERSPACE at 87 (Basic Books 1999).

The standard of reasonable drafting would require that businesses take certain measures to make their contracts noticeable. There are several aspects to this duty to draft reasonably. The first is visibility. The terms should be presented to attract the attention of the nondrafting party. This is the aspect that courts currently require, but often they fail to sufficiently consider the effect of inattentional blindness. Christopher Chabris and Daniel Simons define inattentional blindness as an "error of perception" and explain that when "people devote their attention to a particular area or aspect of their visual world, they tend not to notice unexpected objects, even when those unexpected objects are salient, potentially important, and appear right where they are looking."[35] It is inattentional blindness which makes someone who is preoccupied with counting shirt colors during a basketball game overlook a gorilla pounding its chest in the middle of the court. It is also inattentional blindness which makes website visitors, caught up in the flow of the transaction, ignore hyperlinks and click "I agree" without realizing what they are doing.

The second aspect of reasonable drafting is that the drafting party should make reasonable efforts to present the terms in a way that makes it likely that the other party will *read* them, not simply *see* them. In the Target.com example, the terms might be presented as soon as the visitor clicks on a product category. Thus, a duty to draft reasonably would consider the "look and feel" of the website.

Reasonable drafting also considers word choice. Most websites use the demure wording of "Terms of Use" or "Conditions of Use" or simply "Terms," to provide notice of their online agreements. This language may seem benign to most nonlawyers. Companies should start using language that their users understand, such as "The Contract Between You and [Company]" or "Your Legal Obligations" instead of the more innocuous-sounding "Terms."

A drafter who is trying to get visitors to read legal terms would not place them in competition with activity that is part of the flow of the transaction. For example, a drafter should not place terms via a hyperlink next to an icon that requires clicking to proceed. On Facebook (see Figure 11-2) the link to the terms is placed immediately underneath the sign-up form fields—but the terms themselves are hidden away. In big, bold letters are the words, "Connect with friends and the world around you on Facebook," and "Sign Up—It's free and always will be." The site contains form fields so the visitor can quickly and easily register. Sandwiched between the form fields and the big green "Sign Up" box are, in much smaller font, the links to *the Terms, Data Use Policy*, and *Cookie Use*. If Facebook really wanted its users to read those terms, they would be more visible and contain more information.

[35] CHRISTOPHER CHABRIS AND DANIEL SIMONS, THE INVISIBLE GORILLA at 6-7 (2009).

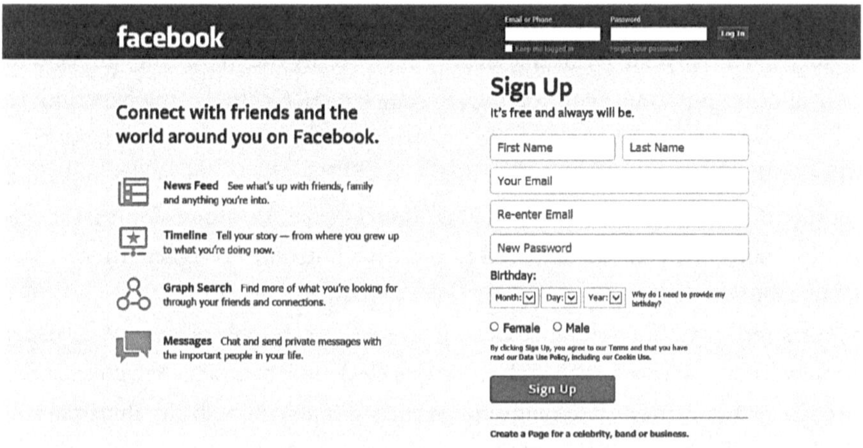

FIGURE 11-2

For example, after "free" they could add in parentheses :"(we don't charge money, but we do use your personal information—please read the *LEGALLY BINDING CONTRACT BETWEEN YOU AND FACEBOOK* to learn how)" Of course they don't do that because they don't actually want their users to learn of their data collection practices.

A drafter who is making reasonable efforts to get visitors to read wrap terms would not engage in online "multiwrapping," which is the placement of hyperlinked legal terms next to click boxes that are designed to conclude a transaction (one court referred to this form as a "modified clickwrap").[36] Facebook states that "(b)y clicking Sign Up, you agree to our Terms and that you have read our Data Use Policy, including our Cookie Use," but it is doubtful that it expects or desires any prospective user to read those terms given their unobtrusive presentation and the prominence of the Sign Up button.

Similarly, in the Target scenario, the "Terms and Conditions" hyperlink essentially competes with the "place order" icon. The juxtaposition of legal terms with transaction completion icons practically ensures that the terms will go unread. Visitors at the end of a transaction process have sunk costs—they have already invested time and energy shopping, inputting information, and developing an expectation for a particular product.After spending time on the site, they want their efforts rewarded. Furthermore, it is not uncommon for a click to another page to result in loss of previously filled data fields. A visitor may be unwilling to click away from the page so close to finalizing the transaction.

[36] Swift v. Zynga Game Network, 805 F. Supp. 2d 904, at 910 (2011).

In addition, where terms are presented concurrently and adjacent to each other, and not sequentially, the terms that are not required by the website design seem to be trivial or unimportant. For example, in *Major v. McCallister*,[37] the hyperlink to the browsewrap was placed alongside a button which completed the transaction, similar to the Target multi-wrap (see Figure 11-1). The placement of the hyperlink alongside the "Submit for Matching Pros" button gave the impression that it was not important. The user was required to press the button to complete the transaction, but she was not required to click on the hyperlink to the terms.

Courts recognize the relevance of font size and paragraph placement in paper contracts. They also consider these factors with electronic contracts. Yet, courts need to recognize that in the online environment there is much more that drafters can and should do to elicit assent. Given that websites are visually oriented, a drafter should use images to encourage visitors to read legal terms. For example, rather than this:

> "By placing your order, you agree to our legally binding contract, which contains "

a website might display this:

> "By placing your order, you agree to our legally binding contract, which contains **warranty disclaimers, tracking policies and limitations of liability.** Click *here* for more information."

The expectations of the parties are influenced by the ways in which electronic contracts differ from paper contracts. The Electronic Signatures in Global and National Commerce Act and the Uniform Electronic Transactions Act have requirements that recognize and account for the differences between paper and electronic contracts.[38] Courts, too, should recognize the differences created by the contracting medium. A duty to draft reasonably should consider the alternatives methods of contract presentment at the disposal of the drafting party. How else could the contract terms have been displayed? Would a reasonable party seeking to elicit knowing assent have presented the terms like this?

---

[37] *Major v. McCallister*, 302 S.W.3d 227 (Mo. Ct. App. 2009).

[38] For a discussion of this contrast, *see* Juliet Moringniello, *Signals, Assent and Internet Contracting*, 57 Rutgers L. Rev. 1307, 1340-41 (2005)(noting that the drafters of these acts recognized that there were differences between electronic and paper records).

The ABA Working Group (see chapter 9) issued fifteen strategies for click-through agreements to avoid "disputes on the validity of the mutual assent process."[39] These strategies reflect reasonable drafting and include "viewing of terms before assent," "assent before access to governed items," "sufficient opportunity to review the proposed agreement terms before proceeding," "continued ability to view terms," "clear and readable terms, in legible font," "consistency" of terms provided on the site, "clear words" of assent and rejection, and "clear method of assent or rejection."[40]

The ABA Working Group emphasized that they do "not purport to set a minimum standard or to identify any exclusive means to obtain valid assent"[41] but that the strategies "recognize the unique factual circumstances that may be presented in electronic settings, which may or may not have a paper analog." The ABA Working Group published its report in 2001—the case law after that time clearly indicates that courts have not required that companies adhere to these common sense examples of reasonable drafting strategies.

Another final aspect of the duty to draft reasonably is testing. There are many ways that companies can test the effectiveness of their contracts. They can conduct focus groups, they can gauge whether users are clicking on hyperlinks, they can send follow-up e-mails, and with the help of eye tracking software, they can determine what users are looking at on a page and for how long. Andrea Matwyshyn proposes a "reasonable digital consumer" standard whereby a company would conduct a "legal usability test" to ensure that users understand online agreements.[42] She adds that by doing this, "companies would begin to view the User Agreement as an integral part of the product and worry about its functionality to the same extent they worry about the functionality of the product itself."[43] But companies will conduct such tests and treat their agreements seriously only if provided with an incentive to do so that offsets the benefits of unobtrusive contract presentation. Imposing a duty to draft reasonably provides companies with that incentive.

Some may object that imposing this new standard is too vague and that companies will be unsure as to how to proceed to meet this standard. First, the existing standard—that of "reasonable notice"—is also vague and constantly moving. The objection regarding vagueness applies any time "reasonableness" is imposed as a standard because reasonableness depends upon context and perspective. To the

[39] Christina L. Kunz, Maureen F. Del Duca, Heather Thayer, & Jennifer Debrow, *Click-Through Agreements: Strategies for Avoiding Disputes on Validity of Assent*, 57 Bus. Law. 401 (Nov. 2001).

[40] *Id.*

[41] *Id.* at 419.

[42] Andrea M. Matwyshyn, *Technoconse(t)sus*, 85 Wash. U. L. Rev. 529, 561–62 (2008).

[43] *Id.* at 562.

extent that context and perspective change, what is reasonable will also change. The flexibility of the standard is a disadvantage, but it is also a very real advantage, especially in the fast-moving area of technology.

In addition, a reasonableness standard is consistent with contract law, which adopts an objective standard in other areas—including with respect to what constitutes adequate notice. The objection that a duty to draft reasonably lacks predictability is misdirected as it is one that has more to do with the standard of reasonableness in general than it does with the imposition of the duty in this particular context.

Others may argue that the imposition of the duty to draft reasonably is too burdensome for the drafting party, which has to consider ways to bring terms to the attention of the nondrafting party. Yet, the burden of ferreting out terms—the duty to read—now falls solely on the nondrafting party. The burden of drafting reasonably merely evens the imbalance that currently exists so that the burdens of digital contracting are more evenly distributed between the parties. Furthermore, a duty to draft reasonably is consistent with how courts have historically treated changes in contracting forms. As Juliet Moringiello observes, "different forms of contracts have historically led courts to refine existing contract rules to accommodate those different forms, often by imposing additional duties on the person offering the terms."[44]

A duty to draft reasonably corresponds to the reasonable notice requirement as applied to paper contracts. Reasonable notice arose in the context of tangible contracts where the drafter's drafting tools and techniques were limited by space. Courts thus focused on font size and whether words were in bold and capitalized. The duty to draft reasonably merely recognizes that there are more tools at the disposal of digital drafters. Judicial focus on the visibility of terms made sense when contract language was limited by paper, and when the consumer was primed to receive a contract, received a tangible prompt that she carried in her hands, and manifested consent by signing. Under these circumstances, it was reasonable to assume if the terms were visible, that a consumer would have seen them and understood they were part of the contract. That assumption is no longer valid in the digital environment where there are multiple stimuli competing for the user's attention and the user is in an environment that is not perceived nor presented as a legal one.

Furthermore, the drafting party is in a better position than the nondrafting party to demonstrate that its conduct was reasonable. The nondrafting party has only her own behaviour and knowledge as the basis for reasonableness. The judge, too, can only speculate as to what reasonable behaviour may be on the part of the nondrafting party. The drafting party, on the other hand, has the ability to test whether users

[44] Juliet Moringniello, *supra* note 38, at 1333.

are actually reading or even noticing terms. It can provide evidence of its testing efforts, thereby establishing that it met its duty to draft reasonably. Furthermore, as Andrea Matwyshyn notes, terms that have undergone user testing may proliferate in the way that coercive terms have proliferated so that "even if only a few influential companies that use digital contracts shift to agreements that reflect usability tested standards, they will be able to instigate the emergence of a new norm in the system over time through lawyers' drafting behaviours."[45]

Reasonable drafting techniques should seek to enhance consumer awareness, even if the adhering party does not have the ability to negotiate terms. In the online environment, a take-it-or-leave-it approach may in fact result in the consumer leaving it. Many of the online service offerings are not necessities—at least, not when they were initially offered. Companies such as Twitter and Facebook had to overcome initial skepticism in the marketplace, as does any company that is offering consumers something new or different. Users had to get accustomed to using these services and overcome whatever concerns they might have had about privacy or security. Although many users would now consider the service offerings of these companies to be necessities, consumer acceptance was not immediate and required reassuring potential users of the benefits of these services. In other words, to require companies to employ drafting methods to enhance consumer awareness of wrap contracts and increase readability of contract terms is not so much about bargaining power as it is about corporate transparency and the prevention of corporate bait-and-switch practices.

Finally, the requirement to draft reasonably is already required by the Federal Trade Commission (FTC). The FTC working paper discussed in chapter 10 perfectly captures the spirit and substance of the duty to draft reasonably. It encourages advertisers to view disclosures in the context of the page as a whole, taking into consideration actual consumer behavior. It notes, for example, that a hyperlink's label—"the text or graphic assigned to it"—affects whether a consumer will actually click on it.[46] It also recognizes that drafters have power and that they have tools at their disposal that nondrafting parties do not. For example, the paper notes that advertisers have ways to measure the effectiveness of disclosures through hyperlinks by measuring click-through rates and evaluating the amount of time visitors spend on a certain page, which may indicate whether the disclosures are being read.[47] It also recognizes that the drafter makes choices, that disclosures "may be displayed on Web sites in many ways."[48] It recommends that businesses conduct research to help them

[45] Matwyshyn, *supra* note 42, at 573.

[46] Federal Trade Commission, "Dot Com Disclosures: Information about Online Advertising" 8 (2000) *available at* http://www.ftc.gov/opa/2000/05/dotcom.shtm.

[47] *Id.* at 9.

[48] *Id.* at 10.

determine whether a particular technique, such as a pop-up window, is an effective method of communication.[49] The paper acknowledges that it is the "advertiser's responsibility to draw attention to the required disclosures."[50]

Wrap contract law, unlike traditional contract law and the FTC guidelines, emphasizes the consumer's duty to read and enforces only very minimal requirements of notice upon the drafter. A party that adheres to the FTC rules and guidelines is most likely meeting its obligation to draft reasonably. Conversely, a party that fails to fulfill its duty to draft reasonably is probably falling short of the FTC requirements.

Finally, I propose a safe harbor, which I refer to as the "turnabout is fair play" rule. Under this safe harbor, a drafting party has met its duty to draft reasonably if it provides notice of terms in the same manner that it allows its users to provide notice to it. For example, Instagram's Terms of Use requires that in order to opt out of arbitration, users must "notify Instagram in writing within 30 days of the date that you first became subject to this arbitration provision." Users must mail in their written opt-out notice to "Instagram, LLC ATTN: Arbitration Opt-out 1601 Willow Rd. Menlo Park, CA 94025," and must include "name and residence address, the email address you use for your Instagram account, and a clear statement that you want to opt out of this arbitration agreement."[51]

Admittedly, few companies will use this safe harbor precisely because the notice requirements they impose upon their users are onerous. Yet, the very existence of such a safe harbor may force realization of the one-sidedness of wrap contracts and prompt courts to reconsider the meaning of what it means to be reasonable.

B. Tailoring Assent

Under current law, contractual assent is an "all-or-nothing" proposition—either a contract is formed in its entirety or it is not. A finding of contract formation means that the nondrafting party has the burden of raising a contract defense, such as unconscionability, to escape enforcement. But as previously noted, courts are generally reluctant to evaluate the fairness of a bargain or the adequacy of consideration. The battle then is often lost at the formation stage—a properly formed contract will be enforced unless the terms are so egregious that it outweighs judicial reluctance to evaluate terms. In addition, there is a feedback loop where wrap contracts themselves affect business practices, surreptitiously introducing or changing terms so that

[49] *Id.*
[50] *Id.* at 12.
[51] Instagram, Terms of Use Http://instagram.com/about/legal/terms/updated/ (last visited Jan. 2, 2013).

by the time the relevant contractual provision is disputed, the practice—such as online tracking or licensing rather than selling software—has been in existence long enough to conform to industry standards, further diminishing the likelihood of an unconscionability ruling.

The problems created by contracts of adhesion in general, and wrap contracts in particular, stem from contract law's failure to provide a middle ground between assent and no assent. A finding of assent leads to a finding of contract formation; on the other hand, a finding of no assent means that no contract was formed.[52] Not surprisingly, courts that wish to uphold a particular transaction or *type* of transaction have been more willing to find assent even in the absence of bargaining power. Assent has thus been construed to mean acquiescence rather than *agreement*, devoid of any requirement of voluntariness or volition.[53] While such a passive notion of assent seems inconsistent with the very reason why we enforce contracts, in fact, it reflects another of contract law's goals, which is to encourage and facilitate economic transactions.[54] Contracts, while important in clarifying the terms of transactions, also stall their progression. Simplifying the contracting process—by discouraging or even preventing negotiations—thus shortens the time from transaction inception to completion. The transaction is thus streamlined by allowing assent to be found even where the contracting party did not have actual knowledge of a particular term.

---

[52] In the absence of a finding of mutual assent, the courts might yet find an implied-in-law, or quasi, contract. Quasi contracts, based in equity, are legal fictions imposed in order to prevent unjust enrichment. *See* Kammer Asphalt Paving Co. v. E. China Twp. Sch., 504 N.W.2d 635, 640 (Mich. 1993); Cascaden v. Magryta, 225 N.W. 511, 512 (Mich. 1929); Luithly v. Cavalier Corp., No. 98-5507, 1999 U.S. App. LEXIS 10653, at *12–14 (E.D. Tenn. May 20, 1999).

[53] *See* Karl N. Llewellyn, *What Price Contract?—An Essay in Perspective*, 40 YALE L.J. 704, 728 n.49 (1931) ("Agreement does not even today carry any… connotation of real willingness. Acquiescence in the lesser evil is all that need be understood.").

[54] *See* Kessler, *supra* note 1, at 630 (noting that "freedom of contract" is both practical and moral). Kessler stated:

> The individualism of our rules of contract law, of which freedom of contract is the most powerful symbol, is closely tied up with the ethics of free enterprise capitalism and the ideals of justice of a mobile society of small enterprisers, individual merchants and independent craftsmen....
>
> With the decline of the free enterprise system due to the innate trend of competitive capitalism toward monopoly, the meaning of contract has changed radically.

Id. at 640. For discussions about the socioeconomic benefits of contracts, see generally A. M. POLINSKY, AN INTRODUCTION TO LAW AND ECONOMICS (Little, Brown & Co. 1983); ROSCOE POUND, AN INTRODUCTION TO THE PHILOSOPHY OF LAW 133–344 (Yale University Press 1954) ("[I]n a commercial and industrial society, a claim or want or demand of society that promises be kept and that undertakings be carried out in good faith, a social interest in the stability of promises as a social and economic institution, becomes of the first importance...."); Lewis A. Kornhauser, *An Introduction to the Economic Analysis of Contract Remedies*, 57 U. COLO. L. REV. 683 (1986).

Another generally accepted contract law objective is the protection of reasonable expectations. *See* Jane B. Baron, *Gifts, Bargains, and Form*, 64 IND. L.J. 155, 157, 190–201 (1989); Roscoe Pound, *Individual Interests of Substance—Promised Advantages*, 59 HARV. L. REV. 1, 1–2 (1945).

If one did not know of a particular contractual term, one could not have assented to such term. In contract law, however, provided that the contracting party demonstrated assent to entering into the transaction,[55] the courts have not much concerned themselves with whether the party had actual knowledge, and thus actually assented to, the contractual term at issue. Instead, as discussed in chapter 8, courts have focused on notice and an opportunity to read the relevant contractual terms.

Courts have imposed a duty to read on contracts of adhesions of all kinds, without distinguishing that these contracts may have different functions—and that in many cases it is *not reasonable* for a party to actually read the terms. The fiction that all contracts are the same derived from the notion of blanket assent, which itself developed out of the objective theory of contracts.

Blanket assent presumably reflected what a reasonable person would believe upon seeing that the other party had affixed his or her signature to a legal document. This interpretation shifted the meaning of assent away from knowledge of what the terms meant to mere awareness that the terms existed. Awareness, in turn, triggered the duty to read and justified the other party's belief that the signing party had assented. This fiction accommodated business interests in facilitating mass consumer transactions where risk assessments were imperative and individual negotiations impractical.

Wrap contracts and wrap contract doctrine have again shifted the meaning of assent away from awareness of terms to the mere existence of terms. Blanket assent applied to wrap contracts means that a party can be held to the terms of a contract without even being aware that a contract exists. As applied to wrap contracts, blanket assent is no assent at all; rather, it is a formalistic requirement that the terms meet certain visibility requirements. These requirements fail to recognize the problems of inattentional blindness online and do not correspond to the likelihood that the user will actually be aware of the terms.

As discussed in chapters 3 and 9, instructive contracts are essentially notices and should not require the consent of the nondrafting party in order to enforce them because they do not involve the transfer of any right or entitlement belonging to the nondrafting party. They are better classified as pure notices but are presented as contracts because the business seeks the nondrafting party's acknowledgment that it understands the policy governing the use of a product or service and will not contest the enforceability of the policy at a later date. Presumed consent makes sense in those situations with only a reasonable notice requirement (i.e. provided that certain visibility requirements are met).

---

[55] With shrinkwrap agreements, the courts have not even required an opportunity to read the contract terms prior to entering into the transaction. *See* ProCD v. Zeidenberg, 86 F.3d at 1447 (1996).

In other situations, however, the drafter exceeds its authority by attempting to negatively affect the nondrafting party's entitlements. A software company may unilaterally set forth the scope of license in a contract. The purchaser adheres to the limits of the license not because she has consented to them but because intellectual property law allows it. Notice alone suffices. The software company may unilaterally establish the scope of use as it owns the intellectual property rights to the software. The software company cannot, however, unilaterally restrict or appropriate the nondrafting party's entitlements without the nondrafting party's consent. If, for example, the software company wanted to prohibit the licensee's right of first sale—an entitlement belonging to the *licensee* - it would need to obtain the licensee's specific assent to that term. Similarly, if the drafter wanted to require the adhering party to agree to mandatory arbitration, it must draft the agreement in such a way as to obtain specific assent to that term. The drafting party should receive specific assent to obtain rights belonging to the nondrafting party that are not directly created from the drafting party's license or promise. In other words, sword and crook provisions (as defined in chapter 5) require specific assent but shield provisions do not.

Currently, the assumption under wrap contract law is that all provisions in a contract reflect the bargain. This assumption does not reflect reality. A consumer may want a particular good or service, but not the ancillary provisions that he or she may not have bothered to read. This does not mean that the consumer should be permitted to set the terms of the bargain nor that she should be allowed to pick and choose the provisions at her sole discretion. What it does mean is that the contract drafter should not be able to get *more* than what was bargained for.

A specific assent approach encourages economic efficiency in transactions by eliminating free-rider provisions. Such provisions are included in nonnegotiated contracts even though their presence or absence would not affect the drafter's decision to offer the product or service. Their inclusion in contracts may reflect a surfeit of caution or a greedy desire for expansive legal coverage at the user's expense. In some cases, it may simply reflect boilerplate carried over from another form agreement. Those provisions that are not free riders, on the other hand, will be called to the other party's attention and will remain in the contract.

Contract drafters faced with the requirement of calling out certain provisions may even delete some of them in order to streamline and facilitate the contracting process and retain customer goodwill. While companies currently compete on the quality of their contracting process, that process fails to reflect the quality of the terms since consumers fail to read them. Where the process is intertwined with and reflects the terms, the quality of the terms is inescapable. Consequently, companies may be forced to compete on the substance of their contracts, making "shopping for terms" a real possibility rather than a hollow claim.

Furthermore, a specific assent approach aids consumer cognition by making important terms easier to find. Currently, the overwhelming number of words contained in form agreements and their unobtrusive presentation makes it difficult to distinguish innocuous provisions from those requiring more scrutiny and contemplation.[56] The act of assenting to certain terms forces the consumer to acknowledge the existence of those terms. The consumer can then assess each term requiring specific consent in her calculation of the costs and benefits of the transaction. The resulting agreement thus more accurately reflects what both parties want and enhances the efficiency of the transaction.

The power to select the wrap contracting form belongs to only one party; nevertheless, often the *nondrafting party* is purportedly making a promise or granting a license to the drafting party. A specific assent requirement requires the drafter to enable the user to indicate the making of that commitment or the scope of that license. If the drafting party wishes to bind the nondrafting party to a sword or crook provision (i.e. a provision extracting an entitlement from the non-drafting party), it must format the wrap contract in a way to permit promise making or license granting by the nondrafting party. For example, if the drafter wants a copyright license to the nondrafting party's content, it must enable the nondrafting party to express the scope of that license by building specific consent into the contract code. Such a requirement brings back the signaling effect that is lost with wrap contracts.

A specific assent requirement ties in to the duty to draft reasonably. The drafter should provide the user with the ability to indicate specific assent in a reasonable manner and take reasonable measures to ensure the effectiveness of a particular format. The drafter can build specific assent into the contract code in several ways. It can require the nondrafting party to click after each promise. For example, to indicate the scope of the license and the indemnification granted by its customers, Amazon could draft the contract as follows:

> If you do post content or submit material, and unless we indicate otherwise, you grant Amazon a nonexclusive, royalty-free [click], perpetual [click],

---

[56] Richard Epstein, on the other hand, argues that those who are less knowledgeable are able to "rely, often to free-ride, on the wisdom of their betters to achieve the terms that make for successful contracting." Richard A. Epstein, *Contract, Not Regulation: UCITA and High-Tech Consumers Meet Their Consumer Protection Critics*, CONSUMER PROTECTION IN THE AGE OF THE 'INFORMATION ECONOMY', 206 (Jane K. Winn ed., 2006.) But as Clayton Gillette points out, in many cases, there are divergent interests among buyers. *See* Clayton P. Gillette, Rolling Contracts as an Agency Problem, in Consumer Protection in the Age of the 'Information Economy' 241 (Jane K. Winn ed., 2006); *see also* Michael I. Meyerson, The Reunification of Contract Law: The Objective Theory of Consumer Form Contracts, 47 U. Miami L. Rev. 1263, 1270-71 (1993) (expressing skepticism that there exists a "small cadre of type-A consumers" that ferrets out beneficial terms to the benefit of the nonreading majority of consumers).

> irrevocable [click], and fully sublicensable [click] right to use [click], reproduce [click], modify [click], adapt [click], publish [click], translate [click], create derivative works from [click], distribute [click], and display [click] such content throughout the world [click] in any media [click]. You grant Amazon and sublicensees the right to use the name that you submit [click] in connection with such content, if they choose. You represent and warrant that you own or otherwise control all of the rights to the content that you post [click]; that the content is accurate [click]; that use of the content you supply does not violate this policy [click] and will not cause injury to any person or entity [click]; and that you will indemnify Amazon for all claims resulting from content you supply [click]. Amazon has the right but not the obligation to monitor and edit or remove any activity or content. Amazon takes no responsibility and assumes no liability for any content posted by you or any third party.

Similarly, companies could draft contracts to permit the consumer to indicate permissible uses of personal information. For example:

Please click on the box if you give us permission to use your information in the following ways:

- **to share with third parties for marketing purposes:**
  - ☐ your personal information
  - ☐ your content
  - ☐ both your personal information and your content

Some critics might object to a multiple clicking approach to specific assent because it is burdensome to consumers. *That is exactly the point.* The goal of a specific assent requirement is not to ensure that users read online contracts; rather the goal is to introduce a transactional hurdle that signals the burdensome nature of the transaction. Although consumers may not read or even consciously note the terms before clicking, multiple clicking and other forms of obtaining specific consent disrupt the contracting process in a way that negatively affect a user's online experience.

Transactional hurdles provide an easier way for users to comparison shop contract terms. Contract terms are part of a business' offering although their invisibility often impedes consumers' ability to compare terms. This is not to suggest that consumers will actually *read* the terms under my approach; rather, they will be confronted with them in a way that affects their online experience—and thus, their relationship—with a particular business.

A business should bargain for benefits received from their consumers rather than assume that such benefits are comprehensively granted with a single click. A website that seeks many entitlements from the non-drafting party as part of an interaction (such as collection of consumer personal information for multiple marketing purposes or a broad license to use user generated content), will be forced to offer a more burdensome contracting process than one that extracts no or few entitlements. For example, a customer who wants to purchase a product from an online retailer will be forced to click to indicate assent to each authorized use of that customer's personal information. The more uses that the website seeks, the more times the customer will have to click. On the other hand, a website that doesn't use customer personal information for any purpose other than to process the transaction will not require multiple clicks from the customer. The customer can then factor in the contracting experience with other relevant information pertaining to the site (lower prices, free shipping, etc.). In some cases, the contracting process may tip the balance away from one provider to another that has a less onerous contracting process.

An alternative to multiple clicking is e-mail consent. A frequent user of a website might submit via e-mail a typed consent to the terms of that website's wrap agreement, thus eliminating the need to engage in multiple clicking each time she visits the website. In order to be effective, the e-mail consent should be typed by the user rather than assented to via a click, thus ensuring that the user is aware of what she is doing and understands the legal nature of the obligations she is undertaking. The user would have to submit new email consent each time the company revises the wrap agreement(s).

Another alternative is "facsimile" contracting software, where an electronic contract is presented by one party to the other as a scanned copy or .pdf version of a legal document. The adhering party is required to type in her name at the end of the document instead of clicking. Some companies already have the capability to provide these facsimile-type agreements. The technical capability exists but companies must be willing to adopt it. Currently, they are reluctant to do so because the absence of signaling works in their favor.

As Russell Korobkin observes, "terms found in form contracts frequently will be non-salient to most buyers."[57] He explains:

> "First, purchase decisions involving products with form contracts are sufficiently complex that buyers usually will be selective in their consideration of

[57] Russell Korobkin, Bounded Rationality, Standard Form Contracts, and Unconscionability, 70 UNIV. OF CHI. L. REV. 1203, 1225 (2003).

product attributes. That is, at least some attributes will be non-salient. Second, relative to other product attributes, form terms are particularly likely to be non-salient because their usual content makes them unlikely to attract buyers' voluntary or involuntary attention."[58]

Incorporating a transactional hurdle in front of certain terms raises the salience of such terms because it affects the consumer experience. A specific assent requirement is more likely to have an impact on consumer loyalty and awareness, thereby making standard form agreements competitive factors in more than a purely rhetorical sense.[59] A transactional obstacle renders a term salient. Website marketers are very aware of the benefits of making transactions as frictionless as possible. In the same way that a consumer is more likely to return to a shopping site that processes transactions with "one click," so too might that same consumer refuse to return to a site that requires numerous clicks to approve onerous legal terms.[60] To require specific assent burdens the consumers, but it also burdens the drafter.[61] The transactional hurdles would likely result in real costs to the drafter in terms of abandoned transactions and defecting users, thereby providing an incentive to the drafter to rethink its contractual offerings.

My proposal is admittedly contrary[62] to the current assumption under contract law that all provisions in a contract reflect the bargain or that manifested assent is

---

[58] Id. at 1225-1226.

[59] To the claim that standard form contracts are unconscionable, it is often the response that consumers are free to shop elsewhere for better terms. In reality, consumers are unlikely to compare several different multipage agreements for reasons exhaustively discussed elsewhere. *See* Melvin Aron Eisenberg, Text Anxiety, 59 S. Cal. L. Rev. 305 (1986); Robert A. Hillman & Jeffrey J. Rachlinski, Standard-Form Contracting in the Electronic Age, 77 N.Y.U. L. Rev. 429, 445–54 (2002); Russell Korobkin, Bounded Rationality, Standard Form Contracts, and Unconscionability, 70 U. Chi. L. Rev. 1203 (2003); Michael I. Meyerson, The Reunification of Contract Law: The Objective Theory of Consumer Form Contracts, 47 U. Miami L. Rev. 1263 (1993).; W. David Slawson, Standard Form Contracts and Democratic Control of Lawmaking Power, 84 Harv. L. Rev. 529, 542 (1971).

[60] *See* Robert W. Gomulkiewicz, *Getting Serious about User-Friendly Mass Market Licensing for Software*, 12 Geo. Mason L. Rev. 687, 695–96 (2004) (setting forth reasons why software publishers should care about better written end-user agreements, including building goodwill with customers).

[61] Robert A. Hillman, *Online Boilerplate: Would Mandatory Website Disclosure of E-Standard Terms Backfire?*, 104 Mich. L. Rev. 837,, 844 (2006).

[62] Although my proposal is contrary to current contract law, it is not the first time an argument has been made in favor of actual assent. *See, e.g.*, Clarke B. Whittier, *The Restatement of Contracts and Mutual Assent*, 17 Cal. L. Rev. 441, 443 (1929) (critiquing the "objective" theory of contracts of the First Restatement and proposing that using "actual assent" as the basis for "mutual assent" except where there has been a "careless misleading which induces a reasonable belief in assent" would lead to better results).

tantamount to blanket assent[63] to terms that are not "unreasonable."[64] The notion of blanket assent may have made sense where contract terms were bounded by their form and the paper upon which they were printed. Blanket assent makes little sense where companies intentionally design contracts to escape user attention and where the terms themselves are weightless, numerous and scattered in different locations.

C. Contract Form, Function and Doctrinal Rules

There is a design principle in architecture that form follows function, meaning that the shape of a structure should be determined by its intended use. I wish to introduce a corollary that should be applied to contracts, which is that function follows form. What this means is that the form of a contract reflects (or should reflect) its function. In other words, the intended use or function of a contract should be determined, or at least signaled, by its form. A browsewrap, for example, should be employed only where the contract is intended to function instructively; it should not be used to impose affirmative obligations upon, or extract entitlements from, the non-drafting party.

Courts should consider the form of a contract in determining the function of that contract and further, they should consider the function of a contract in contract disputes.

The form of a contract, like its function, sets expectations. Therefore, to consider the form and function of a contract does something of fundamental importance—it enables courts to better assess the reasonable expectations of the parties. A court's role in adjudicating contract disputes is to fulfill the reasonable expectations of the

---

63 Karl Llewellyn famously stated:

> Instead of thinking about "assent" to boiler plate clauses, we can recognize that so far as concerns the specific, there is no assent at all. What has in fact been assented to, specifically, are the few dickered terms, and the broad type of transaction, and but one thing more. That one thing more is a blanket assent (not a specific assent) to any not unreasonable or indecent terms… which do not alter or eviscerate the reasonable meaning of the dickered terms. The fine print which has not been read has no business to cut under the reasonable meaning of those dickered terms which constitute the dominant and only real expression of the agreement.

Karl N. Llewellyn, The Common Law Tradition—Deciding Appeals 370 (Little, Brown & Co. 1960); *see also* Hillman & Rachlinski, *supra* note 63, at 461 (defining Llewellyn's notion of "blanket assent" as meaning that "although consumers do not read standard terms, so long as their formal presentation and substance are reasonable, consumers comprehend the existence of the terms and agree to be bound to them").

64 *See* Hillman & Rachlinski, *supra* note 63, at 455 (noting that the current legal approach to standard form agreements supports Llewellyn's view that the law should create "a presumption of assent (or 'blanket assent') to standard terms…. Llewellyn based his framework on the perspective that, so long as the terms are not unfair in presentation or substance, courts should presume consumers' 'blanket assent' to the details they may have ignored.").

party. In wrap contract cases, however, courts have tended to ignore this responsibility and have fixated instead on inventing and applying mechanistic rules of assent in a way that fails to recognize the difference that context and contract form makes to the reasonable expectations of the parties. The rules, which are supposed to help determine reasonable expectations, are too often used to replace it. Contracts, regardless of form, can effectively express the intent of the parties; on the other hand, the intent of the parties is reflected in, and affected by, contract's form.

The interpretation and construction of a contract in accordance with its form and function – the role that it plays in the transaction or relationship - provides a more coherent analytical framework than the 'wrap contracting nonsense which relies upon a fictionalized version of assent. The reasonable expectations of parties depend upon *what type of contract* is at issue. A party signing a commercial lease does not have the same expectations of enforceability as a party clicking "I agree" to the terms of a clickwrap. The drafter of a commercial lease, too, has different expectations than the drafter of a clickwrap. The latter does not actually expect the adherent to read the terms prior to constructively manifesting consent. Neither party to a wrap contract expects the drafter to actually enforce the adhesive terms of the contract; they understand that the contract is instructive, intended to serve as a reference in the event of a dispute. An interpretive framework that expressly considers the form and function of a contract reflects reality and better protects the reasonable expectations of the parties.

Many problems that are associated with wrap contracts specifically and adhesive contracts generally could be resolved by putting teeth into existing rules relating to the construction and interpretation of contracts. The reasonable expectations doctrine, captured in section 211(3) of the Restatement of Contracts, states that, with respect to standardized agreements "(w)here the other party has reason to believe that the party manifesting such assent would not do so if he knew that the writing contained a particular term, the term is not part of the agreement."[65] Courts, unfortunately, have limited the application of this doctrine to insurance contracts. They should instead expand its application to other adhesive contracts.

Another underutilized doctrine is that of good faith. Contract law requires that the parties to a contract perform their obligations in good faith.[66] The doctrine of good faith is intended to prevent improper behavior and preserve the reasonable

[65] RESTATEMENT (SECOND) of CONTRACTS, § 211(3).

[66] As the CORBIN ON CONTRACTS treatise notes, "When unforeseen contingencies occur, not provided for in the contract, the courts require performance as men who deal fairly and in good faith with each other would perform without a law suit." ARTHUR L. CORBIN, CORBIN ON CONTRACTS, section 541 (West, 1952). *See also* Best v. U.S. National Bank, 739 P.2d 554, 557 (Or. 1987)("This court has long stated... that there is an obligation of good faith in the performance and enforcement of every contract.")

expectations of the parties. Courts should recognize that the non-drafting party is unlikely to have read a wrap contract and consider instead the purpose of the transaction or interaction in determining whether a party has acted in good faith. For example, where the drafting party to an adhesive contract has the authority to exercise a right at its sole discretion, such as Facebook's ability to terminate a user's account, the exercise of that discretionary authority should be made in good faith in light of the form and function of the contract. Accordingly, Facebook should terminate user accounts only where the user continues to violate website norms of conduct after fair warning. Similarly, in those jurisdictions that have recognized unilateral modifications as enforceable, a good faith requirement would mean that the drafting party could not make any substantive changes unilaterally to the contract despite any language to the contrary; it may, however, revise the contract to conform to changes in the law, to make grammatical fixes, or to reflect minor technical changes to the website.

In most wrap contract cases, good faith performance will mean that the drafting party uses its discretionary authority only for shielding or instructive purposes. Many wrap contracts contain broad license grant provisions, like the following from the professional networking site, Linked in:

> "[Y]ou grant LinkedIn a nonexclusive, irrevocable, worldwide, perpetual, unlimited, assignable, sublicenseable, fully paid up and royalty-free right to us to copy, prepare derivative works of, improve, distribute, publish, remove, retain, add, process, analyze, use and commercialize, in any way now known or in the future discovered, any information you provide, directly or indirectly to LinkedIn, including, but not limited to, any user generated content, ideas, concepts, techniques or data to the services, you submit to LinkedIn, without any further consent, notice and/or compensation to you or to any third parties. Any information you submit to us is at your own risk of loss as noted in Sections 2 and 3 of this Agreement."[67]

While the above language gives LinkedIn a broad license, a good faith exercise of its rights in this context should mean that the company limits its exercise of rights to shielding or instructive purposes which are consistent with user expectations. A court interpreting the provision should keep in mind that the user has probably not read the provision and that it is rational for the user not to do so. Thus, a good faith exercise of this broad license means that LinkedIn may modify content as necessary to host and distribute user generated content in a variety of mediums. It does not

---

[67] Linked in, User Agreement, *http://www.linkedin.com/static?key=user_agreement* (last visited March 9, 2013).

mean that the company may use such content in its advertising campaigns nor can it alter the substantive content of any user profile. A court should interpret the above license grant provision as a shielding one, intended to protect the company from bad faith claims that it has violated a user's copyright or stolen user submitted content or ideas. It should not, however, be interpreted broadly as giving the company the right to use such content or ideas for purposes other than to host a LinkedIn profile, regardless of any language indicating otherwise.

The doctrine of unconscionability is another devitalized doctrine that could be used in the interpretation and construction of wrap contract terms. In the past, some courts have recognized the potential of the doctrine to invalidate contracts. One court stated that:

> "When a party can show that the contract, which is sought to be enforced, was in fact an unconscionable one, due to a prodigious amount of bargaining power on behalf of the stronger party, which is used to the stronger party's advantage and is unknown to the lesser party, causing a great hardship and risk on the lesser party, the contract provision, or the contract as a whole, if the provision is not separable, should not be enforceable on the grounds that the provision is contrary to public policy. The party seeking to enforce such a contract has the burden of showing that the provisions were explained to the other party and *came to his knowledge* and there was in fact *a real and voluntary meeting of the minds and not merely an objective meeting.* (emphasis in original)."[68]

As noted in chapter 7, however, courts in recent years have been reluctant to apply the doctrine of unconscionability where there has been notice and an opportunity to read.[69] The following section proposes one way to reinvigorate the doctrine of unconscionability.

D. Reinvigorating the Doctrine of Unconscionability

As I was finishing the manuscript for this book, my computer died. I suspect it was some kind of malware that had infected it (and probably something to which I had constructively consented). I went to a nearby electronics retailer. The laptops were displayed on the counters, not in boxes. Little stickers indicated what features were available for each make and model. I selected one that was preloaded with the new

---

[68] Weaver v. American Oil Company, 276 N.E. 2d 144, 148 (1971).

[69] *See* Chapter 7 (c) and related citations.

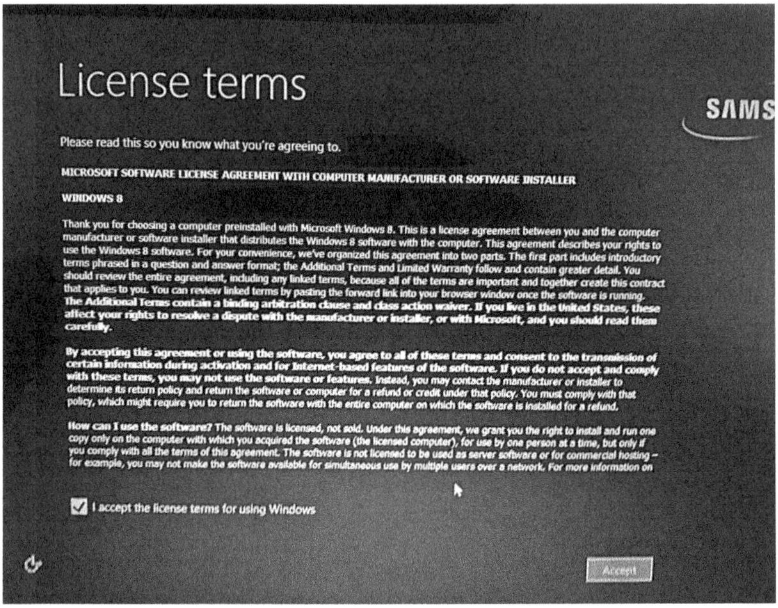

FIGURE 11-3

Microsoft operating system, Windows 8. I told the salesclerk which laptop I wanted and she returned with a plain white box, which I took to the cash register. I paid for my new laptop and took it home. When I booted up my new computer, the first thing I saw was a clickwrap agreement that required me to accept its terms before proceeding. The agreement likely met all the notice requirements set forth in recent wrap cases, including information regarding important rights that were affected. It required the user to read hyperlinked terms, which seem to be accessible only after assent. If I declined the terms, the agreement instructed me to return the software in accordance with the retailer's policy. (See Figure 11-3)

Given that Microsoft's is the predominant operating system, my only alternative would be to return the computer for a refund, if the retailer allowed it. (It's unclear what my options would be if the retailer did not provide refunds or permit returns.) I could have opted for an Apple computer, which uses different software, but based upon my prior experience with Apple, I suspected the license terms would be similar to those offered by Microsoft. I could have handwritten the rest of my manuscript, or tried to find a typewriter, but neither was a real option if I wanted to abide by my publisher's submission instructions.

Resistance was futile. I clicked, "I agree," even though I didn't, not in anyone's eyes but a judge, whose vision was clouded by ill-considered precedent.

Where control in a given industry is concentrated, there is often a systemic lack of bargaining power. Contract terms are imposed in a transaction by the party with greater bargaining power; these terms then become duplicated and standardized within the industry and evolve into industry norms. This type of private legislation has occurred in many industries, including the insurance industry, the consumer credit industry, and the software industry.[70] Unfortunately for the nondrafting party, these terms are often not the best terms. As Douglas Phillips explains in the context of software end-user license agreements:

> Users act quite rationally in declining to read the license, because the costs of attempting to understand the legal significance of the license outweighs the prospective benefit. The result is information asymmetry between the provider and the user. The software provider, as creator of the terms, knows what they say and generally understands their significance. The user, on the other hand, lacks such knowledge. The problem with this asymmetry is that it drives "good" software licenses, from the user's perspective, out of the market. Because users are not able, at reasonable cost, to discriminate among licenses, software providers are left with no incentive to provide more favorable licenses to attract users. Like used cars, software licenses quite naturally tend to be "lemons."[71]

What Phillips observes about terms in end-user software license agreements applies with greater force in the online environment. Digital contracts facilitate the spreading of oppressive terms across different industries. For example, unilateral modification clauses can be found on banking sites, social networking sites, and retail sites. Given the systemic lack of bargaining power, their ubiquity, and the standardized nature of wrap contract terms across industry sectors, notice and/or an opportunity to read terms has little or no meaning—and does not mean that the consumer has acted either knowingly or willingly.

Even where a consumer is aware that she is "manifesting consent" by clicking "I agree," her behavior is not so much an expression of intent to contract as it is a ceding to the reality of her situation—she clicks without reading because she knows that it does not matter what the contract says. If she wants to enter into any transaction online using a computer or mobile phone, she will accept all of the terms of each provider because she has no other choice. The aggregate effect of standardized oppressive terms is a coercive online contracting environment that threatens to

---

[70] *See* Michael J. Madison, *Reconstructing the Software License*, 35 Loy. U. Chi. L.J. 275, 316–19 (2003) (discussing how consumers acquiesce to licensing transactions because they effectively have no other way to purchase software given the evolution of the "licensing norm").

[71] Douglas E. Phillips, The Software License Unveiled: How Legislation by License Controls Software Access at 76 (Oxford 2009).

deprive the consumer of engagement in a significant portion of the marketplace and a major form of civil engagement if she dares to decline the terms. The consumer has no meaningful choice but to click "I agree" if she wants to participate in online forms of commerce, banking, and socializing.

Some may protest that the consumer is a free agent, at liberty to visit another site. Nobody is forcing the consumer to purchase goods from this particular e-tailer, or use this website or software, or so the argument goes.[72] But this argument is based upon a fallacious premise, which is that alternatives in fact exist. In most cases, they do not. In the context of online privacy practices and policies, Jerry Kang states that consent to such terms is "coerced, and not truly voluntary in the marketplace."[73] Widespread adoption of terms means that the choice is not just to walk away from this particular company, product, or transaction—it means to walk away from the online world and nearly all digital interactions.

Some contract terms have become so uniform and commonplace online that the consumer effectively has no choice if she wants to engage in online activity. The lack of choice—common offline but consistently and universally the case online—is often disregarded by courts. For example, in *Fusha v. Delta Airlines*,[74] the court stated that "[t]here are a multitude of other competing internet travel companies that may have much more favorable forum selection clauses and Fusha was free to avail herself of those other companies if she didn't like the terms offered by Airtrade."[75] It is unclear to which travel companies the court was referring. This author conducted a quick search of several travel websites, including the three most popular ones—Expedia, Travelocity, and Orbitz—and found that they all contained mandatory forum clauses.[76]

---

[72] For a criticism of the "economic libertarian" view, see Eric A. Posner, Contract Law in the Welfare State: A Defense of the Unconscionability Doctrine, Usury Laws, and Related Limitations on the Freedom to Contract, 24 J. Legal Stud. 283 (1995).Eric Posner notes that the historical survival of usury laws responds to a basic social problem and that "those who endorse the policy of poverty reduction through the welfare system should support restrictive contract laws." *Id.*at 318.

[73] Jerry Kang, *Information Privacy in Cyberspace Transactions*, 50 STAN. L. REV. 1193, 1265 (1998).

[74] Fusha v. Delta Airlines, Inc., CIV.A. RDB-10-2571, 2011 WL 3849657 (D. Md. Aug. 30, 2011).

[75] *Id.* at 4.

[76] *See, e.g.*, Expedia, Inc., Web Site Terms, Conditions and Notices, http://www.expedia.com/p/info-other/legal.htm ("You hereby consent to the exclusive jurisdiction and venue of courts in King County, Washington, USA, in all disputes arising out of or relating to the use of this Website. Use of this Website is unauthorized in any jurisdiction that does not give effect to all provisions of these terms and conditions, including, without limitation, this paragraph.") (last visited Aug. 24, 2012); Orbitz Terms and Conditions, http://www.orbitz.com/info/win?id=TermsAndConditions#disputes; ("If you take any legal action relating to your use of our site or these Terms, you agree to file such action only in the state and federal courts located in Cook County, Illinois (USA)"), (last visited Aug. 24 2012); Travelocity User Agreement, http://www.travelocity.com/info/info_popup/0,,%7CTERMS_WINDOW,00.html ("any Claims shall be brought in the state or federal courts located in Tarrant County, the State of Texas, United States of America," (last visited Aug. 24, 2012).

Contrary to what courts have too often ruled, choice of terms online is a fantasy that exists only in an alternative contracting universe. Not only does one party lack bargaining power with respect to a particular transaction or party, but one class of parties lacks bargaining power within a contracting environment.[77] It is not a viable option for the consumer to decline the terms of any particular agreement if the consumer wishes to engage in online activity. The party's "assent" is void of volition and merely reflects a refusal on the part of the consumer to resist market forces through self-deprivation that would have profound social and economic consequences.

This situation is quite different from the model contract scenario that is assumed by contract doctrine and differs even from the model adhesive contract scenario. Given the importance of online activity in our daily lives, it is highly unlikely that even the most ardent supporter of contractual autonomy would forego an ill-advised "click" on the basis of principle and an understanding of contract law alone. A refusal to accept standardized contractual terms is simply unrealistic in many types of transactions. Refusing to visit websites or use products and services that utilize wrap contracts means opting out of the use of the Internet, computers, and smartphones and essentially shutting oneself out of important economic and civic activities.

The purpose of contract law is to promote individual autonomy and to ensure the security of transactions, which is essential to the smooth functioning of a credit economy. A coercive contracting environment undermines both these objectives. The position currently adopted by many courts that wrap contracts are enforceable contracts ignores these objectives of contract law and would lead to the socially undesirable conclusion that individuals who wish to decline the terms of a wrap contract should opt out of the efficient online marketplace and the modern economy.

A more welfare-maximizing alternative is to redefine unconscionability so that it reflects the reality of a coercive contracting environment. In most jurisdictions, unconscionability must be both procedural and substantive. It is judged according to a sliding scale, meaning that if there is a high level of either procedural or substantive unconscionability, the threshold for the other will be lower.

---

[77] Professor Addison Mueller noted two factors that together create the modern consumer's lack of effective legal power:

> First, there is an all-pervasive difficulty: our machinery of justice is simply not designed for easy use by the average citizen with a minor claim of any kind....

[Second,] he claims in contract and must use a deck of doctrine that is stacked against him.
Most of his losing cards are colored "freedom of contract."
Addison Mueller, *Contracts of Frustration*, 78 Yale L.J. 576, 578–79 (1969).

I propose that the doctrine of unconscionability be looked at more holistically. Although consistent with the sliding-scale approach, it would not require an express finding of both procedural and substantive unconscionability. Unconscionability in many cases cannot be so easily divided. Courts are generally reluctant to assess the substance of terms. Furthermore, substantive unconscionability relies on norms which may be inappropriate in wrap contracting scenarios. Norms reflected in online terms may not evidence fairness or efficient business practices; rather they may be the product of anticompetitiveness. Standard terms that are adopted by all companies in a market segment result in de facto term fixing that, like price fixing, is suboptimal and eliminates consumer choice.

If the avoiding party can prove the use of a coercive contracting form (i.e. the use of an online wrap contract which she was required to accept in order to proceed with the transaction), unconscionability should be presumed except in two situations. The first is where the relevant term is one expressly permitted by legislative action or by a regulatory agency. For example, warranty disclaimers and limitations of liability have long been recognized under the Uniform Commercial Code provided that certain disclosure and conspicuousness requirements are met.

The second exception is where the drafting party can demonstrate that alternative terms were available. The drafter can do this by presenting evidence that its competitors in the same or similar business offered different terms. In addition, drafters can themselves offer alternative terms and rebut the claim that there was an absence of meaningful choice. The provision of a choice of terms does not mean that the drafting company must provide only consumer-friendly terms and eschew self-interested ones; rather, it means that it cannot threaten the consumer with nonparticipation by proposing an all-or-nothing format with respect to the product or service offered.

For example, let's assume that a term in the contract required consumers to consent to collection of personal information for marketing purposes. All e-mail service provider agreements contain this provision so there is a lack of meaningful choice for the nondrafting party. If, however, an e-mail service provider permits an alternative version of the service—such as providing e-mail without data collection for an annual fee—then there is a meaningful choice. While there may be no alternative to *free* e-mail service without collection of personal information, there is the possibility of receiving the service with payment of a fee. Assuming that the fee itself is not shockingly excessive, the consumer now has a real choice. Yahoo, for example, has two versions of its e-mail services. The free service is slower because it comes with ads; the premium service contains no ads but requires an annual fee. (Unfortunately, this does not mean that Yahoo is not collecting personal information about the user, only that it is not showing the user personalized ads.) By offering different versions of its contracts, the drafter presents a more efficient transaction, one that more accurately reflects the desires of both parties.

Margaret Jane Radin notes that this type of contract customization may pose policy problems, especially since the "opportunity to purchase better terms may seem to exacerbate distinctions between haves and have-nots."[78] The concern is a valid one and not one that this defense eliminates as it has to do with inequitable wealth distributions and socio-economic power generally. As discussed in chapter 2, a primary objective of contract law is not the redistribution of wealth as a stand-alone goal. But contract law does, and should, recognize equitable considerations and fairness principles in the application of its rules. The recognition of environmental coercion in the context of unconscionability aims, in its own small but significant way, to address the problem of unfairness in the marketplace—an unfairness arising from the plethora of factors discussed throughout this book that militate in favor of drafters and against nondrafting parties.

The mere availability of alternative terms raises their salience and makes it easier for customers to determine the value of the rights they are relinquishing. Customers may assess whether the right to opt-out of the mandatory arbitration clause is worth the extra fee. Furthermore, the mere existence of an alternative option draws attention to a term and may raise the ire of consumers. Similar to the way checked baggage fees created a backlash among consumers and allowed airlines that did not charge them to differentiate themselves, the "alternative terms" rebuttal to a claim of unconscionability may ultimately provide an incentive to businesses to expand their offerings and eventually change the way that consumers view their power (and powerlessness) in the online marketplace. These alternatives may alter the coercive contracting environment that currently exists and give nondrafting parties a genuine choice and, consequently, the ability to exercise true consent.

It is important to emphasize that rethinking unconscionability to recognize environmental coercion does not bar any standard terms; rather, it shifts the burden of getting terms approved or proven "conscionable." Businesses seeking to enforce certain terms could do so by mobilizing forces and lobbying their legislators to pass bills permitting those terms, essentially shifting the current system of unilaterally drafted private legislation to the realm of public legislation. At first this may seem like a radical proposal, but upon reconsideration, it should sound very familiar. A common refrain from those who favor enforcing adhesive contracts is that the market will respond—if consumers don't like certain terms, they will (or should) do something about it. More precisely, they argue that unhappy consumers can lobby the legislature or go elsewhere for alternative

---

[78] Margaret Jane Radin, *Human, Computers and Binding Commitment*, 75 IND. L.J. 1125, 1151 (2000).

terms. The latter option typically doesn't exist given the uniformity of online terms. The former is, as a practical matter, a burden more fairly and sensibly shifted upon the drafting companies. If companies expressly want certain terms, such as the ability to track consumer movements online, *they* can lobby their legislators. There are too many coordination and collective action problems with mobilizing adherents to wrap contract who are strangers to each other, geographically dispersed, and have limited resources. On the other hand, companies have a commonality of interest if they are in the same industry. They also have more resources than most individuals and greater experience with organizing campaigns to influence legislators. They are in a better position to effectuate legal change through the political process and often have substantial budgets that allow them to pay for well-connected lobbyists. Furthermore, they are repeat players and have a long-term interest in the enforceability of their contract terms.

Radin has argued that mass market terms cause "democratic degradation," erasing "large swaths of legal rights that are granted through democratic processes and instead substitute the system of rights that the firm wishes to impose."[79] She notes:

> The most obvious democratic degradation is the way boilerplate schemes bypass political debate and procedures. The entitlement regimes that boilerplate schemes delete have been enacted through democratic processes often with extended debate and fierce political struggle while deleting them only requires drafting boilerplate (or indeed just copying someone else's).[80]

My proposed reconceptualizion of unconscionability addresses the problem of democratic degradation by flipping the starting point for enforcement of mass market terms. Rather than the current regime of allowing the drafter to reorder rights and obligations, the drafter must work through the political process to gain legislative approval. Because legislators are appointed through a democratic process, the interests of both drafters and nondrafters are likely to be represented.

---

[79] Margaret Jane Radin, *Reconsidering Boilerplate: Confronting Normative and Democratic Degradation*, 40 Cap. U. L. Rev. 617, 633 (2012). *See also* MARGARET JANE RADIN, BOILERPLATE: THE FINE PRINT, VANISHING RIGHTS, AND THE RULE OF LAW (Princeton University Press 2013).

[80] *Id.* at 634.

12 Conclusion

COURTS ARE FOND of saying that wrap contracts are the same as traditional paper contracts and that they are applying the same rules of contract law to them. Neither statement is true. Wrap contracts are not the same as traditional paper contracts, and courts have not applied the law the same way. A refusal to acknowledge the ways in which digital contracts differ from paper ones is simply unrealistic.

Wrap contracts take the user further away from actual assent than contracts of adhesion; it is not merely the issue of nonnegotiability that is at stake. It is the issue of autonomy itself. The justification for state intervention in what is essentially a private matter is that the parties agreed to it; their consent is the starting point. Without consent, judicial enforcement of contracts is state coercion. Courts justify wrap contracts by claiming that the nondrafting party manifested consent, but their construction of what constitutes manifestation of consent has wandered too far from the truth. Nonconsent does not become consent simply by claiming it is. Consent has meaning in our society and in the law, and it is a different one than that used by courts to establish assent to wrap contracts.

Courts, in their zeal to promote commercial transactions in new environments, have enforced unilaterally imposed rules as contracts in order to protect new business models from unfair practices such as content copying or web crawling and web scraping. They would have done better to delve into these practices directly and enforce prohibitions against them through other doctrinal mechanisms, such as implied contracts, unfair competition, or other equitable doctrines which gave them more flexibility and discretion. By pretending that wrap contracts were "just like" other contracts—that they were contracts at all—courts established precedent that became difficult to escape.

If a contract is properly formed, the escape hatches are few and far between. The most common escape hatch is the defense of unconscionability, meaning in most cases both procedural and substantive unfairness. But unconscionability leads courts back to the snake pit they tried so hard to avoid, which is having to assess the fairness of terms and the adequacy of consideration. The consequence is that most of the time, courts enforce properly formed wrap contract terms.

At this point, it is too late to turn back. The genie is out of the bottle, and there are too many cases proclaiming that wrap contracts are "just like" paper contracts and that consent can be constructed rather than knowingly given. But all is not lost if we turn once again to what makes contract law effective in an evolving marketplace—its flexibility and dynamism, captured in doctrinal adjustments that rehabilitate existing rules.

Wrap contract doctrine has shifted and distorted the focus of contract law. Contract law and contracts should promulgate the intent of the parties and ensure the security of transactions. These twin objectives are captured in the role of the courts in contract disputes—to enforce the reasonable expectations of the parties. Unfortunately, the way the standard of reasonableness has been applied by courts in wrap contract cases fails to reflect societal norms or majoritarian realities; rather, it reflects a judicially constructed notion, and one that assumes an idealized view of business incentives.

Drafters should not be free from social expectations and norms of behavior, which is not to say that they can't contract out of them. But they must do so in a way that conforms to contract law. They can establish the terms of their contract, but they can't change what it means to call something a contract. They can set the rules of the transaction but they can't change how those rules must be set. The offeror is the master of the offer, but not of the universe.

Currently, the focal point of inquiry in mass consumer contracts is the consumer, when it should be both parties. While notice must purportedly be "reasonable," the test does not take into account whether it is in fact presented in a reasonable manner. But it makes little sense to analyze the reasonableness of the offeree's conduct given that in many cases, it is perfectly reasonable for the offeree *not* to read the terms. This is so because in most cases, the legal concept of notice is meaningless as applied to the typical, reasonable consumer.

Courts construe notice in a way that makes no sense to the average consumer. Most consumers don't pay attention to the words "Terms of Use," even if they are positioned at the top of the page. This doesn't mean consumers are unreasonable or imprudent. On the contrary, there are too many contracts, and too many terms contained within them. It would be socially undesirable for all consumers to actually read each contract they "agreed" to—the economy would grind to a halt. One study estimated that it would cost the average American Internet user 201 hours or the equivalent of $3,534 a year to read the privacy policies of each website that he or she visits.[1] If every time you downloaded music, checked your e-mail, or paid a bill online, you read the terms of the various wrap contracts you encountered, you would not have time to engage in productive work, recreational activities, or relationships. Modern life, in other words, would break down if we treated wrap contracts just like other contracts.

The contracting of everything has conditioned nondrafting parties—typically consumers but also businesses—to throw up their hands at any attempt to participate in the bargaining process. The perception is that the system is rigged and contributes to a generalized feeling of frustration and anger and even, in some cases, irresponsibility toward one's contractual commitments. A contract is made by the parties and enforced against them—but it reverberates and affects nonparties. Broken promises have negative externalities. Parties may feel justified in breaking promises they never intended to make, which leads to a breakdown in trust. Wrap contracts may contribute to consumers' feelings of helplessness and anger at their inability to control business practices.

Given the importance of contracts in a credit economy, they should be treated much more seriously than they are. Contract law is flexible enough to accommodate changes in the contracting environment, but with wrap doctrine, the rules have been twisted only in one direction, toward the desires of drafting businesses. A solution to the irrationality of wrap contract doctrine must recognize the drafting party's role and responsibility in creating the form of the contract and the contracting environment. There is much more that can be done to make online contracting more effective—and companies are in a better position to do that work than consumers.

The doctrinal adjustments suggested in chapter 11 recognize the power of drafters over contracting form and environment and more evenly balance the burdens associated with each. These doctrinal adjustments have broad applicability and their use is not limited to wrap contracts, but they may be more relevant to such contracts for the simple reason that form matters. A failure to recognize the difference that form makes takes us as a society further away from what an agreement has traditionally meant, and sends us tumbling down the rabbit hole where contract law is as arbitrary as the Red Queen's rules.

---

[1] *See* Aleecia M. McDonald & Lorrie Faith Cranor, *The Cost of Reading Privacy Policies*, 4:3 I/S: A Journal of Law and Policy 540, at 562 (2008).

Table of Cases

Index